U S S R

SAMSUN

GARESUN

RIZE

TRABZON

GÜMÜSHANE

KARS

IMRANLI

AGRI

DOĞUBAYAZIT

SIVAS

GEMEREK

ERCIS

MUS

AHLAT

Lake Van

VAN GUZELSU

KAYSERI

MALATYA

BITLIS

GÜRPINAR

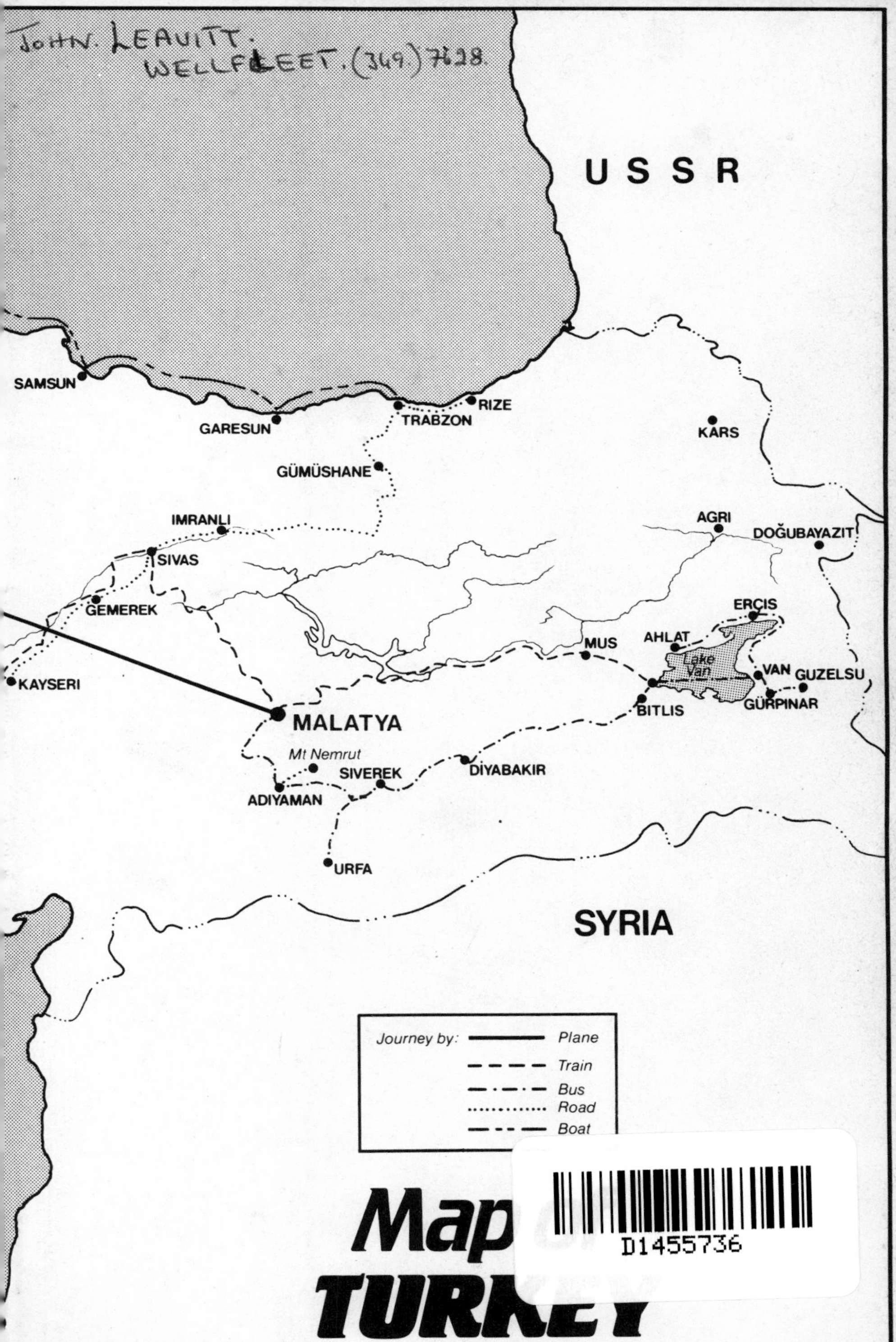

Mt Nemrut

SIVEREK

DIYABAKIR

ADIYAMAN

URFA

SYRIA

Journey by:	
———————	*Plane*
– – – – –	*Train*
–·–·–·–	*Bus*
··············	*Road*
–··–··–	*Boat*

Map of
TURKEY

A TRAVELLER IN
TURKEY

A TRAVELLER IN
TURKEY

DANIEL FARSON

ROUTLEDGE & KEGAN PAUL
LONDON, BOSTON AND HENLEY

First published in 1985
by Routledge & Kegan Paul plc

14 Leicester Square, London WC2H 7PH, England

9 Park Street, Boston, Mass. 02108, USA and

Broadway House, Newtown Road,
Henley on Thames, Oxon RG9 1EN, England

Typset in 10/12 pt Linotron Times
by Inforum Ltd, Portsmouth
and printed in Great Britain
by The Thetford Press Ltd,
Thetford, Norfolk

Library of Congress Cataloguing-in-Publication Data

Farson, Daniel, 1927–

A traveller in Turkey.
Bibliography: p.
Includes index.
1. Turkey—Description and travel—1960–   —Guide
books.   I. Title.
DR416.F37   1985   956.1   85–14634

ISBN 0–7102–0281–4

Dedicated to Mrs Gulsen Kahraman,
Turkish Tourism Attaché in London, who
in helping me plan these journeys has
become a valued friend, providing the
perfect introduction to her country

In addition to all the Directors of Tourism
in Turkey who went out of their way to
help me, I should like to express my
special appreciation to Mr Yelman Emcan
in Ankara, Head of Promotion of Tourism
in Turkey, for his encouragement and
assistance in making these journeys
possible.

NOTE

Apart from a separate visit many years ago, these journeys took place over the last three years. Purely for simplification, I have assembled them together while making the chronological order obvious but incidental.

North Devon 1985

Contents

Introduction   (1)

Information   (5)

1   Of mosques and minarets   (7)

2   Flower Sellers' Alley   (9)

3   The Pera Palas   (14)

4   Exploring Istanbul   (17)

5   My first guide to Turkey   (21)

6   Eating your way through Turkey   (33)

7   From Istanbul to Trebizond   (38)

8   A Turkish bath   (48)

9   Across the Turkish Alps, over the Zigana Pass   (50)

10 A beautiful death in Gumushane   (53)

11 A lunar landscape on Earth   (56)

12 Wild Flowers in the dining car – taking the train to Van   (65)

13 Losing a guide in Diyarbakir   (81)

14 Losing a kilim in Urfa   (86)

15 Climbing to the vainest man on Earth   (93)

16 Driving back from Nemrut   (98)

17 Tarsus – but what's in a name?   (101)

18 The Tomb of the Fearless King   (105)

19 My second guide to Turkey   (114)

20 A city in silence   (123)

21 Luxury in Antalya – at the Talya Hotel   (123)

22 From Antalya to Marmaris – the new Riviera   (128)

23 A Grecian plot in Turkish waters   (134)

24 Kekova – history in the water   (140)

25 An avenue of eucalyptus   (146)

26 The Greek shadow   (147)

27 The Greek island of Symi   (149)

28 The woman who kicked a tortoise   (154)

29 The man who blazed the trail – Eric Richardson of the YCA   (161)

30 A first look at Dalyan   (164)

31 Abidin Kurt   (169)

32 A rough road to Datca   (178)

33   Cnidus – and the sexy statue   (182)
34   Bodrum, and Dursun the sponge diver   (185)
35   The *Maya* – available for charter   (188)
36   Aphrodisias – and the triumph of Professor Erim   (193)
37   Pamukkale – Yusuf and the dead birds   (197)
38   Return to Dalyan   (203)
39   Bad news in England   (207)
40   Farewell to Dalyan   (209)
     Index   (215)

Illustrations

between pages 30 *and* 31

1   The Galata Bridge in Istanbul
2   The entrance to the Dolmabahce Palace
3   The author with Mr Hasan Suzer
4   A ferry down the Bosphorus
5   Three old men in Giresun
6   The church of Sancta Sophia in Trabzon
7   Mustafa in the square at Trabzon
8   The Sumela Monastery
9   At the top of the Zigara Pass
10 The sacrificial slaughter of a sheep in Gumushane
11 The extraordinary rock formations in Cappadocia
12 Some of these conical shapes are known as 'fairy chimneys'
13 The holes in the tufa stone are houses
14 A family on the train to Tatvan
15 The early Armenian church on the island of Akdamar in
    Lake Van
16 Carvings depicting scenes from the Bible decorate the
    outside of the church
17 The main street of Van
18 The seventeenth-century castle of Hosap near Guzelsu
19 The bridge below the fortress
20 'Joe – the Turkish crossing-sweeper'
21 The stone heads at the top of Mount Nemrut
22 A lion at Nemrut
23 Hercules, looking up to Mithridates I
24 A Turkish woman leads a camel, donkey and dog through
    the woods near Ozuncaburc
25 The genuine and little-known tomb of the Fearless King
26 The phallus carved at the base in honour of Priam
27 Young wrestlers at Finike

28   A woman weaves a kilim on her loom at the top of the hill
      above Kale
29   The harbour of Kas
30   One of the sarcophagi stranded in the water near Kekova
31   Luxury at the Talya Hotel in Antalya
32   Termessos – the mountain city which defied Alexander
      the Great
33   The 'land', across the river from Dalyan
34   Lycian tombs carved in the rock at Dalyan
35   Dursun Mutlu, the sponge-diver
36   In Turkey a woman's place is often in the field
37   The frozen falls at Pamukkale
38   The Stadium at Aphrodisias
39   The massive Medusa head at Didyma
40   The Temple of Hadrian in the Street of the Curetes, Ephesus
41   Abidin Kurt, the indispensable guide to Dalyan
42   Guests leaving the wedding party at Candir

Maps

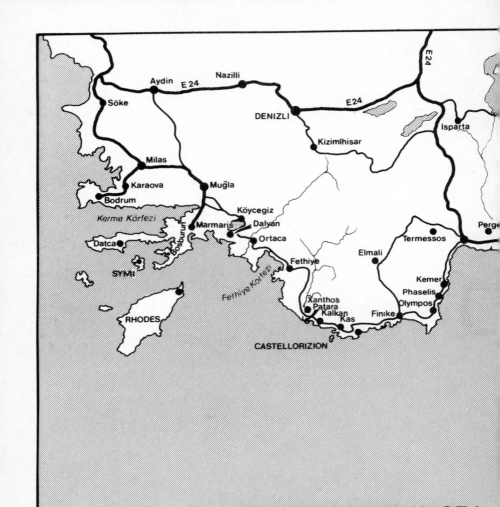

Southern coastline of Turkey

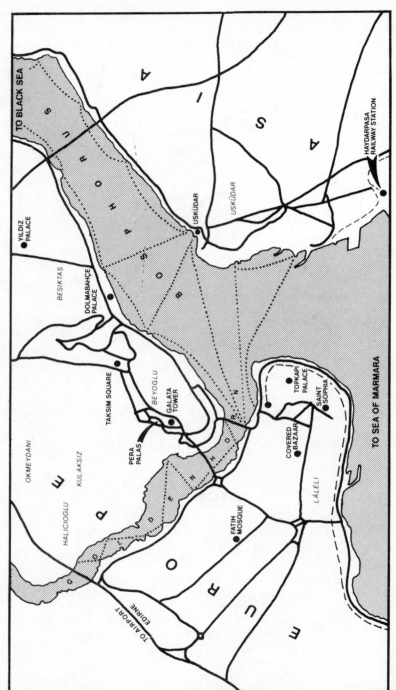

Map of Istanbul

Introduction

There is a lady in the village where I live who hides her vulnerability behind a formidable façade, firing questions as if they are statements.

'You've been away,' she told me accusingly. 'On holiday.'

'Not really,' I apologised, 'more of a working trip, writing travel articles. With any luck a book might come of it.'

Unimpressed, she continued, 'You've been in Turkey. That was brave of you.'

'Not at all. It's a marvellous country.'

'I thought it was primitive and dangerous.'

'Everything the British think about Turkey is the opposite of the truth,' I replied. 'The Turks are the nicest people in the world, in fact I'm searching for a piece of land where I can build a house.'

'What an extraordinary thing to do. You don't speak Turkish.'

'No,' I admitted, 'it doesn't seem to matter. I met a number of Turks who spoke perfect English. They have a sense of humour too, like ours at its *best*.' She frowned suspiciously but did her utmost to be pleasant: 'What exactly did you *do* on your holiday.'

'I watched the sacrificial slaughter of a sheep in Gumushane,

I danced with the groom on his wedding night in a mountain village,

I went mad on the strongest wine in the world in Urgup,

I attended a circumcision party in Antalya, and

I climbed to the tomb of the Fearless King which has a giant phallus carved on the outside, not that it's in the least offensive . . .'

The poor woman shuddered: 'It doesn't sound my sort of place at all but I hope you'll be happy if you find your Turkish paradise.' This was gracious in the circumstances and I thanked her. 'I think I've found the perfect place if I can buy the land. That's why I'm going back.'

*   *   *

On my first journey to Turkey in 1982, I left with an eagerness to be away from England.

My livelihood as a freelance writer seemed more precarious than usual and I had become the centre, albeit unwittingly, of a scandal in the West Country village where I live. I had written an article for the *Evening News Magazine* assuring Londoners that spring in the countryside is not necessarily the idyll they imagine: that it is harder to buy fresh vegetables, like spinach, than it is in Berwick Street Market; that fish is scarcer by the sea; that far from the bliss of solitude there is a constant din of helicopters or guns being fired to alert the gallant lifeboat crews as visitors are swept out to sea. As for those invigorating strides across the countryside, all too often they are stopped abruptly by barbed wire and signs which warn trespassers that they will be prosecuted. These are backed by irate farmers who threaten to shoot your dogs if they so much as bark at one of their nervous sheep.

All this was written tongue-in-cheek. Anyhow, the page was surrounded by little cartoons so it was obviously meant to be funny even if I failed. My own village was not named, but someone in London cut the page out and sent it to a woman who made an instant identification and showed the wretched thing to someone else who had it Xeroxed though the humorous border was deleted.

Suddenly – and especially among those who never read the article for themselves – it was rumoured that I had 'declared war' on the village. The irony that I have written more glowingly about the place than any writer before or since was forgotten in the instant. The climax was reached with a front-page attack in the local paper including an interview with a local woman who declared she would like to throw me over the quayside, and this was sustained by the editor with a correspondence over the following weeks until a stone was thrown through a window and two boys shouted as they cycled past, 'hates the place but still lives here.'

There is no point raging against injustice, and the tiny storm had an element of farce, but this was another reason why I was anxious to go abroad, and possibly live there permanently if I found that proverbial place in the sun on a Greek or Turkish coastline where I could build a house and plan a garden, write my books and run a little bar or taverna on the side. There is no deceiver like the self-deceiver.

I am either blessed or cursed by a monstrous naivety. Once a BBC producer turned on me in Transylvania demanding, 'Don't you think it's time you grew up?', while a friend has accused me of preferring 'the fantasy to the reality'. I am guilty on both counts. I am still waiting to grow up. When I read that someone of fifty-three has suffered some calamity or even died, I murmur 'Poor old thing!' ignoring the fact that I am five years older. The day I do finally grow up and lose my absurd optimism, I shall wither. So I set off in pursuit of my piece of paradise with the innocence of a child – or an absolute fool.

I left England on 1st May, 1982. My destination was Istanbul but first I flew to Salonika in the north of Greece where a man urged me not to continue my journey to Turkey, warning me of the dire consequences which befall anyone who crosses the border, with cars denuded of their tyres and people of their money. As the person was connected with Greek tourism I cannot be certain if his fears were genuine or simply part of his job, but the Grecian hatred of the Turks is so fanatical it is almost second nature to decry them, except that this man was English and should have known better.

As I told the lady in my village two years later, most of the British assumptions about Turkey are the opposite of the truth. The Turks are the most generous and trustworthy of people. Later, on that first journey when I walked along the quayside in Marmaris counting the last of my money, a young man ran after me holding a 1,000 lira note which I had dropped, not a vast amount but a fair slice of a weekly wage for him. What made it particularly gratifying was his obvious pleasure in giving it back.

Anyhow, I disregarded the warnings and continued by bus to Kavala where I took the ferry to the island of Thassos.

This was the wisest prelude to any journey I have made. I started to relax the moment I stepped ashore at Prinos and drove by bus through groves of shimmering olive trees while the driver played bazouki on the radio and the sun shone overhead. This was the start of spring when the air was so invigorating that I walked that first afternoon to Makryammos, the most fashionable beach in summer with an entrance fee of £1, but now it was closed and no one stopped me when I wandered down for my first swim of the year. The next morning I took the bus the short distance to the hillside village of Panayia where I had my breakfast of yoghurt and honey in the small square before I found a path which led me down beside a leaping stream to the curve of white sand. I plunged into the surf and swam in the pale, translucent sea and could have done so naked with no one around to protest at such a spectacle, apart from the fish. I ate some of these later in the afternoon at a simple taverna a few yards from the water after the freshest taramosalata I have tasted, instead of the usual travesty of yesterday's mashed potato dyed pink. With a

Greek salad enriched by oil and herbs, and a bottle of chilled retsina, this incomparable meal cost me less than £4. Afterwards, the woman who owned the place took me inside the modest Blue Sea Hotel alongside, where an old-fashioned room with immense wooden furniture would have cost me £6 a night if I had stayed for a week. This end of the bay with a modern shop and a few small hotels further on is known as Skala Potamias and I thought I could stay here happily for a month or two and spend the time swimming, writing and eating taramosalata. Perhaps *this* was the very paradise I was searching for? Already! On my second day in Thassos? Impossible! Yet, looking back on this northern Greek island three years later I realise how lucky I was to enjoy its magic before the crowds descended for the summer. Unlike most of the islands in the Aegean, Thassos is lush. The foreground is alpine with meadows and pine forests, a gentle impression belied by the lizards which scurry into the green field, the olive trees, and the distant outline of the mountains blurred by a smoky haze which remind one that this is a Greek island after all.

In such an atmosphere I felt so fit on my third day that I rented a bicycle as I had done on Samos once before when I strapped the machine on the roof rack and took it off again at the highest point on the island in the mistaken belief that the road must go down hill all the way. This time there was no roof rack on the bus so I hired a folding bicycle which was a novelty to me but seemed to make sense until I hauled it out of the boot near the mountain village of Potamia. In doing so I found that the screw which held the contraption together had fallen off. I signalled frantically to the bus but it vanished round the corner, so I broke off a piece of wire from a nearby fence and made a splint which I was rather proud of until I felt the bicycle shuddering underneath me as I raced downhill expecting it to jackknife at any second and hurl me headlong onto the asphalt. After this, I pushed the wretched thing and though this was hardly the progress I had in mind it is a perfect way to see a new landscape for you can hear the birds and insects, smell the flowers and the pines, and observe the details which escape you when you rush through by car. Finally I reached a small bay of white sand halfway round the island at a place called Aliki with no more than a few stone cottages and ancient ruins on one side of a small peninsula. How perfect, I thought, to own a taverna in such a place. I seized the chance for a swim before I caught the last bus which took me back round the other side of the island to the capital of Limenas where I was staying, with a detour to a remote village in the centre followed by a long wait at Prinos where the driver waited for the ferry and bought me coffee to compensate for the delay. It is 60 miles around the island and the bus journey costs a couple of pounds. As we waited at Prinos, hordes of schoolchildren from the mainland chattered like crickets, clutching their transistors which were tuned to different stations while a few with headphones gyrated silently on their own as if they suffered from St Vitus's Dance. Their enjoyment was so evident as they waited for the ferry to take them back that I could not begrudge them a decibel.

That night in Limenas I met two girls from Darlington. One was redheaded and though she had only been in the sun for a few hours she was crimson and she knew it: 'I can feel the blisters throbbing neath my cheeks.' She had a lovely northern accent and really did say 'Eee!'

I admired their spirit. They had taken the Magic Bus from Victoria Station armed with lettuce, bread and half a dozen boiled eggs, and had driven through Belgium to Munich, Austria and Yugoslavia, arriving at Salonika where someone told them there were no buses to Kavala three hours away, a cruel lie for they leave every hour from the outskirts of the city. So they took the train to Drama joining up with a team of Greek footballers who adopted them as mascots and persuaded them to continue to the town where they were playing. Fortunately they won, 5–3, and the girls were full of their adventure: 'Eee! We had a real good time we did, except the manager told us to be in by ten, that was the worst part.' Afterwards I wondered if she meant the manager of the hotel or the football team. The Darlington girls were a sign of the fun to come for they were looking for jobs to last them through the summer. We exchanged addresses, as one does so eagerly on holiday with promises to keep in touch which are rarely fulfilled, so I was pleased to hear from the redhead several months later: 'Thassos gradually got busier – in July and August it was like walking through a London Street on a Saturday afternoon, almost unbearable. September was fairly quiet, and when we left in October there were only two cafés open. We really had a marvellous time.'

As for myself, I had arrived at the right time of year before the madding crowd. When I left the island at dawn the next day on a ferry carrying tree trunks, a slab of marble and empty beehives with a few lingering bees, I looked back at the receding shore with a surprising sense of gratitude. Nothing much had happened, but the island had given me rest and contentment, exactly what I needed.

Information

Thassos appeals to young and old alike, depending on the time of year you go there. Young people love this island and Greeks flock there from the mainland, and Germans too, for the first-rate camping sites, sunbathing and swimming, and the lively disco nightlife in Limenas in summer.

Tours are organised by *Young World Holidays*, 29 Queen's Road, Brighton (0273 23397). If you make your own way from Salonika to Kavala I recommend the *Hotel Oceanis* where the owner, Yannis Papadoyannis, spoke perfect English and made me welcome.

At Limenas I stayed in the *Hotel Timoleon* on the quay opposite the jetty where the ferries arrive, causing a certain amount of noise which was compensated by the friendliness of the staff who brought me fresh orange juice and strong coffee on my balcony in the morning. There are many smaller hotels in the streets behind where you can make your own choice.

The *Blue Sea Hotel* at Skala Potamias is class C but all rooms have a private bath and lavatory. The telephone number is 0593 61482, and it is run by Mrs Kalogiannidou. I look forward to returning there myself.

1 Of mosques and minarets

Rather than retrace my steps to Kavala, I took the earlier ferry to the mainland port of Keramoti where I boarded a bus to Xanthi, a town with a bustling, eastern flavour which appealed to me, and managed to buy a seat on the special coach to Istanbul. This haphazard sequence worked like clockwork until we reached the frontier where everything stopped. We had to change buses and waited interminably before our replacement arrived. For once I did not care, though usually enraged by the slightest delay. I was refreshed by Thassos, ate the fruit I had bought in Xanthi, and read a book which absorbed me. Also, I was enjoying the adventure of going somewhere new. My only worry was the thought of arriving after dark.

One of the Turkish immigration officials, with an extraordinary nose which ran parallel to his face instead of away from it, took an interest in me that was equally curious, asking me to stay at his home in order to teach him Shakespeare.

'You like Shakespeare?'

I admitted that I did, but at this moment he noticed the date of birth in my passport and exclaimed, 'It's not possible! You cannot be so old?' Thereupon he lost interest in both myself and Shakespeare, but I thought it immensely flattering that he should have mistaken my age so dramatically in the first place.

Finally the new bus arrived and we moved off, past the great mosque at Edirne built for Selim II by the greatest of all the Turkish architects, Sinan, who was eighty-five when the building was completed in 1575 and declared that this was his masterpiece, surpassing his mosque to Suleyman the Magnificent in Istanbul. I caught a glimpse of the great dome and the four exquisite minarets rising into the sky around it and thought of Richard Hannay's comment on this perfect balance when he arrived in Constantinople and 'saw what I took to be mosques and minarets, and they were about as impressive as factory chimneys'. I hope that John Buchan was indulging in a sly piece of humour when he wrote this in *Greenmantle*, but I am far from sure. We arrived too late for me to judge for myself, missing that first, breathtaking impression, and for some reason I was dumped on the outskirts of the city where I found a taxidriver who had not heard of the Pera Pelas Hotel, the oldest and most splendid hotel in Istanbul. We found it at last; I booked in, and headed for Flower Sellers' Alley.

2 Flower Sellers' Alley

The name sounds colourful but the flowers are banked in a street around the corner and the scene is as black as a Gustave Doré engraving of one of those drinking dens off Ratcliffe Highway in the East End of London over a hundred years ago. Cats crouch furtively on the corrugated sheets which protect the people below from falling masonry, for the surrounding houses, so grand when they were young, are now crumbling facades. In one window I thought I glimpsed a patch of colour as someone crossed a room, but afterwards the place looked so abandoned I decided it must have been an illusion. Otherwise most of the windows are barricaded and the houses at the end of the alley have a shuttered look as if the contrasting gaiety below is unbearable to watch, with hundreds of men drinking, eating, singing and dancing to a weird cacophony of musical instruments. There is a constant surge of movement through the central passage which is scarcely 5 feet wide, lined with the tables and chairs from a chain of different restaurants.

The colour comes from the atmosphere. The place has such strength it can afford a graciousness too: inside one restaurant an old man moves silently around the room, nodding courteously as he sits at other people's tables and helps himself to their dishes of *mezes*, sufficiently varied to provide a meal in themselves. He is known as The Philosopher and once he was rich, entertaining his friends in this same place, so it is taken for granted that he will be looked after in his turn. I was made welcome, waved towards an empty place at one of the crowded outside tables where dishes of *mezes* were pushed towards me to pick at before my *shish* arrived from the restaurant. I do not smoke but blessed the precaution of buying duty-free cigarettes which enabled me to offer a golden packet of Benson & Hedges in return. The days when Turkish cigarettes were so superior that you found the slim, white packet with the crescent moon on the tables of our stately homes are over; today they are so inferior that English cigarettes are accepted gratefully where money would offend (since 1985 they are more available).

A constant procession thronged the alley, of strolling musicians and pedlars, some with baskets of stuffed mussels, another with a box of inner soles for shoes. A boy passed with packets of chewing gum, looking so forlorn that I gave him a 100-Turkish-lira note and was touched when he returned a few moments later and offered me a single stick as a gift which I accepted with pleasure while he smiled, no longer so forlorn.

The music ricocheted as each table vied with the other as if in competition. A man from Kars near the Russian border leapt into a narrow space and started to dance, shooting his feet forward until at last he stumbled and fell on the ground. His friend seized an accordion and the dancer recovered, sank to his knees and kicked out with even greater abandon while his companions rose to their feet clapping their hands like machine gun fire. A tiny woman in a patterned dress stopped at my table to strum a strange-looking instrument, a cross between a vast banjo and a colander, the noise as hideous as herself for she had a gigantic nose and was almost bald but she had the most beautiful smile so I smiled along with her until my attention was caught by a grey-haired man in a ragged coat who sat down with a sigh on a portable stool and opened his violin case tied up with string. His face reminded me of someone – a squashed countenance with his mouth pressed so tightly against his nose that his cheeks bulged outwards, then I realised – an ancient, Turkish Popeye. After removing his violin, he resinated the bow and started to tune it in the din, holding the instrument against his ear to hear the notes. Another man with a violin threatened to join us, prompting our own Menuhin to fiddle madly in order to establish his claim, and the rival moved on. To make a bolder impression, Menuhin started to sing as he accompanied himself but it was the saddest, faintest noise and he abandoned the attempt as the group at the table behind us started to chant in unison. How could his delicate sound compete in such an uproar? But it did a moment later, when a man opposite sang a passionate ballad and his friends called for silence as they listened in rapt admiration. Menuhin seized the moment and sidled up beside him playing with a devotion that could not be denied.

My *shish kebab* arrived and a place was found for it on the table covered with glasses and empty bottles. The window into the restaurant was open – a man looked out and I feared he was going to be sick but he fell asleep instead.

Usually I detest noise, yet this chaos was soothing. The exuberance appealed to my sentimentality with strangers making lifelong friendships in a moment, if only to be forgotten by the morning.

Everyone appeared to be celebrating.

At the end of the passage I was startled to see a man upside down and when I stood up for a better look I discovered this was a tumbler balancing on a chair balanced on a table. The atmosphere grew more abandoned and the sound of chanting swelled from the inside of the restaurants too . . . then all hell broke loose – the tumbler disappeared but chairs and tables rose in the air instead, hurled by two men who were fighting each other though not yet visible. People came running towards us trying to get out of the way as the fight zigzagged down the alley, like the stampede of men chased by the bulls at Pamplona. The waiter seized the dishes from the edge of the table and I pressed myself against the wall as the protagonists hurtled in our direction. Then they appeared, flailing in all directions, until they were pulled apart and led off bleeding profusely, and shouting angrily with half-hearted attempts to escape from their protectors and strike out again. The waiter returned with the dishes; the musicians picked up their instruments; everything continued as before. The interruption had lasted a matter of seconds.

Curious to see the inside of the restaurant, attracted by the sound of the music, I moved to another table inside to listen to a gigantic Turk called Kemmoni Hasan, playing a small violin with magnificent anger, accompanied by his son and another man whom he bullied like the prima donna that he plainly was. And rightly so, for this man was an artist and he knew it. When he stopped the noise broke out boisterously as before at a central table where a group of men were celebrating some special occasion, possibly the wedding of the drunken young man who staggered from table to table touching his glass of raki against those of strangers who welcomed him like a long-lost brother.

Two men sat at the table beside me with a mound of chips in front of them, one of which was thrust into my mouth in spite of my protests. One Turk was drunk, alternating between frozen gloom and hysterical happiness, while his tall, moustached friend demurred when asked to join in the singing at the central table and looked disappointed when they did not persist. Sure enough, when they asked again, he allowed himself to be persuaded and was kissed furiously by the 'groom' as he stood up and started to chant in a deep voice like a joyful gargle. Two men at the central table rose to their feet shaking their tambourines above them. Hasan watched all this impatiently, waiting to continue his performance but once persuaded, the tall singer was not going to stop and his chant was taken up by the others who started to clap their hands violently, cheering him on, forming a circle which started to dance around the room. As the circle spread, the waiter pushed my table against the wall and I recognised with irritation an English voice behind me. I turned round to see a peculiar middle-aged man with a Turk who was little more than a boy. The reason the English man looked peculiar was his hair – or the pretence of it. To describe it as thatch would be an insult to the cottages of the West Country, but this was the impression. Not even a thatch made of straw but more the plastic variety imported from the Continent. It glistened in the light and I wondered if it was courage which made him wear such a toupée, foolhardiness, or misplaced vanity.

In spite of this absurd roof, he was a nice man with the jovial face of Doctor Doolittle in the original illustrations of the book by Hugh Lofting, and he introduced me courteously to his companion, Ahmed, whom he had met on the boat from Izmir to Istanbul. Ahmed nodded, shining with pleasure, interested at everything around him, including his thatched friend, evidently proud of their relationship. I could not help speculating on how innocent this might be.

Thatch revealed that he came from Leeds where he managed a shop which dealt in leisurewear but was thinking of retiring to spend half the year in Istanbul and half in Ibiza.

'It's such a shame,' he sighed proudly, 'this is my last night and Ahmed has to sit for his exams tomorrow so he must go home early.' He said this affectionately, apparently pleased to put the boy's interest first.

'A little time yet,' he added as he looked at his watch.

'Examination,' Ahmed confirmed. 'In Turkey university big problem. In England easy. I go to Oxford for the university.' He grinned hugely. Good lord, I thought, what has Thatch been telling him? 'Oxford difficult too,' I warned him, falling into pidgin English.

Further talk became impossible as the dancing men chanted as if their hearts were breaking, stopped by a sudden cry for silence as an elderly man rose to his feet and started to declaim. For a moment I thought they would be impatient with such an interruption but they were deeply moved, clapping furiously when he came to the end of a passage before they allowed him to continue. This delicate tension was broken by the lurching arrival of a German I had noticed outside. He had a silly face, a ginger beard, and the nastiest shorts as if he had spent days staining them deliberately.

'Music!' he yelled, prancing in front of the orator before he slapped Hasan, the violinist, on his massive back. The orator sat down and I thought Hasan would start to play but he shook his head impassively.

'Oh dear,' said Thatch, 'why do the Germans have to spoil everything?' In the silence his voice rang out and the German youth swung round and his bloodshot eyes raked our table. Concluding that I was not the enemy he turned on Thatch instead.

'You do not like Germans?' he demanded.

'As a matter of fact I rather do,' Thatch answered calmly. Then, with fatal bravado, he added, 'but I don't like bloody Germans who spoil the fun for everyone else.' Inflamed though he was, the German got the drift of this all right and his glare swung from Thatch to Ahmed and back again. I knew it was going to happen, and it did. With a cry of triumph he grabbed the thatched toupée and flung it on the floor, running out of the restaurant.

With surprising tact, Hasan gestured imperiously to his accompanists, raised the violin to his chins, and started to play. Within a moment the chanting continued as if the incident had not occurred – nor had it, for them.

Thatch sat there motionless. I assume he had used some fixative to keep his roof in place for now his scalp was scratched and slightly bleeding. He was, as I should have expected, an ordinary, bald man, who looked much the same, but it was a shock nevertheless.

Ahmed picked the toupée off the floor and put it on the table. He was no longer smiling but it seemed to me that his obvious distress was caused by his friend's humiliation, rather than his own.

Thatch picked up his thatch which looked as lost as a fox on tarmac and went upstairs. I smiled at Ahmed but there was little I could say, even if I had spoken Turkish. When Thatch returned, complete with 'hair', the boy went upstairs in his turn.

'Would you like a drink?' I asked.

'I think I'll break my rule and have a raki,' said Thatch. He let out a terrible sigh: 'Poor Ahmed, poor, poor Ahmed.'

'I doubt if he cares a jot,' I lied.

'Oh no, I'm sure he doesn't,' said Thatch airily, 'but it makes all the difference to *me*'.

He tapped his hairpiece sadly: 'You see, Ahmed never guessed.'

Flower Sellers' Alley closes down at midnight as other places start to open. Thatch drank his raki and left with Ahmed who faced his exams in the morning. The chanting ceased, the Turks kissed each other on the cheeks as they said goodbye, so I paid my bill and left as well. The fun for the night was over.

3 The Pera Palas

When I booked into the Pera Palas that first evening, the entrance hall was strewn with chattering Japanese and the marble columns were plastered with posters. I have seen neither since. The Pera Palas has become my favourite hotel in Istanbul, the one I shall always return to though I was disappointed to look out on a brick wall in the morning instead of the Golden Horn. I could have been in Bootle. Once I despised the traveller who demands to see his room beforehand; now I ask for one of the splendid rooms on the middle floors.

The Pera Palas is a grand hotel. It is not the smartest in Instanbul and far from the newest, and, above all, it is not international with all the blandness that involves. In the Pera Palas you know you have arrived in Turkey.

'I wish to God I could lay my hands on the place,' a rival hotelier told me once, and I murmured a silent prayer that such a fate will not befall it. He would 'do it up'. I am sure he would keep it Turkish, even Ottoman, but he would do so with a vengeance with waiters dressed as eunuchs in the Harem bar and barmaids as Circassian slaves in the Sultana coffee shop. The mock glitter would replace the genuine tarnish, for I have to admit there is a sense of former splendour in the Palas where the wallpaper in the bar is slightly faded and the bar itself so high you almost need an alpenstock to climb on to the stool. This bar is downstairs with no rooftop panorama, but I have spent some of my most entertaining hours in Istanbul perched on one of those stools or seated with a group at a table.

The bedrooms have old-fashioned furniture and large beds with massive wooden headrests, instead of the clinical anonymity of most hotels today, and the bathroom is as massive as a suite. Breakfast downstairs is Turkish with little choice apart from slices of cheese and sausage, and there is no beauty parlour for the ladies. That is the charm of the Pera Palas. As the manager told me unctuously, 'We think of our guests as friends instead of door keys.'

The hotel was built in 1892 for the first passengers off the Orient Express who were brought by sedan chair from the station. Today you can see the original chinaware with the initials of the *wagons lits* in a glass case in the room off the great Middle Hall, the pride of the Pera Palas, an orgy of baroque in brown, yellow and gold with a high ceiling inset with domes and 'windows' and one of the largest chandeliers in the world. Drinks are served as well as coffee. When I entertained a sophisticated Turkish couple one evening they were amazed for they had never been inside the hotel before, just as most Londoners are unfamiliar with the elegance of the Ritz or the Connaught.

At the end of the room lies the most beautiful lift in the world, a graceful fantasy of open ironwork in contrast to those metal caskets which hurl you skywards in the best hotels. This lift rises as sedately as an elegant lady who has curtsied. One evening I noticed a young Irishman who had stopped over in Istanbul on leave from his job in Kuwait, still sitting there when I returned a few hours later.

'It's the lift,' he explained, 'I can't take my eyes off it.'

The names of the people who have ridden in this gilded cage over the years indicate the special nature of the place: Sarah Bernhardt; Mata Hari; Edward VIII; and Greta Garbo, who was no stranger to grand hotels. Agatha Christie is alleged to have started her *Murder on the Orient Express* in her bedroom upstairs. In 1983 I flew in from Dalaman on the same plane as Jacqueline Onassis and was impressed to find her checking into the Palas as well, without a bodyguard in sight.

The most honoured guest was Kemal Ataturk who rented a suite when he was an army officer. His rooms are preserved and shown off proudly if you ask to see them, with an Indian screen, Chinese drapes and signed photographs. The clock is stopped at five past nine, the moment he died on the morning of 10th November, 1938. I was told this had been prophesied by a fortune teller though she gave the time as *seven* minutes past nine. 'You see,' the manager informed me, 'his soul had left him two minutes earlier.'

A few years ago the hotel went into a decline due to a workers' strike which lasted a year at a time when other hotels were booming, but there has been a recovery since then with the walls repainted in their original colours of white and pale green, and though the prices rise slightly every year the Palas keeps to the policy of charging the lowest rates of the first-class hotels.

In addition to that fabulous lift, there is another fixture which symbolises the continuity of the Pera Palas. This is the impressive figure of the owner, Mr Hasan Suzer, a tall, handsome man from the south of Turkey with the distinction of a diplomat, and I imagine that diplomacy is a vital ingredient in running a great hotel. Mr Suzer observes everything and everyone with the watchful eyes of the hawk he resembles. We do not speak each other's language except through an interpreter but we forged a rapport, probably because this formidable man senses that I admire his hotel, and also through drink which is a language in itself and needs no understanding. He plies me with exotic tastes when I sit at his table, a Pera Palas cocktail of pomegranate, grapefruit, orange juice and Mahlip, a marvellous Turkish vermouth which is made in a distant town called Tokat and is hard to find in the shops.

I should not mind falling unconscious at his feet after a surfeit of Mahlip, for he would understand that, but I should hate to cross such a man in business, yet – and this twist seems typical of the Pera Palas – it must be the only hotel in the world where a share of the profits go to charity. Mr Suzer gives a percentage to children's welfare, another trustee contributes to education and the third to health. When you pay your bill you have the rare satisfaction of knowing that part of your money goes to children.

On my last visit I was disappointed to see no sign of Mr Suzer but the next morning when I settled at the reception desk I was presented with a bottle of Mahlip which he had left as a parting gift. American hotels like the Hilton are much the same all the world over. The Pera Palas in Istanbul is unique.

4 Exploring Istanbul

Having arrived after dark, I set out the following morning to explore the city on foot, walking down the hill to the right of the Pera Palas to the two bridges which span the Golden Horn. In between is the fish market with the gaping mouths and anguished eyes of species I had never seen before brought from the various coasts of Turkey, from the Black Sea to the Mediterranean.

As I reached Galata I was rewarded by the sight of the sun rising through the city's haze creating a fusion of grey and pink, with the first hint of sunlight reflected on the shimmering water already busy with boats. Above them the outline appeared of slender minarets and massive domes, as if suggested by a watercolour without a detail clear. In that smudged second my eyes – if not my camera – caught the beauty of Istanbul.

There is something especially moving about a man-made scene. A range of snow mountains is the affirmation of nature, but a building like St Paul's or the Queen's House at Greenwich, or a skyline like that of Venice, New York or Istanbul, is *our* justification – man's own defiant finishing touch. In St Mark's Square one Sunday afternoon listening to the municipal orchestra playing *Sheherazade*, I found myself in tears from the elation of such surroundings. The powerful shapes of Istanbul's skyline are sterner by comparison but I am thrilled every time I see them. This is partly due to the feeling that you are crossing from Europe into Asia though of course you are doing nothing of the sort for the Golden Horn is no more than an inlet and a tarnished one today. Asia lies on the other side of the Bosphorus and looks considerably less Asian than old Stamboul.

It is hard not to loiter near Galata Bridge. Men sell silvery fish displayed in baskets and others line the rails of the bridge itself dipping their lines in the hope of a smaller catch themselves. Amazingly they do succeed, and if you go down the steps at the far end of the bridge you will find a couple of primitive barbecues where you can sit by the water's edge while they grill you the fish that has just been caught. I have heard this compared more favourably to Tourkolimani (coincidentally the 'Turkish Harbour') near Athens, 'where they take the fish from the freezer', but my fastidiousness prevents me from eating any fish from these waters however 'fresh'. Indeed, I should think the fish themselves must be thankful for their release from these polluted waters as dark and dank as a great big sewer. Yet the fish exist, and I have no such qualms in the Bosphorus itself.

It is claimed that Galata Bridge gave its name to the card game, dating from the days when two English families lived on opposite sides of the Golden Horn but joined up in the evening to play their own version of whist. Because of the danger in crossing at night, they took it in turns saying, 'It's your turn to bridge.' An unlikely story except that the source is the impeccable Fodor.

Crossing the bridge to old Stamboul – and I relish being able to write such a sentence – you are confronted with the Yeni Cami, the New Mosque completed in 1663. Centuries of dirt from the coal-burning ferries have muted its elegance and I look forward to the day when this landmark will be included with other buildings which are being cleaned at the moment.

There is no denying that Istanbul is a dark and dirty city but so are London and Manchester, and when the grime is blasted away by jets of air the stone is revealed as delicate in colour as it was at birth. Then you realise how often the architect's inspiration has been obscured by adjacent buildings which diminish the proportions, and the dirt which conceals the texture. One advantage of being a photographer is the instinct which prompts one to look above eye level and appreciate a building which you might have ignored.

To the right of the New Mosque, an open space leads to the entrance of the Misir Carsisi – the Spice Market or Egyptian Bazaar – which is more of a general market now though spices and herbs can be found there in the stalls and shops which line each side. Upstairs, just inside the entrance, is Pandeli's restaurant beloved by tourists though I find it disappointing and prefer the Liman to the right of the bridge on the other side at Rihtim Caddesi (*Caddesi* means street), for lunch only, which has a better view of the waterfront, a calmer, airier atmosphere, and more interesting food.

From the Spice Market you can walk up to – or perhaps it makes more sense to walk *down* from – the great covered bazaar known as the Kapali Carsi.

It would be wretched to go to Istanbul without seeing the great architectural splendours of St Sophia, the Topkapi, the Blue Mosque or the mosque to Suleyman the Magnificent designed by Sinan, the finest Turkish architect of all, who combined immense proportions with perfection.

On such visits I wish I knew more. Far from despising the groups who whizz through Turkey in their luxury coaches on cultural tours, I envy them their expert guides and admire their advance homework which enriches their appreciation. Unfortunately the discipline of groups is not for me, and my waywardness is certainly not for them, but I realise this is one area where I am the loser.

Conversely, I relish the alternative excitement of such eccentricities as the Dolmabahce Palace which needs no special understanding. Anyone with an eye for the outrageous should go there.

It was built in the 1850s by the architect Balian in a style that could be described as Turkish-Indian baroque, a fantasy sugarcake of a palace from the outside, layered with icing, and as rich as a Christmas pudding inside and as hard to swallow. This effect is deliberate, an attempt to move away from the Turkish tradition of the Topkapi to a new style which would make the home of the sultans more acceptable to western eyes, unaware that westerners far prefer the exotic mystery of the 'East'. This was the last home of the sultans until it became the residence of Ataturk who used the apartments, which are still preserved, when he stayed in Istanbul, away from his new capital at Ankara. Even now, the ferryboats on the Bosphorus outside sound their hooters at the hour of his death.

After walking through the ornate gardens with real and artificial swans, you enter a triumph of kitsch with glass bannisters and chandeliers and gifts of Indian ivory tusks and polar bear rugs sent to the sultans, all in the worst possible taste. The Ambassadors' waiting room is plush and red, with gilt chairs and resplendent drapes, and every item of furniture is on such a gigantic scale that it seems out of all proportion, like the details of a set which have been magnified to reduce the size of the human beings inside it, for a film like *The Incredible Shrinking Man*. A glass chandelier from Queen Victoria to the Sultan Abdul Aziz weighs four and a half tons, and the Ali Baba vases could hide a family, let alone a man.

Hideous gifts from Queen Victoria abound and the guide informed me gravely that she was in love with the sultan. I noticed a portrait dated 1879 of Edward VIII in uniform: 'Presented to his Imperial Majesty the Sultan Abdul-Hamid-Khan Emperor of the Ottomans from Albert Edward Prince of Wales as a Token of Friendship.'

After passing through a music room to a bathroom in white marble which was used by the sultan 'after he made love', we ended up in a vast hall nearly the size of St Paul's, with a garishly painted dome and musicians' gallery used for religious feasts. It came as a relief to step down to the terraced gardens beside the Bosphorus. On a lesser scale, Dolmabahce might be a joke. Taken so seriously, this is a wondrous folly.

Close by, as an antidote, is the Naval Museum with replicas of the galleys used by the sultans complete with figures of their oarsmen and themselves, and the wooden figurehead of a lion which preceded the Imperial Boats. Also a rowboat, so small it might have been a child's, designed especially for Ataturk, carved most beautifully out of teak or mahogany. This was shown to me with considerable pride by Yusuf, my first guide to Turkey.

5 My first guide to Turkey

'I am number one man in Istanbul,' Yusuf Erkman informed me when we left the tourist office after he had been chosen as my guide. 'Twenty per cent of Istanbul knows me. I do not know them. Funny! My mother was a countess, my father was a count, I am son-of-a-gun.'

'You certainly are,' I agreed warily.

Wiry and swarthy, with the eyes of a practised interrogator, Yusuf exuded intrigue like a character from a film about the Casbah or the Grand Bazaar in Cairo, and I became his sweaty Sidney Greenstreet following in the wake of his Peter Lorre. He claimed he had lost his voice a few days earlier in Venice after travelling with a Japanese film crew on the new Orient Express, but this was hard to believe for he never stopped talking. To Yusuf, interruption was the spice of conversation, so long as the interruption came from himself.

At first I was dismayed by the stridency of his company. This was the first time I had been treated to the luxury of my own personal guide, and I began to realise what a delicate relationship this can be: if the guide is too clever, overwhelming the ignorant visitor such as myself with his superiority, moving at a breathless pace with no time to stand and stare, let alone sit and drink, this could ruin a visit. Fortunately, Yusuf and I developed a sardonic understanding based on mutual suspicion which changed to grudging respect as I began to appreciate his intimate knowledge of Istanbul where you have to be tough in order to rise to the surface. That marvellous, hovering skyline of mosques and minarets distracts the eye from the dark desperate alleys below thronged with hustling people, where Yusuf seemed at home. Indeed he descended on places with such authority that I wondered if he belonged to a secret, international police force and at one exasperated moment I asked him, 'How many men have you killed?'

'I prefer to make crime,' he replied mysteriously, then, to show he was joking, added, 'My wish is for the advancement of humankind and world culture.' He came out with lots of phrases like that.

A man of many roles, nothing was beyond his intelligence, nor had any human experience been denied him. Not only human, but extra-terrestrial too, though he was only permitted to hint at the proof he possessed of visitors from space. This reticence, which was so uncharacteristic, implied that he had been involved personally in this close encounter – and was sworn to secrecy. Had they landed, listened to Yusuf, and departed swiftly?

Disconcertingly, many of his wildest claims proved true. Allegedly fluent in sixteen languages, he had written a guide book to Istanbul in Japanese.

'You did not realise?' he rebuked me when he noticed my surprise. 'I *am* part-Japanese.' When a Turkish girl who worked in the architectural department of the government brought me a magnificent poster of one of the wooden houses she is trying to preserve, Yusuf nodded his approval: 'Yes, I took that photograph myself.'

'*You* did!' the girl and I exclaimed simultaneously and sounded so incredulous that Yusuf modified his claim: 'I held the camera for the photographer.' But I discovered that he had taken several of the colour shots for the brochure of the Pera Palas where I was given further proof of his versatility as he sketched me on a pink piece of paper in the Middle Hall.

'I did not realise you were an artist, too.'

'My pictures are everywhere in Spain.'

'The Prado?'

'Certainly not,' he rebuked me indignantly, 'all in private houses.' He signed the portrait with a flourish, 'El Turco', presumably the equivalent of El Greco, and I have kept it in case any fleeting twinge of vanity should ever rise in me again, for I would be reminded of the rosebud lips of Oscar Wilde, the mirthless eyes of Edward Heath, and a look of horror all my own.

'Lifelike,' I shuddered with the awful realisation that it was.

'Of course,' he smiled, accepting the compliment. 'No problem.'

As a guide, Yusuf could not be faulted. He protected me from the occasional beggar, pushing him out of the way with a volley of abuse, and shook his fist alarmingly at small boys who wanted to ask about my camera. He bullied the staff at the fashionable Facyo restaurant at Tarabya on the Bosphorus, but in doing so provided a banquet starting with giant prawns from Iskenderum in the south, followed by turbot from the Black Sea. As I drank the excellent Doluca dry white wine and looked out on the Russian tankers looming in the distance, with jaunty tugs thrusting through the choppy currents in the foreground, I began to look more kindly on Yusuf too.

One evening I asked Yusuf to join me at Rejans, a restaurant which several people had recommended. We had some difficulty in finding the place at the end of an alley off the main road to Taksim Square (Olivo Cikmazi 17, by Istiklal Cad. 244, near the Galatasaray), and my first impression was one of disappointment – plainly, Rejans had seen merrier nights.

It must have been an invigorating place when two White Russian sisters came here after their escape from the Russian Revolution, and started a restaurant for their compatriots. I wondered if my father had eaten here when he came to Constantinople and wrote that the nightlife centred around three places: 'The Turquoise restaurant, where every waitress was said to be a Russian princess (available) and usually was; the Rose Noir cabaret, where naughty Turks and hopeful-to-be-naughty Europeans collected; and Maxim's, an all-night cabaret run by an American negro, Thomas, who had married a Russian refugee of noble family, and had two *café-au-lait* babies.' My father described the scene when a White Star liner docked at Constantinople with a shipload of wealthy American tourists and the Russian waitresses jumped into Turkish bloomers ready to receive them. 'The tourists entered Maxim's like a chorus themselves, rushed to the tables around the dancing floor and stared at the bloomered dancing girls.

"Very Turkish!" explained their guide-interpreter. "Just like a harem – what?" Half an hour later he stood up and looked at his watch. "Ladies and gentlemen – this concludes our trip to Turkey. Ship sails in twenty minutes. All aboard for Jerusalem and the Holy Land – we now follow footsteps of the Master!" Thomas salaamed them out, bowing with pressed hands – "Good bye Effendi" – then he took off his fez and became a nice Mississippi negro again.'

Surprisingly Maxim's exists today. I have not been there myself, but judging by the description of the Irishman who admired the lift in the Pera Palas, it remains remarkably unchanged with a belly dancer carried in on a massive tray, displayed to a 'sultan' who examines her shortcomings as she is laid out before him. No one could accuse Rejans of catering shamelessly to tourists, though there is the gimmick of plunking down a bottle of lemon vodka (the bottle has a small lemon inside it) on the table, snatching it away again when the owner thinks you have had enough. As I savoured my pirozhki, I looked around me and wondered what Rejans would be like at the height of the season, crowded with people and full of life. . . . An eerie sensation engulfed me . . . not *déja vu* but the

real thing: I *had* been here before. Twenty years earlier I had come
to Istanbul on a journey which had proved so abortive that I had
relegated the incident to the back of mind in order to forget it.

It makes me uneasy to remember it now, but there was an unlikely
moment in my life when I was rich enough to own a car. Not only a
car but a salaried driver to go with it, for after passing my test I knew
that cars and myself were a lethal combination to be kept apart.
  The reason for this fleeting wealth was simple: my parents had
died, leaving me some money, and I had a successful job in
television as an interviewer for Associated Rediffusion in the early
days of ITV. After one of my programmes, *Living for Kicks*, a
magazine stated, 'Currently the talk around TV studios is: after
this, Dan can demand the biggest salary any TV star ever had.' This
lulled me into a fatal complacency and when AR turned down my
suggestion for a series on the First World War, describing it 'as dull
as yesterday's newspaper', I took six months' unpaid leave in order
to see the war graves at Flanders for myself, which only confirmed
my faith in the idea. Afterwards we drove to Paris and Marseilles
where we caught the boat to Istanbul. For some years I had been
enchanted by the names of Antalya and Alanya on the map, and it
was my intention to drive to the south of Turkey. A sillier way to
choose a destination could hardly be imagined, but this was my
objective. One obstacle prevented it: my driver, a massive East
Ender with the gentleness of the very strong, who had never been
abroad – and *hated* it. He disliked the food, the way the French
spoke French, everything distressed him. Above all, he missed his
girlfriend in Brentford with a torment which was painful to watch.
  We never reached Antalya. After driving for two days through
pouring rain from Istanbul to Izmir, he suffered a small nervous
breakdown and had to be flown back to London and his girlfriend.
Looking back, I can appreciate what an ordeal it must have been :
driving through a foreign country, unable to speak the language or
read the signs, literally sick from the food, and heartily sick of
myself for I regarded friction as an essential part of travel. When I
returned to England he continued as my driver exactly as before and
Turkey was never referred to, but at the time I was left in Izmir – the
very point where the real exploration was about to begin – with a car
I could not drive which I put on board an Italian ship full of
Germans heading for Piraeus. When we docked I paid a taxidriver
on the quayside to look after it until I met an English woman who
seized the chance to drive the car home while I flew back to my job
to be told, sheepishly, 'We've heard the BBC are doing a series on

the First World War so you may have been right after all.' Soon
after this I resigned.

So a journey which seemed so promising, with ample money for
once and no emotional distractions, ended in disaster. Even my
brief stay in Istanbul had been a disappointment due to a military
curfew with gunboats patrolling the Bosphorus, and a hurried
dinner in a crowded restaurant which did not seem particularly
Turkish. It was, of course, Rejans.

Would I have found my paradise if I had reached Antalya? I
doubt it. I was not ready to appreciate Turkey then. But now that I
had no car, no driver, and little money, I was ripe for the experience
and eager to see what I had missed before.

Yusuf never let me down until the moment of my departure. As I
waited for him in that splendid hall in the Pera Palas, I thought I had
caught him out at last when he failed to arrive. In my anxiety as it
became time to leave, I was hardly aware of the discordant music
coming from a distant room until it grew so overwhelming that I
stopped to listen – someone was playing the piano very badly. El
Beethoven? It had to be, and was.

'You did not know I am musician?' Yusuf looked up proudly as I
hurried in.

'No, but I recognised your touch.'

When the time came to say goodbye, he seemed sorry to see me
go and I suspected that behind the bluster he was just as vulnerable
as the rest of us. I was relieved by the return to arrogance as he
shook me clammily by the hand with the instruction that I should
ask for him again should I return to Istanbul: 'I will be happy to have
the happiness to be your guide-friend, and be sure I'll be the best in
Turkey.'

Information

Istanbul

Landmarks
Santa Sophia: If, god forbid, you have to rush through Istanbul with
time to see one landmark only, it should be Santa Sophia which is
one of the wonders of the world today. Outside it is simply impressive; inside it is stupendous. The sense of space is unsurpassed even
by St Paul's whose dome is actually larger. This effect is due to the
lack of clutter, with a clean sweep from the great supporting
columns – some of which were taken from the Temple of the Sun at

Baalbek – to a series of smaller domes mounting to the highest overhead. The mosaics date back to the sixth century when the Byzantine emperor Justinian built the church to replace the cathedral which had been burnt to the ground in the Nika riot. The Turks converted it into a mosque and the mosaics were concealed by plaster in the last century, scrupulously uncovered in this one by an American obsessed with Byzantine art, revealing the brilliant colours we see today.

In 1935, Ataturk converted Santa Sophia into a museum, breaking another link with the past while bringing Turkey into the present.

If you are planning to visit Santa Sophia or other landmarks on your own, make certain they are open beforehand for they close, confusingly, on different days. Santa Sophia is closed on Monday.

Topkapi is closed on Tuesday. With the finest situation in Istanbul, on the point where the Golden Horn joins the Bosphorus, the Topkapi deserves a morning or an afternoon on its own. A palace has existed here since the time of Constantine, but it was Mehmet the Conqueror who enclosed the original site in 1457, six years after he occupied Constantinople. For the next four hundred years this was a city inside the city, an Ottoman Vatican, the seat of government with the Sultan's Harem and courtrooms, housing several thousand people. Going around the exotic labyrinth today, one can see the richness which surrounded the sultans but also sense the suffocating restriction of their lives, well conveyed by Eric Newby in his book *On the Shores of the Mediterranean* (Harvill Press, 1984).

As Newby explains, the rule of the sultans was absolute for they governed an empire which stretched from the Atlas Mountains in Morocco to the Caucasus. This accounted for the layers of hierarchy inside the Topkapi where visitors were killed if they happened to set eyes on a woman in the Imperial Harem, and even the eunuchs wore high collars to prevent them from looking left and right. The White Eunuchs were the elite and volunteered; the Black Eunuchs who supplanted them were castrated by monks who razored 150 negro boys a year, burying them up to their haunches in warm manure afterwards which might explain their melancholy disposition. In the reign of Murat III there were as many as 800 Black Eunuchs in the Harem, and several hundred rooms in the Harem altogether. Today no more than twenty-five are open to the public but these are evidence enough of the fabulous decorations, tiled courtyards and coloured glass windows, occasionally relieved by a touch of humanity like the murals of food painted in the hope of tempting a sultan's son who had lost his appetite.

The Topkapi is extravagant compared to the ultimate simplicity of the architect Sinan. After the hothouse atmosphere you can relax in the excellent open-air restaurant alongside, though the only alcohol is beer.

The Grand Bazaar, or *Kapali Carsi*: In spite of its size and the thousands of shops, it is so well designed you can find your way about easily. Whole streets are devoted to a single trade – coppersmiths, carpetmakers, etc. – but if you are going specifically to buy it certainly helps to go with a Turk for the price drops instantly.

The market is centuries old, built by Sultan Mehmet II, and has been destroyed by fire on a number of occasions – as recently as 1954 – but always rises again and remains much the same.

Afterwards, you can take the road lined by modern shops which leads down to the Spice Market below, with *Pandeli*'s Restaurant at the far end and Galata Bridge beyond.

Nightlife

Do not expect a readymade district waiting for you, like Soho in London, St Germain or Montmartre in Paris, or the Plaka in Athens, lined with amusing little bars. In Turkey drinking is accompanied by eating, so most of the fun is found in restaurants, ranging from the rougher atmosphere of Flower Seller's Alley, to the smart, seafood restaurants at Tarabya, to the newer restaurants on the way to the airport.

If you wish simply to drink, the rooftop bars of the modern hotels, the *Hilton*, *Sheraton* and *Etap*, off Taksim Square, offer sensational panoramic views and though the prices are more expensive you have the chance of meeting people who speak your own language if you are on your own. A number of bars, only used by men, open at midnight in Siraselviler Caddesi off Taksim. If you want cabaret, with belly dancers and 'atmosphere', it is best to go to the places where this is laid on professionally for tourists like *Maxim's* and the *Galata Tower*, rather than the more half-hearted versions in various back streets which cost much the same, though you may have the compensation of finding yourself alone instead of surrounded by tourists. For genuine atmosphere, you will have to look extremely hard and enlist the help of Tukish friends. Istanbul used to be famous for a gypsy quarter where you arrived around nine at a private house. You were served food and drink and everything appeared ordinary to the point of boredom until eleven o'clock when the food was removed from the low tables, which you sat beside on cushions, and the girls came on and started to remove their clothes. The old men – probably their fathers and uncles –

hammered and wailed on their musical instruments, reaching a crescendo as the girls stood naked and jumped on to the tables, grinding and bumping to the music. Little was left to the imagination, and at this point the customer grabbed the girl he fancied and was led to a back room to indulge in strange Turkish delights.

Sadly, the gypsy shebang closed down after the last declaration of martial law. The authorities believe that the old tradition gave a bad image to Istanbul, but I expect it will recover if only in a neutered form for the benefit of tourists.

Hotels

The *Pera Palas*, Mesrutiyet Cad. 98–100, Tel: 145 2230 telex: 24152 pera tr. My personal favourite.

The *Divan Hotel*, across from Taksim Square. Tel: 146 40 30. Though I have eaten in the first-rate dining room, I have not stayed here but have received good reports. It seems to provide the answer if you have an aversion to the large American type hotel.

The *Sheraton Hotel*, Taksim Park. Tel: 148 90 00. Telex: 22 729 sher tr. Instinct advises me against the style of the Hilton and Sheraton class hotels, but this is inverted snobbery for they are, at least, professional. I have stayed at the Sheraton and found the rooms impeccable, the service efficient, and the rooftop bar attractive with sensational, panoramic views. The open-air pool is superb. The lower floors are well designed and airy. The obvious charge that you might be in Detroit is not valid: when I was there the downstairs lobbies were thronged with Turks visiting one of the fairs held throughout the winter, selling Turkish produce, leading to a street of shops which stay there permanently. The food is a welcome surprise, far from the international blandness I expected, and an Ottoman restaurant was in preparation which will specialise in reviving Turkish dishes. This initiative and the undeniable vigour of the Sheraton in Istanbul is due to the general manager, William Bauer, an ambitious young American who plainly knows his job and likes it. He is an admirer of Turkey and the Turks, like myself, which is how we met.

So, what is the problem? As someone pointed out, 'At the end of the day you have to go to the cashier.' By British standards, the prices are extremely high and unless you check them carefully beforehand you might be in for a shock. This does not apply to those who are rich enough to book into Hiltons and Sheratons the world over, never searching for an alternative.

The *Dilson*, just off Taksim Square, is less expensive. Tel: 143 20 32.

Books on Turkey

Fodor's Guide to Turkey deserves its popularity, is full of surprise and interest and better written than you might expect. *The Traveller's Guide to Turkey* by Dux Schneider is my own favourite. *The Companion Guide to Turkey* by John Freely is not a guide in the hotel/timetable sense, but covers the country in greater detail. Mr Freely (misspelt as Freeby in *The Times*, which was an unfortunate error to make where a travel writer is concerned) is an expert on Turkey, already distinguished for his book *Strolling in Istanbul*, written with Hilary Sumner-Boyd. I am told that copies of the latter still exist in the international bookshop near the bazaar.

On a more archaeological level, the books by the late George Bean are outstanding: *Turkey Beyond the Meander, Lycian Turkey, Turkey's Southern Shore*, and *Aegean Turkey*. There is also *Ancient Civilizations and Ruins of Turkey* by Ekrem Akurgal (Istanbul 1978). *The Lycian Shore* by Dame Freya Stark I took with me on my first journey and it proved the best of company. Though published in 1956, it evokes the coastline gloriously. Then there are classic travel books like Rose Macaulay's *Towers of Trebizond*, and the recent *Journey to Kars* by Philip Glazebrook. I owe a considerable debt to all these books, not only for their information but also for the pleasure the writers have given me.

For specialists, visiting eastern Turkey, there are *Eastern Anatolia and the Urartians* by Professor Afif Erzen, and *The People of the Hills* by C.A. Burnley.

I would recommend any visitor to read one of the biographies of Kemal Ataturk, which will help to put the modern history of Turkey in perspective and explain why he is revered in Turkey today. Above all, take a Turkish phrase book or dictionary.

Otherwise, I should not burden yourself with more than two books when you are travelling. Conversely, this is the chance to take the classic English novel which you have always intended to read. It is strangely satisfying, under an alien sun, to read a book which evokes the flavour of England. During my journey to Van, *Bleak House* was my solace and constant companion, enriching every day.

Travel companies

As Turkey becomes the new pleasure ground, more and more travel agencies are offering holidays. Rather than make a list, I recommend the following which impress me as outstanding.

Sunquest is long established as far as Turkey is concerned, due to the personal interest of A.E. Kilic, the managing director. The choice of coach tours is imaginative and covers many of the places mentioned in this book. A friend of mine, the writer Donald Rumbelow, travelled on the Crusader Tour and wrote to me afterwards, 'Turkey was wonderful! The Crusader Tour is well worth taking. I found it tremendous value for money. As it was April it was right at the beginning of the season. Hardly a tourist except for the occasional coachload of Germans. Most of the roads were deserted. We covered 1,200 miles in the fourteen days. This seems a lot but actually there was plenty of time for stops and sightseeing.' Out of season, the Crusader can cost as little as £439 for two weeks, confirming the claim that it is 'tremendous value'. Sunquest goes to the furthest corners of Turkey: Ani, near Kars, Dogu Beyazit, and Van. Their Grand Tour takes three weeks, costing a little more than £700. Obviously you should write for the latest catalogue which reveals the variety of the holidays now on offer, including Bareboat Cruising (on your own) and the Istanbul-Kusadasi Cruise. Sunquest's choice of hotels is outstanding, including the *Divan* and the *Pera Palas* in Istanbul, and the *Talya* in Antalya. One of Sunquest's Two Centre holidays, dividing your time between them, would be ideal. Address: Aldine House, 9–15 Aldine Street, London W12 8AW. Reservations: Tel: 01 749 9933. Telex: 23619.

Swan Hellenic, famous for their Art Treasures Tours of the World, have a nineteen-day tour of eastern Turkey which goes three times a year, going to many of the places referred to in this book. Unashamedly deluxe and elite, the cost is £1,161 but the coach party I encountered at Lake Van had the benefit of a lecturer and were overjoyed by the smoothness of their journey. Address: Beaufort House, St Botolph Street, London EC3 7DX. Tel: 01 247 0401.

Falcon could be invaluable if you want 'low-cost flights' to Turkey, going straight to Dalaman Airport from Gatwick. As the prices vary throughout the year, you should contact Falcon direct and might receive a bargain.

Falcon Sailing offers Independent Charter, Flotilla Cruising, and a Villa-Flotilla, with a week on shore and then afloat.

Falcon Holidays are based in Bodrum and Marmaris where the hotel is the excellent *Halici* which I have stayed in myself and can recommend as the best inside the town of Marmaris. Prices range from £268 (out of season) to £371 in August for two weeks. Car hire can be arranged, or you can take advantage of the excellent Turkish bus service – one of the most efficient and cheapest in the world – to explore the coast.

1 *above*: The bustling Galata Bridge in Istanbul which crosses the Golden Horn

2 *left*: Lioness and cub guard the entrance to the Dolmabahce Palace built in 1853 as the last residence of the Sultans

3 *left*: The author with Mr Hasan Suzer in front of his hotel, the Pera Palas in Istanbul

4 *below*: A ferry down the Bosphorus, beside a row of traditional wooden houses in Istanbul

5 *right*: Three old men in Giresun, embracing on the feast day of Bayram

6 *left*: The church of Santa Sophia in Trabzon built in the middle of the thirteenth century, with exceptional frescoes inside

7 *below*: Mustafa in the square at Trabzon, with Kemal Ataturk behind him

8 *right*: The Sumela Monastery, a cliff-face eyrie glimpsed between the trees below, famous for their twenty-six shades of green

9 Three pictures taken at the top of the Zigana Pass in the Turkish alps

10 *left*: The sacrificial slaughter of a sheep in Gumushane

11 *below*: The extraordinary rock formations in Cappadocia – churches at Goreme

12 *right*: Some of these conical shapes are known as 'fairy chimneys' but there are alternative descriptions. The effect is due to the layer of harder volcanic lava on top of the softer tufa, protecting the conical shapes as they were whittled away by erosion

13 *below*: It takes the eye some time to register the astonishing fact that the holes in the tufa stone are houses

14 *above*: A family on the train to Tatvan, with wild flowers picked from the fields during one of the stops

15 *below*: The early Armenian church on the island of Akdamar in Lake Van

16 *above right*: Carvings depicting scenes from the Bible decorate the outside of the church, remarkably well preserved after a thousand years

17 *below right*: The main street of Van with the down-to-earth air of a frontier town

18 *above left*: The seventeenth-century castle of Hosap near Guzelsu on the way to Iran

19 *right*: The elegant bridge below the fortress is 500 years old

20 *above right*: 'Joe (far left) – the Turkish crossing-sweeper' at the *garaj* in Diyarbakir in front of one of the buses taken by the author

21 *below right*: A monumental vanity, the stone heads at the top of Mount Nemrut. The last fell several years ago, the others have been hoisted upright

22 *above left*: A lion at Nemrut, roaring at the sunrise

23 *below left*: Hercules, looking up to Mithridates I, the father of Antiochus who erected this relief in his memory

24 *above*: A Turkish woman leads a camel, donkey and dog through the woods near Uzuncaburc inland from Silifke

25 *above*: The genuine and little-known tomb of the Fearless King

26 *left*: The phallus carved at the base in honour of Priam

27 *above right*: Young wrestlers at Finike, also famous for its oranges

28 *below right*: A woman weaves a *kilim* on her loom at the top of the hill above Kale with the waters of Kekova below her

29 *above*: The harbour of Kas curving round protectively with the tilted lighthouse at the end and the Greek island of Castellorizon beyond

30 *below*: One of the sarcophagi stranded in the water near Kekova

31 *above right*: Luxury at the Talya Hotel in Antalya. The sea is reached by a lift from the swimming pool above

32 *below right*: Termessos – the mountain city which defied Alexander the Great who turned away

33 *above*: The 'land' across the river from Dalyan

34 *left*: Lycian tombs carved in the rock at Dalyan, probably from a scaffolding lowered from above

35 *above right*: Dursun Mutlu, the sponge-diver, in front of his charter yacht, the *Maya*, with the castle of Bodrum in the background

36 *below right*: In Turkey a woman's place is often in the field and this plough near the road to Bozborun was drawn by cows instead of oxen

37 *left*: The frozen falls at
Pamukkale caused by the
calcium deposits from the hot
springs above Hierapolis
nearby

38 *below left*: The Stadium:
one of the landmarks
uncovered by recent
excavations at Aphrodisias

39 *right*: The massive Medusa
head at Didyma, cracked but
still malevolent

40 *below*: The entrance to the
Temple of Hadrian in the street
of the Curetes, Ephesus

41 *left*: Abidin Kurt, the indispensable guide to Dalyan

42 *below*: Guests leaving the wedding party at Candir on their way to collect the bride from Ortega

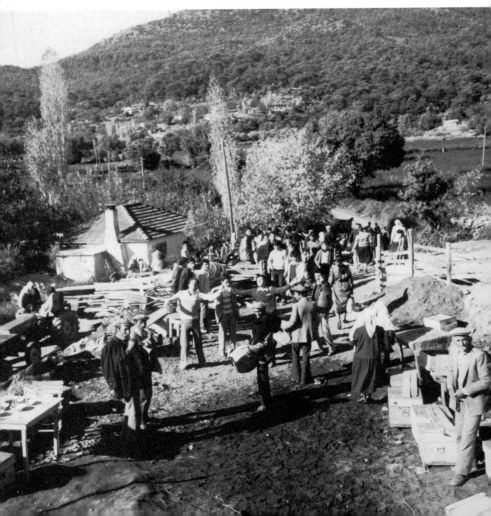

Falcon, 190 Camden Hill Road, London W8 7TH. Reservations: Tel: 01 221 6298 (charter), 221 0088 (scheduled). Also at Brazenose House, Brazenose Street, Manchester M2 5BH. Tel: 061 831 7000; 5 Royal Exchange Square, Glasgow. Tel: 041 204 0242.

Luggage
Once you have packed, unpack and remove at least a third of what you planned to take. If you need anything, you can always buy it in Turkey and items such as leather are cheaper anyhow. Only take what you can carry. You can buy useful carrier bags in Turkey, stronger and larger than our own, for things you wish to bring back.
    Do take: a bathroom plug; a box of tissues; ample film for your camera; and one of those mosquito machines, if you can find them, which you plug into the wall.

Tourist offices
There are tourist offices in most towns in Turkey. I have found them exceptionally helpful. Usually the directors speak English and the reproductions in the various tourist leaflets prepared by the Ministry of Culture and Tourism are so enticing that they encourage you to go in search of the original sites yourself. The main bureau in Istanbul is at Mesrutiyet Cad. 57, Galatasaray. Tel: 145 68 75. There is also an office at the entrance to the Hilton Hotel. If you need advice in London before you go, the Turkish Tourist Office is at 170–3 Piccadilly (first floor), London WIV 9DD. Tel: 01 734 8681.

Restaurants
The *Abdullah*, on a hill above the Bosphorus, is probably the best in Istanbul. It was closed when I went there for lunch, so it is wise to check in advance and make a reservation for it is several kilometres out of town. Even looking at it, I could recognise that this is exceptional. A low building overlooks the gardens where they grow their own vegetables – on a hot day it would be a treat to eat in such surroundings. Address: Emirgan Koru Cad. 11. Tel: 163 64 06 or 163 52 91.
    The *Facyo* restaurant at Tarabya is where Yusuf ordered a banquet by the Bosphorus which first convinced me of the range of Turkish seafood. I have been told that this attractive restaurant has 'gone off', but by now it should have come on again. Address: Kirecburnu, Tarabya. Tel: 162 40 01.
    Palet 3, also at Tarabya, one of several restaurants bearing that name. I was taken there on my last visit by two close Turkish friends and enjoyed a memorable dinner, mainly of seafood. Specialities

include baked shrimps, seafood soufflé – and fish salad. Also, outstanding smoked fish, served like smoked salmon. All this with music and entertainment too. Tel: 162 08 93. There are three *Palet* restaurants, *1*, *2* and *3*, named after the owner's pastime as an amateur artist.

The *Domani* restaurant, also near Tarabya, on the Istanbul side, has the advantage of your being able to lunch on the wooden balcony overlooking the water which laps a few inches below every time a ferry moors at the nearby jetty. Exactly the jolly, unpretentious type of restaurant I had been hoping to discover for myself. Reached from the bus which stops near the *Carlton Hotel* on the main road, or by ferry. Address: Sevki Gurses Iskele Cad. 14–16, Yenikoy. Tel: 162 10 94.

The *Sulukale* has been recommended to me, with 'gypsy' atmosphere.

Lavatories
It might seem odd to include lavatories after restaurants, though I suppose this is a natural sequence. Undeniably, going to the lavatory is one of the hazards of travelling in Turkey for plumbing has declined since the days of the Romans. Also, the procedure is not what we are used to. The idea of washing ourselves afterwards is alien, and the practice of putting used paper in a basket or bin strikes some people as distasteful. Even so, to avoid blocked pipes, it is vital to respect this request.

Then, in these days of unisex, there is the confusion of the illustrations on the doors. I met a languid though fiercely heterosexual Englishman in Ankara who admitted his dilemma: 'I wore high heels at several balls at Cambridge, but I've *never* smoked a pipe! Where am I supposed to go?'

A warning
If you are travelling in early summer, be aware of the end of Ramadan, a variable date which marks the end of fasting. I arrived once in Bodrum to find the streets clogged with people, the bars overflowing, and no accommodation apart from a plank in a corridor next to a communal lavatory in a small house where scores of young Turks seemed to sleep in shifts. More seriously, the banks were shut for the four days of the public holiday. My indispensable Giro Post-Cheques saved me as usual, for Turkish Post Offices remain open until eleven at night, even at weekends.

6 Eating your way through Turkey

When I arrived in Istanbul a leading gourmand and newspaper editor, Ridvan Mentes, invited me to the elegant restaurant in the Divan Hotel and introduced me to 'the leading *maître d'hotel* in Turkey' who surprised me with the claim that Turkish cuisine is the third best in the world, after French and Russian. This is a bold boast, disregarding the infinite variety of Chinese dishes, but it becomes less so when he told me that the Ottomans brought paprika to Hungary and coffee to the gates of Vienna, where the army used the sacks of the coffee beans as sandbags.

Ironically, Turkish coffee, known the world over for its richness, is one of the few products which needs to be imported today, unlike tea which is grown at Rize on the Black Sea. Otherwise, Turkey is self-supporting and this is the secret of Turkish cuisine – its freshness. In England 'fresh' can mean 'thawed' or 'just opened'; in Turkey there is no such thing as yesterday's food. Every tray in the restaurant's glass cabinet is made that morning, and the Turks are dismayed by our travesty of *doner kebab* which we allow to linger in the kebab houses of Soho until the meat begins to curl. To make it worse, we use pork instead of lamb. Ideally, it should be goat or veal.

Turkey is now the larder for the Middle East and when I approached the Xanthus Valley a few weeks later it looked like a plain splattered with ponds until I descended and found these were polythene sheets covering thousands of greenhouses which grew tomatoes. One of the most delightful features of Istanbul is the presence of kiosks at almost every corner where they squeeze you any fruit in season: orange, grapefruit, even strawberry; or the national drink of *ayran* resembling buttermilk, a yoghurt mixed with water. In the south, you see bananas growing on trees beside the road.

If you like the taste of yoghurt, olive oil and garlic, and the use of aubergine and green pepper, you will relish Turkish food. It is not so much the cooking as the presentation of the produce which is different, enhanced by herbs and spices. Best of all are the *mezes* which introduce every meal, the small dishes of cold appetisers which fulfil that description yet provide a meal in themselves, especially at lunchtime.

This is where a word of warning is helpful: do not order too much too soon. There are no licensing hours in Turkey, no cry of 'last orders', no hovering waiter who glares at his watch as he waits for you to leave. It is never too late to have lunch in Turkey unless it is time for dinner. The only haste will come from yourself, and a meal in a Turkish restaurant should last several hours if you are in good company.

Never make the mistake of ordering every course simultaneously, for if you do it will all arrive at once. The Turks do not think in terms of separate courses, so order as you eat.

Unlike the British hors d'oeuvres trolley where you point to various wilting concoctions – a dry sardine, a limp lettuce leaf, and some tinned sweet corn – receiving a dollop of each, you will be given the whole dish of *mezes* to yourself in Turkey. So if there are two of you, or more, it makes sense to share a dish and afford a greater variety. If one taste proves so delicious that you want more, you only have to order it. The difficulty lies in resisting the temptation to order too many dishes from the wide selection which includes: a pureé and other forms of aubergine such as the cold, braised *imam bayildi*, which means the 'priest fainted' because it was so delicious; the classic *cacik*, cucumber with yoghurt and garlic; beans of every description; *dolma*, vineleaves stuffed with rice and pinenuts; *biber dolma*, stuffed green peppers; even a *tarama*, for the Turks claim that every Greek dish came from them. These dishes, which manage to be sharp yet subtle at the same time, provide the ideal food on a hot day, eaten under a trellis of vines in the open air. They are one of the reasons for travelling through Turkey. If you live in London it is impossible to recapture such an atmosphere, but I urge you to go to the Topkapi restaurant in Marylebone High Street which serves a wide selection of *mezes*, including the marvellous Circassian chicken which is a national dish though hard to find in Turkey. This would give you a chance to experiment with the complementary tastes and note the names of those you like.

Not only is it possible to eat well in Turkey, but the cheapest is frequently the best which is not the case in Britain where the caffs serve some of the most revolting fry-ups in the world.

The difference between the grander *restaurant* and the simpler *lokanta* is a fine one. There is a salutary story concerning a customer who ate in his favourite lokanta every day until he was called away on business. When he returned a few months later he was dismayed by the increase in his bill and asked what had happened.

'When you were here last,' the waiter informed him proudly, 'we were a lokanta. Now we are a *restaurant!*'

Part of the fun in Istanbul is discovering your own, small kebab lokanta, as I did when I was attracted by the smell of barbecued meat and the glimpse of a friendly atmosphere in the Ocakbasi, down some steps at 52 Siraselviler, off Taksim Square. Small succulent pieces of lamb, served with a tomato paste of herbs and spices accompanied by a bottle of lager, cost me less than £2 on my first visit in 1982.

On my brief visit, in November 1984, at the furthest point of the Datca Peninsula among the ruins of Cnidus, a group of workmen, the only people there apart from a small garrison of soldiers, waved to me to join them as they ate their lunch on the ground. No sandwich box for them, but different types of bread, cheese and yoghurt, and a choice of several dishes laid out on plates. Because the quality of the produce is universally high, even the simplest meal is astonishing by British standards.

The only risk is a slight monotony which can be avoided if you make your choice as varied as possible, while seizing on the best. Whenever possible, I started the day with yoghurt and honey (*yogurtlu bal*) for Turkey has the freshest, homemade yoghurt I have tasted, particularly delicious when made from goat's milk. A cleaner taste can hardly be imagined, the perfect antidote to a night on the raki. Mixed with a local honey, like the dark, pine variety you can buy in the market at Marmaris, with some fresh fruit such as melon or peaches, this is the height of luxury for me, preferable to the traditional Turkish breakfast of white cheese and black olives. Tea is the universal drink throughout the day (pronounced *chai*) and the green tea made from sage is well worth trying, but tea is never served with milk. I ask for *limon* and hope I am not given a glass of neat, acid juice as I was in Datca, but just a slice. Turkish coffee is sublime, served in the tiniest of cups and preferably accompanied by a glass of water (pronounced *soo*). If you want it *medium* sweet, ask for *orta*. If you must resort to Nescafé, do so in private. It exasperates the harassed restaurateur when a family descend with their own tin and demand jugs of boiling water as if this is their right.

At lunchtime, the incomparable *mezes* are matched by a hot appetiser called *borek*, deep-fried pastries filled with cheese and spinach, or sometimes meat, rolled up like a cigar – hence *sigara boregi*. On my first day in Marmaris I spent an entire afternoon consuming these, washed down with cool white wine – the combination was irresistible, though I have noticed that even tepid food tastes marvellous in the open air.

Kebab is the universal meat dish and there are many varieties. My favourite are the small pieces of lamb – *sis kebab* – which you can find everywhere, even in the bus depots, and the excellent meatballs – *kofte* – also served on skewers. The *Adana* kofte is highly spiced, and worth trying if your palate is jaded. *Cumin* is used consistently.

When you tire of kebabs there is a magic word to remember though I seldom saw it on the menu – *sauté*. If you ask for a sauté of lamb (there is usually lamb in the glass cabinet which you can point to) the word should produce a tasty goulash with onions, tomato and herbs. In Cappadocia, they have a stew served in individual pots with the addition of green pepper including the hot variety. In both cases, the best side dish is *rice*, larger-grained and tastier than the packets we are used to in Britain.

Chicken is the obvious alternative. If you have the chance, try the Turkish speciality *Cerkes tavugu*, prepared for the sultans by the Circassian (hence Cerkes) girls in the Harem, who were apparently the most beautiful of all. But even if they were hideous this dish should have won the sultan's heart. Basically, it consists of pieces of chicken pounded together with a walnut sauce, the result of hours, if not days, with a pestle and mortar which release the oil from the nuts. In the luxurious Buyuk Efes hotel in Izmir it is served like paste but I prefer the small pieces of chicken in the version served at the Koru Motel at Pamukkale, one of the few places where I found it on the menu. Back home I made my own, speedier version with the blender: boiling the chicken and cutting it up into small segments, adding a small cupful of the stock to half a pound of shelled walnuts in the blender, with a slice of white bread soaked in milk and squeezed dry, a teaspoon of paprika and a clove of garlic, blending them together briefly, and served cold, though not chilled. It worked marvellously.

Another advantage is the range of fish from the various coastlines, from *hamsi*, the small anchovy, and *palamut*, like a big mackerel, from the Black Sea, to red mullet from the Bosphorus, bass from the sea of Marmara, and giant prawns from Iskenderum in the south of the Turkish Mediterranean. Cold mussels stuffed with rice are a feature in Istanbul – *midya Dolmasi* – and I am assured that the clams taken from the water at Tarabya can be trusted too. If you go to the markets, most of the gaping mouths and distraught eyes are unfamiliar, though I recognised sole in Izmir. I recommend sturgeon and swordfish whenever you can find it.

There are numerous sticky cakes for the end of the meal, though I prefer a mixed salad of local fruit and nuts mixed with honey, or simply a slice of melon.

Though Turkey is a Moslem country, drink is less restricted than it is in England except for the fast of Ramadan when even a glass of water is forbidden in the middle of the day in the eastern regions of the country. In many ways the nicest drink under the Turkish sun is an Efes beer, a lager which makes Tuborg pale by comparison. Turkish gin is vile, but vodka is good and can be drunk with one of the excellent bottles of fruit juice available. *Vodka ve vishne*, vodka and cherry juice, is a favourite combination. There is excellent wine, especially the white *Villa Doluca, Cankaya*, or the slightly cheaper, and to my taste better, *Kavak*.

Raki, of course, is the national drink, the equivalent of ouzo with an aniseed base, sometimes described as 'Turkish dynamite'. I love raki; it hates me. There have been mornings when I have vowed to end the affair, but I have always gone back. Most Turks have the sense to limit themselves to a couple of glasses, unless they are celebrating, which they usually are, and it is vital to eat copiously if you are going to indulge in more. There are several brands: *Yeni raki* is the most popular, but if you are buying a bottle as a gift or want to bring one home, choose the brand with the red label which is more expensive but noticeably better.

The Turkish for 'cheers' is pronounced *sherry-fay*, one of the first words I learned.

7 From Istanbul to Trebizond

The ship was just the right size. The *Izmir* was built in Bremerhaven in 1955, weighs 6,000 tons and carries three hundred passengers, though there seemed far fewer, so it was not an impersonal cruise ship but a working boat where it was easy to find your way around.

The usual dockside delay was no hardship as I studied my fellow passengers, many of them peasants who seemed to be transporting their entire homes in sacks, and once on board I had a stroke of luck: due to some mistake over the bookings, my cabin was occupied and I was transferred to the suite reserved for the President of the Shipping Line. Never averse to comfort, I made no argument as I was taken to my state room, which led to a spacious cabin and the grandest luxury of all: a bathroom with a massive bath which even sported a plug.

Leaning over the rails when I went on deck, I found my bearings for the first time in Istanbul as the *Izmir* moved away towards the opening to the Sea of Marmara. With that astounding frieze of mosques and minarets behind us we sailed out of the Golden Horn and turned north towards the Bosphorus. On the European side I recognised the distinguished outline of the Pera Palas on the hill above, the two towers of the Etap Hotels, the Sheraton below Taksim Square and the lower shape of the Hilton further on.

On the Asian side, at a greater distance, lies Uskudar, better known to us as Scutari with Florence Nightingale's lamp preserved in the Sultan Selim barracks where she ran her hospital in the Crimean War. Interested in graveyard sculpture, I had been to the British cemetery which is dominated by a memorial to herself and the British killed in that war. Like so many graveyards on foreign soil, it is beautifully maintained with a surprising variety of tombstones in addition to those I expected. The tomb to General Mariau Lanciewicz, described as the 'ex-dictator of Poland', who died at Haidar Pasha in 1887, is decorated appropriately with canon balls, while that of an English teacher, Evelyn Imrie, born 1924, died 1975, suggests a mystery for she became the headmistress of the

English High School for Girls in Istanbul in September 1974 yet killed herself six months later. I wondered what had gone so tragically wrong. The graves which moved me most were those for the young: Warrant Engineer Samuel Scot RN of *HMS Ark Royal* who died on 5th June 1920 – 'His sun had set while it was still day' – and Julian Henry Layard, the Assistant Military Attaché to the British Embassy at Constantinople who died of typhoid fever while on duty with the Turkish forces in 1870; and, younger still, the Hindu and Sikh soldiers of the Indian army who died in 1919 and 1920, remembered by rows of crosses frequently bearing the name of Singh.

The *Izmir* gathered speed, hugging the European shore, past the confectioner's palace of Dolmabahce, underneath the gigantic spans of the only suspension bridge in the world to link two continents. It was built by a British-German consortium, opening in 1973 in time for the fiftieth anniversary of the Turkish Republic with an astounding total of 34 million cars crossing between Europe and Asia in the first twenty-eight months, earning 523 million Turkish lira in toll fees which paid for the entire construction. The mind boggles when you realise that before 1973 all such traffic crossed by ferryboat. Now a new bridge is being contemplated from Topkapi to Uskudar though I hope this never happens for it would mar the isolation of this magical promonotory.

It is hard to explain the exhilaration of sailing up the Bosphorus when there are rivers and waterways of comparable size in other parts of the world. Probably it lies in the constant distractions and contrasts: scattering a shoal of tiny fishing boats with indignant hoots on the ship's siren, while colossal Soviet tankers glide by whose captains and crew must eye these waters with a jaundiced jealousy. In places the straits are so narrow, a mere 500 yards compared to 3,000 at Buyukdere, that I could recognise the grand old wooden houses, the *yalis*, I had seen on a previous ferry trip, darkly stained and derelict yet still impressive with their spacious windows and wooden balustrades, sometimes three stories high with a central attic roof to add the extra height which makes their proportions so pleasing to the eye.

The Bosphorus is 30 kilometres long, Russia's outlet from the Black Sea to the Sea of Marmara, past the Dardanelles and finally into the Mediterranean. It is intensively alive with boats of every variety above and fish below; dolphins are less frequent nowadays after senseless slaughter but can still be seen, and one winter a bear was sighted on a passing ice floe, or so I was assured by Yusuf.

We turned into the Black Sea, once a brackish lake, purified today by the fresh water pouring from the Danube, Don and Dnieper, and the first surprise is the discovery that the name is the literal truth for the water is as black as quink. Alerted by a jolly burst of music from the loudspeaker which remained mercifully silent otherwise throughout the voyage, I hurried down to lunch.

Food is the vital interruption of every voyage and the dining room on the *Izmir* proved encouraging with tables laid out with glistening glass, cutlery and linen napkins, and vases of fresh carnations. The service was unobtrusive and the food better than I dared to hope with four courses for dinner including fish, a vegetable such as fresh green beans or stuffed pepper, as well as meat and dessert, refreshingly unpretentious compared to the thawed out Sole Véronique or Duckling à l'orange served from plastic bags in British restaurants today, and tastier too. Including tea you can have a total of seven meals for an all-in price added to your ticket of little more than £15, surely the best value offered by any ship in Europe. The wine, of course, is extra.

That evening I wallowed in my bath, the water enriched by a sachet of badedas which I discovered at the bottom of my sponge bag, and all the grime of Istanbul and a residue of raki poured out of me. I fell asleep in the president's palatial bed a moment later with a sense of deep contentment.

As we approached Sinop the following morning, I was invited to the Captain's bridge with none of the usual intimidation of chains to block one's way or signs proclaiming STOP. On the contrary, Captain Huseyin Eyupoglu welcomed me as if he was the host of a successful cocktail party, talking and laughing with a group of Turkish passengers standing on the deck alongside. An alert and cheerful man, he could have been the animated conductor of a Viennese orchestra and at one point dived towards a small boy who had broken free and was tottering determinedly towards the wheel with the obvious intention of assuming the command himself. Gently but firmly, the Captain turned him back. Such informality would not be tolerated on the run down the Mediterranean but the Black Sea coast is unspoilt by tourism. Captain Huseyin told me that no more than fifteen British passengers travel in the busy months of July and August, and virtually none in the kinder months of May or September.

Unlike the British who are reluctant to sing the praises of their countryside, the Turks declare the beauty of Turkey with disarming pride. 'This land is for someone who loves nature,' the Captain told me, pointing to the shore and the hills immediately behind. 'You will find pools and rivers but few restaurants and facilities.'

Immensely good-humoured, Captain Huseyin was tactful too and treated a young cadet in the gleaming white uniform of the mercantile marine with the exaggerated respect due to a twenty-two-year-old though the youth was hardly lacking in self-confidence. Attaching himself to me as we went ashore, the cadet proved as self-possessed as Yusuf, kissing his friends on the quayside and along the street, peacock-proud as he told them he was going to the training school in Samsun to become an officer. He had eyes like melting chocolate.

As soon as I left the long arm of Sinop's jetty I understood the Captain's point about the lack of 'facilities'. Once inside Sinop and I was practically through it, down the main street busy with cobblers and barbers – the most important men in Turkey for they know everything – and out the other side of the narrow peninsula overlooking an attractive bay. On other coasts this superb situation would have been seized for a holiday village or a restaurant at least, but here it was wasteland used for an abandoned dump, with the rusting frames of bicycles.

Simple though it is, Sinop will become popular soon enough and I should not be surprised if foundations were rising on that dump already. There is a touristic hotel and several restaurants and if I had not been on the *Izmir* I should have liked to stay there myself for the isthmus is attractive and redolent with history from the days when it was named Sinova by the Assyrians. Though it seems an impregnable fortress surrounded by water on three sides, it has changed hands with surprising frequency, occupied by the Hittites and the Persians, the Romans, Byzantines and Ottomans, and in spite of the protected harbour the Turkish fleet was destroyed there in 1853 in a sudden attack by a Russian squadron which sank every ship but one, drowning or killing 3,000 Turkish sailors. Public opinion in Britain and France was outraged and hostilities were declared officially four months later, the start of the Crimean War.

The massive walls of the fortification still dominate the town with a prison famous for its dungeons where the prisoners were chained and put in fetters, sometimes up to their necks in water. As the guide sheet remarked, 'This is very discouraging things for the prisoners to escape.'

Before I returned to the *Izmir* I sat down with the pristine cadet who regarded me as a foreign attribute to impress his friends in a pleasant tea garden shaded by willows, near the quay. As it was impossible to order a beer, I settled for a mixture of boiling water, a squeeze of lemon and two sugar lumps served in a glass too hot to handle, and by the time this arrived the *Izmir* hooted a warning that it was time to leave.

Every journey should have a disappointment, and mine came at Samsun, our next port of call. The dockside which stole the trade from Trebizond is industrial and interminable so I needed a taxi to take me into the town itself. Due to an out-of-date guidebook with photographs of cunning duplicity, I expected a quaint little fishing village by the sea though I should have checked this picturesque image against the population of 150,000. I ate my dinner in a bleak, open-air complex which had just been used for a trade fair but was all too deserted now. Though a glimpse of the centre of town showed it to be a fraction more lively, I was relieved to go back on board the *Izmir* where I poured myself a bath at once using the last of the foaming badedas which postponed the horrid realization that the water was being sucked from the harbour below, as foul and stinking as a cesspool. I leapt out and waited, towelled, shivering and filthy, until we were safely out at sea when I ran a second bath and washed myself clean.

Giresun, where we docked the following morning, was different again with an eastern atmosphere enhanced by the first day of Kurban Bayram, a religious holiday which lasts for four or five days when sheep are sacrificed to Allah. This is the second Bayram festival; the first, known as Seker (sugar) Bayram, marks the end of the fasting of Ramadan, two months and ten days earlier.

Going ashore I found that most of the shops were closed because the owners were visiting their families. Children were dressed in their Sunday best, and the crowds inside the mosques overflowed into the streets where men embraced and kissed each other with special warmth or, in the case of someone older, were kissed on the hand which was raised to their forehead as the younger man vowed, 'I obey you always.' In one courtyard outside a mosque, a solitary, legless man squatted on the stone after the others had gone, counting the money they had left in his cap.

The sense of celebration was blunted when I met a Dutch passenger who was appalled by what she had seen a moment earlier – a sheep with its throat cut, the blood pouring down the cobbles of the narrow lane. The slaughter is supposed to take place in a back garden, but if the people are poor the street has to do instead.

'Damn!' I exclaimed, with the instinctive regret of the photographer who has missed a scoop. Inexplicably, I had left my camera in the cabin. Hurrying back from the ship, I found that the cobbles had been washed clean and the only sacrificial sheep was a cheerful animal led on board a small fishing boat to be killed at sea. Unaware of its fate, it munched contentedly at a plate of food put on deck by one of the fishermen as a last supper.

Back on the *Izmir* Captain Huseyin and his crew were sharing the sweets and cakes which are part of the feast day's ritual, while a message of goodwill from their union was relayed over the loudspeaker. As we continued our journey in the afternoon the ship sauntered along the coastline, which could have been the shore of some Italian lake with a green foreground broken by occasional villages with hills climbing steeply behind. I had the luck to get into conversation with a Turkish husband and wife, Inal and Gulen Atac, who were travelling to Trebizond on the way to their annual visit to their home in Gumushane where Inal was born.

When I told him of my disappointment at missing the sacrificial slaughter that morning, Inal explained that this takes place over several days and invited me to stay the night at his home on my way south where he was going to sacrifice a sheep for his neighbours. This cheered me up greatly.

Leaning over the rails, absorbing that beautiful coastline and about as relaxed as it is possible to be, Inal told me about his grandfather who had been finance minister in Ataturk's government. I had been wondering why the Russians missed their chance in failing to take the Bosphorus as retribution after the First World War, and he explained that the Revolution which separated the Russians from the Allies had brought them closer to Ataturk's concept of a Turkish Republic. I was glad to learn more about this extraordinary man, in many ways the most formidable figure of the twentieth century, having replaced an ancient oppression with a modern state. The personal courage of Kemal Ataturk is legendary and undeniable, and I admired the way that he was a fallible human being too, with a lusty appetite for life.

Born in 1881 in Salonika, Mustafa Kemal graduated from the military academy in Istanbul and led the Turkish army in the defence of Gallipoli, routing the British and Australian expeditionary forces with the combination of brilliant strategy and ruthlessness which enabled him to maintain his own regime when he became the first President of the Turkish Republic in 1923. The British cannot conceive of the reverence with which the Turks regard him, unless we imagine a leader combining the audacity of Churchill and the sanctity of the Queen. Every village has his monument, every office his photograph. 'He was everything,' said Inal Atac. He added, softly, 'He still is.'

Ataturk's summer house on the Black Sea lies outside Trebizond, a white Italianate building with the hint of a grand Swiss chalet, set in splendid gardens with flowerbeds surrounded by pine trees which have grown so tall they partly obscure the view of the town below. The house was presented to the President by the grateful citizens of Trebizond, and though he only came here twice it is now a museum with photographs of Ataturk including several with Edward VIII on his visit to Turkey when he was Prince of Wales. The Turks rather than the tourists visit this monument to their leader, peasant woman with shawls and soldiers with shaven heads. Their gentle awe is impressive.

We reached Trebizond early in the evening. *Trebizond!* What romance that name evokes, though it is known as Trabzon today. I should have been warned by the treachery of my guide book and my mother's disillusionment when she fulfilled a lifetime's ambition and took the Golden Road to Samarkand to find a dirty, dull town which bore no resemblance to the image raised by Elroy Flecker. In the same way, I had been lulled by Rose Macaulay's *The Towers of Trebizond*, unaware that this marvellous book has more than its share of fantasy, savouring her descriptions literally: 'Still the towers of Trebizond, the fabled city, shimmer on a far horizon, gated and walled and held in luminous enchantment.' Alas, the towers of Trebizond today are those of a flour mill and an industrial chimney.

After that initial shock I fell in love with the place, the most sympathetic of all the Black Sea towns I went to. The Hotel Ozgur, crowded with the usual visiting football team, this one from Malatya, overlooks the main square which is lined with trees ranging from palms to pines, with a statue of Ataturk in the centre flanked by beds of red flowers and tea gardens which open at seven in the morning. This is the heart of Trabzon, large enough to provide a peaceful oasis in the traffic, and I drank my coffee there the next morning. A soldier lay asleep at the next table, a sack at his feet; a man nearby was writing a letter; another fondled a glass box containing perfumes and potions. A family sat down with the women wearing colourful headscarves, no rush, just a way of passing time with tea, coffee or a beer. A small boy approached me dressed in his best clothes for Bayram, almost a uniform with grey flannel trousers, smart blue blazer and shiny black shoes.

His shyness was delightful, overcome by his curiosity as he tried out his few words of English. His name was Mustafa.

'How are you?' he asked with considerable effort.

'Very well, thank you,' I replied gravely. The bossy waiter tried to shoo him away as if he was a cat, but I held him with the offer of a Pepsi. Afterwards, being photographed in front of the statue of

Ataturk was excruciating for Mustafa as he tried to control a sneeze, and finally succeeded. Then it was clenched fists, a wondrous smile, and I left the happier for having met him.

Because it was Bayram, most of the restaurants were closed. In the evening I stopped two Turks in a car beside the curb to ask if they knew of one which was open and it turned out that they ran a kebab house in Barking. Before I could hesitate, I was bustled into their car and driven at a furious pace out of town. We drove interminably and I began to grow anxious for they were tough-looking men and it was rash to get in a car with complete strangers in a part of northern Turkey where the Lazes are notorious kidnappers. It occurred to me also that they might be taking revenge for some injustice they had received at the hands of the English in Barking.

At last we hurtled into a smart open-air restaurant with a bandstand beside the sea where the Turks ordered a bottle of raki and started to tell me about their kebab house, explaining that they had been forced to return to Turkey for their national service. That accounted for their alarming, shaven heads. Now my anxiety was due to the quantities of food which kept on arriving, including the excellent Black Sea fish, palamut. I thought it was time to call for the bill and discovered they had paid it already and would not accept a lira towards it.

As they dropped me off at my hotel, one of them told me, 'Do not write that we are bad people.' How could I?

The lay-out of the old walled city is spectacular, with a ridge between two deep ravines suggesting that the ancient name of Trapezus was based on the shape of a trapeze.

Today, the finest building is the Church of Ayia Sophia 3 kilometres from the centre of town, on a flat piece of land overlooking the sea. Even here the photographs deceived me though they were postcards taken recently, showing the church on a windswept barren plateau. Yet one of the most attractive features is the informal garden with shrubs and trees and buttercups in the grass which enhance the church itself which was built in 1250. After the fall of the Comnenus Empire in 1461 it was converted to a mosque and is now a museum. The frescoes were covered with whitewash until a hundred years ago, and then with a thick plaster which damaged them further. They were restored as recently as 1957 and the scenes are still magnificent, especially the 'Casting out of the Devil'. The sculptured frieze in the south porch represents the story of Genesis with an eagle, the Comnenus symbol, perched on the arch above.

The Church of Sophia conveys the grandeur of the past when Trebizond was a Byzantine stronghold for two hundred and fifty years, the last Christian outpost in Asia after the fall of Constantinople, surviving for eight more years until the city was besieged by Sultan Mehmet II in 1461 and the Emperor David Comnenus surrendered.

Trebizond prospered on the trade from the Black Sea to the east, providing the gateway to Armenia when it was a free Roman city, and the transit point in the early 1800s for the camel caravans which crossed the mountains on their overland route to Persia. Ten thousand Persians lived in the city before 1914, with a large Greek population expelled by Ataturk. The last invaders were the Russians who occupied the city in the First World War, making advance arrangements for a visit from the Tsar, but when the Bolsheviks took over they stopped the exports to Batum and Trebizond started to decline as a commercial centre. The Russian border lies ominously close today with a Turkish military zone starting at Hopa beyond Rize. It takes an hour to drive from Trabzon to Rize along a pleasant coast road with ample opportunities for a swim including the sandy beach at Arakli where the water is so clear I could see the small crabs scuttling over the sand underneath. From the *Izmir* the water did appear to be black, but here it could have been the Mediterranean. I lunched in the open-air Plaj Restaurant beside the sea, watching the Turkish families who were celebrating the holiday playing ball with their children and their dogs in the shallow sea. This was a hot day towards the end of September but it had been raining heavily the week before and at times the Black Sea is so rough that even though the rocks on either side act as breakers the few hotels are flooded.

The day when it becomes predictable will be the end of travelling for me, but I doubt if this will happen in Turkey. Of all the misleading photographs in that wretched guide, that of Rize was the most enticing, a Turkish version of Clovelly in the middle of the last century, but Rize is a city with a bustling market and a vast square where stalls sell corn on the cob, and *two* statues of Kemal Ataturk nearby, one in a great white cape. The most unexpected feature in Rize is the Botanical Garden at the top of a steep hill where Turkish families enjoyed their afternoon tea at tables under exotic palm trees with a panoramic view over the city. The view on the other side proved more sensational with lines of green terraces which provide Turkey with most of its tea. These were started by two Englishmen at the beginning of the century, and could pass for Sri Lanka now. Turn round and you are back in Turkey.

By now I had acquired a guide, Koksal Basaran, and a young taxidriver called Osman, always laughing, ready to venture anywhere. When I expressed my astonishment at Rize's Singhalese tea plantations, Koksal gave a superior smile: 'East is east, and west is west,' he explained, 'but Turkey is something else.'

Information

Trabzon

Sailings
Reservations can be made beforehand with the representatives of the Turkish shipping line in London: *Walford Lines*, St Mary Axe, London EC3A 8BB. Tel: 01 283 8030. The *Izmir* left Istanbul at 10.00 on Thursday, arriving at Trabzon on Saturday at 13.00. Prices are so cheap that I recommend travelling Special First Class or even Lux. Though prices might have risen, they should be around £50 each including food. The freight of cars is reasonable too.

Hotel
Hotel Ozgur. Highly sympathetic with a helpful reception, a pleasant restaurant and a bedroom with private bath which overlooked the square. Tel: 1319 2778 3064.

8 A Turkish bath

On my last evening in Trabzon I had a Turkish bath. Like abstinence, this is something one should experience but I cannot recommend it. A Turkish bath is exactly that for the Turks go there to wash themselves clean. This is not a luxury but a sheer necessity for their domestic plumbing is deficient, to put it as kindly as possible, which explains the row of taps outside of every mosque where men perform their ablutions. In the days before the advent of the less romantic sauna, Englishmen revelled in their Turkish baths, proceeding from rooms which were hot, hotter and almost unbearable, half-glimpsed figures vanishing into the steam, sweating out the impurities for which they had paid so dearly. There was something aristocratic about the Turkish bath, especially that in Jermyn Street, frequented by princes of the realm and even a foreign king, Carol of Romania, who woke up there with such a hangover after a binge before a royal coronation that he insisted on taking his white-jacketed attendant with him to give him support in the procession. The crowds assumed that the man was an admiral or a foreign minister at least and the grateful king awarded him the highest sash and order his country could bestow afterwards. Or so the story goes.

The real Turkish bath is 'something else' altogether. I arrived feeling fit and hoped to leave fitter. As I entered the inconspicuous *hammam* off a side street, everything seemed in order with the promise of a bath, douche and masaj. I deposited my wealth and the *tellah* gave me two thin, striped towels and a pair of wooden clogs, apparently called *nalin*, on which I clip-clopped precariously to a cubicle where my doubts began. Off it was a tiny washroom with a marble seat and washbasin. No heat, no steam. I rang impatiently for the *tellah* who reappeared and threw several bowls of boiling water over me as I tried to explain that I wanted the steam room which did not appear to exist. After an especially scalding splash my cries persuaded him to run some cold water into the basin and he went to work with a vengeance. Soap is a crucial part of this ordeal as one is smothered in suds with no thought of eardrums or eyeballs and at last I could appreciate that look of abject misery when a dog is forcibly shampooed. As I had bathed my way across the Black Sea in my stateroom, I found this purification unnecessary and gestured to the man to stop. To my relief he threw more bowls of water and wiped off the residue of bubbles with a flannel, but then came the worst assault of all. Wearing a rough hand pad or mitten, which would make a loofah feel like velvet, he scraped my skin so violently that I could feel it coming off, especially those layers of sun tan acquired so arduously.

'*Masaj!*' I yelled unwisely, 'that's all I wanted, apart from steam.' The word *masaj* was recognised and he kneaded a few muscles at a vulnerable point on my shoulders to show that he understood and waved me towards the marble slab though this was far too small to lie down on. I was about to protest at the absurdity of a *sitting* massage when he pounced.

The truth had dawned already that I was badly out of condition, also that even the fittest of the British have bodies like jellies compared to those of the Turks who are built of teak. Even so, I was unprepared for the excruciating pain inflicted by this unassuming, silent sadist who squeezed my skin as if he was trying to break it, struck my spine with such a volley of blows that I thought he had broken it, and finally twisted my limbs to the point where I could hear them crack.

'Enough!' I gasped in surrender and at last the man withdrew. After dressing with difficulty, I limped back to the Hotel Ozgur and staggered into the foyer sweating profusely at last. I slept badly that night for my skin was so raw it was sensitive to the slightest turn of the sheet and it took two days before I recovered.

Other people will have better experiences of the *hammam*, at least I hope they will, for they differ from town to town. Suspecting I had been unlucky, I persevered and tried again with varying results: the *hammam* in Marmaris was little more than a washroom; in Istanbul, where there are eighty *hammams* to choose from, the building was famous and certainly impressive but the masseur almost finished me off for good; the best was at Kusadasi which was smaller but just as beautiful to look at, with the luxury of real heat at last in the central *hararat* steam room.

If you are looking for the 'trouble' promised by Fodor who advises, 'You *must* go with a Turk of the same sex or you are bound to get into trouble of some sort or another,' you will be disappointed. If you hope for the tickling tiny fingers of the Thai massage parlours you will be dismayed. If you are a masochist you may be satisfied.

9 Across the Turkish Alps, over the Zigana Pass

I said goodbye to the Newcastle family who had travelled on the *Izmir*, the only other British passengers. The father, who looked as if he was in his twenties, worked for an English-owned factory in Istanbul but instead of returning home for his annual holiday he was taking his wife and two redheaded children on an exploration of central and eastern Turkey in order to understand the country better. Promising to let me know what he thought of Kars near the Russian border, they drove with a flurry of waves out of the main square on their way to Erzerum.

My first stop was Sumela, one of several astonishing monasteries to the south of Trabzon. This northern district could be described as the Turkish Alps: the valleys were lush with rivers racing under the arches of ancient bridges and herds grazed peacefully on the green slopes near wooden chalets raised on stilts. Childhood memories were stirred as I was reminded of similar scenes when driving through Bavaria, Austria and Switzerland with my parents.

After 30 kilometres we reached Macka, derived from the word Macuka which means *stick*, used by the peasants to defend themselves in the past, and turned left down the Altindere Valley for Sumela. The road to Sumela is noted for its twenty-six shades of green, and I could well believe it.

Sumela, 54 kilometres from Trabzon, is astounding. At first it is hard to make it out, perched on a mountain ledge so high it is barely discernible between the branches of the trees with their leaves in the different shades of green. Then I spotted the ancient monastery pressed so tightly against the sheer cliff it might have been painted, yet this inaccessible eyrie was once the most important monastery in Asia. The legend that a Greek monk, the Blessed Barnabas, saw the place in a vision and sailed from Athens in AD 385 with the icon of the Virgin Mary painted by St Luke to place it inside a cave in the mountain face seems no less crazy than any logical explanation for choosing such a perch. But it became so important that Alexius II of the Comnenus dynasty chose it for his coronation as the Emperor of Trebizond in 1349.

Eager to discover what lay behind that sheer facade which is nearly 4,000 feet high, I crossed the bridge over the river and started to climb the steep track which ends at last with a set of ninety-three steps cut into the rock. Today it requires an effort to comprehend the community before the Greeks were expelled by Ataturk in 1923 and the wooden structure of the roof was destroyed by fire in 1930 once the monastery was abandoned. Now it is crumbling and pitifully in need of the repairs which are carried out under the guard of a few soldiers. The frescoes inside the church which date from 1740 have faded, and the doors and windows are gaping holes; there is rubble everywhere which one has to scramble over to see the colossal bird's eye view of the valley from the open arches. It is tempting to close your eyes to the dereliction and the vandalism of today's visitors who scratch their names on the frescoes in search of immortality in the most pathetic form of vanity, and let your imagination soar instead. The place must have been sublime, secure in its solitude and safe from attack, which is why it was chosen in the first place, regardless of the monkish dream. The significance of Sumela as a civilised centre for culture and religion, with three chapels, immense dormitories, corridors and courtyards, and a library which was world famous for its thousands of books in the fifteenth century, becomes comprehensible if you think of it as a *peaceful* stronghold, and then is deeply moving.

Down again beside the river, Turkish families were laying out their picnics on the tables provided by the forestry department with open barbecues where they could cook their kebabs or the small mountain trout bought from the fish farm on the way. I was ravenous after the climb, and Turkish hospitality is unequalled, so I was tempted when one family insisted that we join them after I took photographs of their children, but it was time to continue our journey to Gumushane through the Zigana Pass and as we climbed the zigzag roads and hairpin bends with even Osman losing his constant smile I was thankful we were doing so in daylight.

Anyone who thinks of Turkey as a barren land would be astonished by this alpine landscape, for though the peaks of the mountains are bare, there are forests below, and the bottom of the valley is green and dotted with clusters of small villages, each with its minaret, which makes the distant scene look friendly rather than remote. The shades of green were broken by the autumn colours of yellow, brown and bright red ash. Dust was raised by the thundering lorries with eyes to ward off the evil eye painted above the headlights. Even the mudguards were decorated. This must have been a formidable trek in the last century when it served as the overland route to Persia, or further back in the time when the Greeks were defeated in the battle of Cunaxa in 401 BC and Xenophon led his army of 10,000 mercenaries in an epic retreat, describing the moment when they caught sight of the Euxine (as the Black Sea was called) on their way from Persia to Trapezus. His soldiers shouted out in triumph, 'Thalassa! Thalassa!' – 'The sea! The sea!' – and passed the word down the column. As Xenophon wrote in the *Anabasis*, 'Then suddenly they all began to run, the rear guard and all, and drove on the baggage animals and the horses at full speed, and when they had all got to the top, the soldiers, with tears in their eyes, embraced each other and their generals and captives.'

Did this occur at the top of Zigana Pass? Certainly it is high enough. The air became keener and the slopes were covered with falls of white and pink flowers like tiny tulips, and then we reached the summit of a few houses where newly killed lambs were hung outside for travellers to choose their joints, while the severed heads were scattered in sinister profusion at the back. We selected our cuts and cooked them ourselves on the open barbecue where they burnt at an alarming speed and proved excessively tough, partly because this was today's kill and was cut in a way we were not used to, but Osman devoured every morsel and though I was disappointed that the lamb was not tastier I put it down to a good experience.

With no knives or forks, I used my hands which I cleaned afterwards in the village fountain, and walked down a muddy track where irate mothers called their children inside when they saw my camera, while a man sat on a wooden chair, a bandage round his head, with the elegance of a dandy posing for his portrait, the mountainous landscape as the 'backcloth' behind him.

10 A beautiful death in Gumushane

We crossed the Zigana Pass. The lush coastline with the tea plantations at Rize, and the twenty-six shades of green of Sumela, were left behind as we plunged down the gorge of Harsit Cayi towards the town of Gumushane, entering the plains of Asia which stretched interminably, where herds no longer grazed on favourite slopes but moved with their nomadic shepherds following the seasons.

Gumushane (pronounced Gooma-sharni) means Silver House, named after the silver mines mentioned by Marco Polo. The modern town was adopted by the wealthier citizens of Trebizond as a summer resort after the old town, 4 kilometres away, was destroyed in the Russian occupation of 1916. Though its popularity as a resort escaped me, the home of Inal and Gulen Atac (pronounced Att-ash) was the most attractive house I stayed in during my travels in Turkey.

Educated at Trinity College, Cambridge, Inal has a heartfelt affection for England, as I have now for Turkey. It was through him that I started to comprehend the Turkish hospitality which is inviolate for it applies to everyone. Osman, my taxi driver, was prepared to drive down the road to look for accommodation on his own but he was included as a matter of course.

'He is my brother,' Inal explained simply. We were all 'visitors from God'. I was to experience this again at a peasant's hut during my search for the tomb of the Fearless King, and though it was primitive by comparison the hospitality was no less gracious than Inal's. It is a way of life we have forgotten, in the south of England, at least. Perhaps, in the wilder regions of eastern Turkey, a visitor from God would be killed without compunction after leaving the house if he has caused offence, but while he is under the same roof he is honoured.

Inal is one of those rare people who actually believe that they owe something to life. He is respected as a dedicated, highly efficient businessman, representing the British firm of Glaxo in Istanbul with considerable success for Britain, yet he is the personification of courtesy, greeting me with a generosity I can never repay, attentive to his servants, with a love for his family which is unconcealed. There is a reason for the special closeness of the family today: a few years ago, Gulen was injured so severely in a car crash that she was left in a coma with little chance for recovery. Refusing to accept this, Inal flew her to Zurich after she had been unconscious for two months and if his wealth ever needed justification it had fulfilled it now, for after expert treatment Gulen regained consciousness and has now recovered. 'It was worse for them,' she says, 'I knew nothing about it.'

The atmosphere at Gumushane that evening was one of particular happiness. The splendid wooden house is 106 years old, and Inal's grandfather, his father and himself were born here. He returns every year if only for a week, the annual event for the elderly caretaker whose eyes were bright with excitement, his hands stained from the juice of the walnuts he had been collecting in the orchard. The rest of his year is devoted to looking after the property and preparing for Inal's visit, chopping firewood, attending the beehives, picking the fruit from the orchard for the homemade jams. This was as close as I shall get to Chekhov – the fine old wooden house, the retainer who reminded me of Firs, the orchard outside which included cherry trees and a copse so dense you had to force your way through it. A few years back Inal gave a corner of the land to a relative who sold it to a construction company, to Inal's bitter disappointment. They were starting to build and I glimpsed the scaffolding rising up beyond the pine trees at the bottom of the orchard. Now the town council want to take some land on the other side to widen the road. I could feel the stain of 'progress' advancing, hear the axes.

None of this threatened when we arrived in the dark shortly after eight and were taken to our rooms, removing our shoes before we crossed the white scrubbed wooden floors. Reverentially, Inal showed me the room where Ataturk slept on a visit to his finance minister which has been preserved as a monument ever since, and afterwards we sat down to a banquet at the long table on the wooden verandah under a trellis of vines which serves as a dining room when the weather is warm. Consuming course after course, we washed down the good bottle of raki we had brought with us, a woefully inadequate contribution compared to the quantities we drank before the night was over.

Yoghurt was welcome on the morning after, accompanied by a colourful variety of jams prepared by the old retainer and his wife:

apricot, plum, cherry and rose petal which recalled a long-forgotten taste, made so simply from rose petals mixed with sugar and placed in the sun which turns it into jam after a week. The petals had fallen from the roses which surround the house and all the fruits came from the orchard except for the strawberries which 'Firs' had bought in the village. I mixed my yoghurt with honey from the comb, followed by hard boiled eggs, tea and coffee.

When breakfast and the buzz of conversation drew to a close, Inal invited me to watch the sacrificial slaughter of the sheep which had been bought by 'Firs' a few days earlier. The idea of this ritual shocks the sentimental British, and daunted me until I saw it for myself. This was no cobbled back street in Giresun where the animal might have been frightened, this was a pastoral setting in a clearing under the trees with banks of yellow and pink flowers behind where the tethered sheep was munching at the grass contentedly. While the women stayed in the background, Inal murmured a quiet prayer as the retainer caressed the animal and cut its throat with one swift stroke of the razor-sharp knife. The animal's body kicked and shuddered as the blood poured out but it could have known no pain. When I described the ceremony as 'beautiful' on my return to England, people could not accept it, but I see nothing to regret in this ancient tradition which marks the end of the fast of Ramadan. After the slaughter, the carcass was blown up like a balloon to make it easier to dissect, and the meat was distributed that afternoon to the poorer families who can rarely afford it. As many as thirty people received one of the portions which were laid out on tables, and every part of the sheep was used including the skin which was salted and rolled up as a gift.

Compared to the horror of the abattoir with the smell of blood terrifying the animals as they are dragged to their slaughter, this was a beautiful death in Gumushane.

11 A lunar landscape
on earth

One day I hope I shall take the road to Erzerum and Kars in eastern Turkey. Lord knows what I shall find for I have received conflicting reports, but from what I can gather Kars is undeniably a tough, almost a terrorist town with a hotel which everyone agrees must be rated as one of the worst in the world. Kars also has the dubious distinction of being the only town in Turkey where the police disclaim all responsibility for anyone who is rash enough to venture into the streets after dark. Inal Atac discovered this in the autumn of 1984 when he hired a bus to take his wife and two other families from Gumushane on an exploration of the eastern regions. Finding the 'best' hotel in Kars unbearable he started to walk towards the second-best in the certainty that this could not be worse, but after several yards he heard footsteps running behind him with shouts that he should stop. 'You're insane,' they told him when he explained. 'You may be bitten in the hotel but you'll be shot in the street.' So they stayed in the 'best' hotel sleeping in their clothes for the sheets were too dirty to be touched, using their spare clothes as pillows. It sounds like the hotel described as 'sub-standard' by Malcolm Cowen, the Newcastle man who had sailed on the *Izmir*, who wrote to me later, 'Kars is the most depressing place ever, dust everywhere, grey buildings and people.'

Yet I met some indomitable English ladies who stopped at Kars on their Swan Hellenic 'Art Treasures Tour of Eastern Turkey', and though they shuddered at the memory of the 'best' hotel they assured me that Kars itself was an unforgettable experience: 'If you haven't seen Kars,' they told me smugly, 'you haven't seen Turkey.' In his delightful book *Journey to Kars*, Philip Glazebrook wrote, 'As I walked back through the dark streets, amongst those inexplicable ruined walls and empty spaces of Turkish towns, where rubbish heaps stirred with rats, and when I saw the frosty stars look down on the outline of the black citadel, I never was less disappointed with reaching an objective in all my life.' You could hardly praise a place more highly than that and it suggests that the dangers after nightfall are exaggerated, but Glazebrook had chosen Kars for his final destination so I imagine that he was damned if he was going to be disappointed in anything, though even he had to ask the hotel porter to clean his room 'of the rubbish and filth accumulated on every surface' before he set out to explore the citadel.

The position of Kars made it a national fortress, besieged over the centuries by the Russians who occupied the town in 1828, 1855 and 1878 when the area was ceded to Russia officially at the Congress of Berlin. In 1915, the expedition of the Turkish General Enver Pasha, Ataturk's political rival, was defeated with a shattering loss of 78,000 men, but only six years later Kars returned to Turkey in the War of Independence.

If you go there read John Buchan's romantic description in *Greenmantle* and Glazebrook's account of the famous siege in 1855 during the Crimean War when a gallant Turkish garrison of 15,000 men held out against an attack of 40,000 Tsarist troops. The Turks were supported by a British garrison under the command of General Sir Fenwick Williams who became known as the 'Hero of Kars' and was honoured by London as a Freeman of the City and by Parliament which granted him £1,000 a year for life. This was his reward for the epic defence which lasted for five months 'when every living creature in the place had been eaten, and horse soup was a delicacy reserved secretly for the dying'. Yet, at the same time, war was conducted with an exaggerated courtesy. While the Russian General, Mouvarieff, waited, killing 8,900 men in a single raid, he intercepted a copy of Carlisle's *Diary in Turkish and Greek Waters* which had been posted to the British Medical Officer, and after reading the book he had it delivered to the besieged town with his apologies. Accepting the surrender after a decimating attack of cholera inside the citadel itself, General Mouvarieff told his British counterpart, 'You have made yourself a name in history, and posterity will stand amazed at the endurance, courage and discipline which this siege has called forth in the remains of an army.' Glazebrook adds a caustic postscript, revealing that the Turks were less impressed by their allies whose tactics lost them both the town and the army and who took the glory with few casualties themselves. One of the British soldiers received the VC.

I assumed that Kars today was little more than a muddy village until I checked with my maligned Fodor and discovered that this is a city with 35,000 people, though still a windy frontier town, 6,000 feet high, with the citadel on the rocky summit overlooking the winding river. King Abas I made Kars the capital of Armenia in the tenth century before he transferred the capital to Ani 50 kilometres to the east, where more than 100,000 people lived until the Mongol invasion. Today it is a ghost town lying so close to the Russian border that you can see the machine guns in the towers. You need a military permit to go there which should not be too difficult if you persist, though Glazebrook was regarded with such suspicion that he abandoned the attempt.

Leaving Gumushane the mountains reminded me of the foothills of the Atlas in southern Morocco with their red soil and strips of green along the bottom of the valleys beside the dried-up beds of rivers and streams. Soon this impression was dispelled by the trees, largely pine, becoming increasingly abundant, with others in vivid autumnal yellow and orange as if they were on fire. Then we left the forests behind and approached the Anatolian plains whose immensity diminished our car to the merest speck. Everything here is on such a colossal scale that it should be forbidding, yet this is not the case: there are reassuring signs of humanity in this vastness, men threshing, women sitting in the shade of a tree surrounded by sheep, the tents of the workers on the road. It is easy to imagine the camel caravans which crossed here once or the solitary horseman moving across the plain to knock on a stranger's door in the darkness as 'a visitor from God', to be given food and the owner's room for the single night. Even the red-brown hills in the distance looked deceptively soft, as though a giant could plunge his hands inside them as if they were pillows when, in reality, they are brick hard and dry, consisting of baked earth and thistles. Even so, I had no difficulty in believing that we were crossing one of the earth's faults towards Erzincan where 40,000 people were killed in the earthquake of 1939.

We took the turning away from Erzincan towards Sivas and stopped thankfully at a small village where a glass of cool water was more welcome than champagne. Inspecting his taxi anxiously, Osman discovered that one of the tyres needed changing and when I helped him remove the spare from the back I saw that every piece of luggage was impregnated by a covering of dust.

When we moved off down the stretch of smooth tarmac which we had reached at last, we applauded as the taxi gathered speed and Osman grinned with relief after the tracks he had endured. A moment later, in the sudden wind, the layer of fine dust in the back swept over us turning our hair white before its time.

Now the plains were so flat that a lake resembled a sheet of glass suggesting a depth no greater than an inch, reflecting the bilious hills in its mirrored surface.

Sivas and Kayseri resemble Birmingham and Sheffield in so far as few people would go there just for the fun of it, yet I suspect they might prove infinitely rewarding if one did just that. Sivas is a bustling city with a population around 150,000 where we stayed the night and, dutifully, went the next morning to the Gok Medrese, the locked doorway topped by twin minarets, a glorious example of Seljuk design. Then we drove to Kayseri, known as Caesarea under the Romans, and once the capital of Cappadocia before the birth of Christ.

The Cappadocian plateau must be the maddest, vastest lunar landscape on earth and I cannot understand why film companies have failed to use it as a setting for their science fiction epics. With weird formations in a landscape like dissolving icecream, it looks as if a volcanic eruption had melted the landscape freezing the tormented shapes as they started to re-emerge. And something like this *did* happen. Mount Erciyers, 12,848 feet high and now extinct, covered the area with lava thousands of years ago which stiffened into pumice or tufa stone. Over the centuries, the erosion of wind and rain twisted the shapes like sculptors into the conical towers we see today. Then came man, for pumice is easy to mould yet hardens once it is exposed to the air, so the rocks made perfect dwellings in a district where building materials such as wood are scarce. This is the greatest shock of all, once your eyes accept it, that the holes in the rocks are door and windows and that these are *homes* where people have lived since 3,000 BC, and the caves still used as coolers for such fruit as lemons which can be stored for months and remain preserved. The Hittites were among the first inhabitants, but the main influence came from the Christians who settled here after they fled from Arab persecution and carved a refuge complete with elaborate churches, richly decorated with frescoes.

Some of the massive rocks with a slab of tougher stone perched precariously on the top are referred to archly as 'fairy chimneys', though Fodor describes them as 'looking for all the world like a cap rakishly pulled down over one eye'. To my sardonic eye they look so unmistakably phallic that at first I thought they must have been carved to achieve exactly that effect, but, instead, they are simply freaks of nature. *Simply*! Nothing could look more bizarre, certainly nothing I have seen in my travels. And far from being isolated they stretch for miles.

Some of the earliest Christian rock dwellings can be seen at Zelve with the ruins of a Byzantine church as well as a Moslem mosque at the entrance to the valley, a honeycombed cliff with caves both natural and man-made where people lived as recently as 1950 until they were evacuated because the caves became unsafe. The first shock is replaced by admiration for the people who exploited a natural upheaval turning it to their advantage as they carved their communities literally out of the rock.

Goreme is another place which has to be seen to be believed, a centre of ancient Christianity with a religious school and numerous churches. Compared to those at Sumela, the frescoes in these churches are remarkably vivid, more so than the dim light suggests, dating as far back as the fifth century. To the expert, the smallest, faintest surviving fragment must be infinitely rewarding but these can be appreciated by anyone for their colours and the simple composition of scenes which are instantly recognisable like 'The Last Supper' in the Dark Church of Karanlik Kilisse with a huge fish resting on a dish surrounded by Christ and the Apostles. 'The Crucifixion' is splendid too, not just for the craftsmanship but also for the devotion which must have been involved and the touching simplicity of the decorations on the surrounding columns.

This troglodyte civilisation above the ground is strange enough, only surpassed by the subterranean cities underneath where the Christians descended when the Arabs swept in from the east. Their peak, with a population estimated between 30,000 and 60,000 people, occurred around the seventh century until the Arabian hordes were driven off by the Byzantines. In the eleventh century, the Seljuk Turks took over but left the Christian communities alone.

These underground cities are amazing with churches, ventilator shafts, water tanks and labyrynthine passages. Derinkuyu, 29 kilometres south of Neveshir, means 'Deep Well', and it has seven stories reaching a depth of 85 yards. Kaymakli, which is connected to Derinkuyu by several kilometres of tunnel, was probably the grandest Christian city of catacombs in the world with halls, kitchens, cisterns, wine vats and chapels. In spite of such amenities life must have been ghastly once they sealed themselves in after rolling gigantic millstones against the openings with no smoke allowed to escape for fear of discovery.

I went below for a few minutes, bent double as I crouched my way along the narrow tunnels which descended to one of the lower layers, and if I had never suffered from claustrophobia before I did so then. If I had been a Cappadocian Christian, I should have preferred the risk of pillage, carnage and rape in the open air, compared to the suffocating existence below.

There is so much to see above with every valley revealing yet another extraordinary formation that you should allow time to explore it leisurely with the chance to absorb the variety. Urgup proved a useful base, a lively little town surprisingly unspoilt by the tourists. This is partly because many stay in the Turban Holiday Village just outside, as we had to do, which suffers from the inevitable impersonality created by coach tours of chattering visitors who descend like locusts demanding this and that from the staff who will never see them again and remain indifferent. The lack of the human touch is all the sadder because the complex of buildings is well designed and suitably de Chirico in this surrealistic landscape.

Even the walk down the hill from the Turban is rich in surprise, the white modern buildings in the foreground contrasting with trees in the trellissed courtyards and poles for electric light, backed by the troglodyte homes honeycombed in the rockface behind. The occasional transport that passes along the cobbled street is usually donkey often piled high with some sort of greenery followed by a woman with a stick or scythe who glares when she spots a camera. Another woman in a headscarf and blue-patterned dress over brown-patterned baggy trousers stared at me suspiciously from her doorway, retreated and slammed the metal door behind her. Donkey transport graduates to donkey-and-cart and from there to tractor-and-cart piled high with produce for though the earth is hard, and the heat in the summer must be devastating, the ground is surprisingly fertile.

A slender minaret provides the familiar landmark ahead, concentrating the view of the valley and surrounding hills. At this time of the year, in late September, the evening air is warm and the light is clear and devoid of glare.

The director of tourism for Urgup, a lively man full of information, joined me for dinner at a lokanta where the eager English-speaking waiter told me of a place with music. This idea grew increasingly attractive after several glasses of the local wine called Cubuk, a cheap and violent vintage, the start of a wild evening which ended in a large room with a Turkish band and crowds of men drinking raki in huge quantities, rapidly. This was the sort of place I had been hoping for in Turkey, away from the tourist track, and I blessed my good luck though the director looked hesitant as room was forced for us at a table near the stage. He had the courtesy to ask me to dance, a custom which may disconcert the British but is natural in Turkey and, indeed, unavoidable in a country where women do not dance with men except in the international night clubs in Istanbul. Turkish men do not hesitate to dance with each other, working themselves into a frenzy, but nowhere could have been less 'gay' than that room in Urgup though the only woman was the burly singer. The director, who was as fat as myself, started to sweat profusely, for the atmosphere was hotter than any hammam, and another dancer cut in, an immensely strong young Turk with a black moustache who urged me on with cries of 'Good! Good!', teaching me some sidesteps too. Then his younger brother who looked slightly mad, alternating between scowls of hostility and beams of ecstasy, insisted on dancing with me himself. How good I was! Or so I thought. I am one of those inveterate, show-off dancers convinced they have natural rhythm while making absolute fools of themselves. And this was my sort of dance with arms flailing, body shaking and feet kicking in a crazy, drunken Turkish fandango. 'Good! Good!' cried the Turkish brothers as I sank to my feet like a Russian Cossack, waving my arms in the air until I fell over. As I staggered back to my chair, I noticed, and greatly resented, two German tourists arriving at the other side of the club, also persuaded to dance which they did with smirks of self-satisfaction, twirling their fingers with odious flamboyancy, prancing around like clowns making a spectacle of themselves – *exactly* as I had done. A mirror for narcissus. But a moment later I forgot them as I danced with *both* of the brothers at once – *brilliantly!*

After that the evening veered pleasantly out of control: the English-speaking waiter joined our table where he had to squeeze himself next to the tourist director who took offence – time telescoped most curiously – the police arrived and I was seized by the two brothers and swept off to Neveshir in their car. 'My God,' I thought, as they raced along the road ignoring my protests, 'rape at last, at my age!' only to be dropped at a ghostly hotel which they thought was my destination, driving me all the way back to the Turban without a murmur of complaint. After writing their address, the brothers drove off with cries of everlasting friendship. A marvellous night though the tourist director looked ashen the next morning when I called to say goodbye and drove off to Tarsus on the way to Mersin and the Mediterranean.

Information

Kars

If you wish to continue to Ani, the local tourist office should be able to provide you with the necessary military permit.

Ani

A ghost city well worth visiting for the astonishing Armenian churches still in good condition. Noted for the 'thousand and one' churches altogether, the most famous is the cathedral which became a mosque in 1064 reverting to Christianity in the thirteenth century.

Dogubayait

Another 'must' if you are travelling through eastern Turkey, the fairytale mosque of Ishak Pasha which looks so ravishing in the photographs, an Arabian Nights' Palace apparently floating on the plain below Mount Ararat.

Sivas

Hotel
Turistik Otel Kosk. Modern, comfortable and satisfactory. It has 44 rooms with baths. Address: Ataturk Cad. 11. Tel: 1150 1473.

Kayseri

Once the Roman Caesarea and the capital of the province of Cappadocia, right in the geographical centre of Asia Minor. Today it is famous for its shops and bazaars where the bargaining is so notorious that Turks who haggle over their purchases are labelled 'Kayserians – sharper than the Jews'. Yet the black and white tablecloths I bought here were cheaper than anywhere else.

Urgup

The *Turban Urgup Motel*, just outside the town. Some of the drawbacks I experienced may well be ironed out by now for the place was new, the trees were waist-high and the pool not yet completed. Even so, I urge you not to send your washing to the laundry. The advantages are all the excellent modern facilities.

Guzelgoz Pansiyon (named after the owner, Mustafa Guzelgoz) was recommended to me, a simple pension for little more than £1 a night though doubtless more today, clean, with a shower and place to cook.

Urgup/Goreme

Restaurant
7 kilometres from Urgup and 800 yards from Goreme, there is an underground restaurant called *Kaya* camping and restaurant run by Sahin Kaya which is unashamedly for tourists but probably good fun if you happen to be in a group. Carved out of the rock in the old

style, there are two storeys and each floor holds 300 people. Obviously the music and atmosphere are carefully contrived but I doubt if it is any less jolly for that.

Avanos

Shopping

This is a small town founded by the Seljuks 13 kilometres from Urgup which is famous for its pottery, carpets and marble souvenirs. I bought several of the small round pots which are used for the local and delicious stew which I enjoyed at the *Merkez* restaurant in Neveshir called *Guvec*, small pieces of lamb with tomato, hot pepper and aubergine. Though a bore to carry back, I find them invaluable for soup today.

Onyx: whole shops are devoted to onyx in various forms such as ashtrays. They are cheaper here than elsewhere so if you like onyx you would be advised to buy here rather than wait. A friend advised me to visit one of the onyx factories, adding, 'It's sweat shop conditions with a short life for the workers, most of whom are young boys. As they work at their machines the dust chippings spray upwards into their faces. We reckoned most of them would be dead of lung disease by the time they reached their forties.' I took his word for this and did not visit an onyx factory. It put me off the onyx too.

Hotel

Hotel Venessa. This is a new hotel and looked comfortable with 73 rooms with showers and balconies with views over Cappadocia. Plainly this is for tourists with a bar, disco and laid-on 'folklore dancing'. Tel: Avanos 201.

12 Wild flowers in the dining car – taking the train to Van

(Before continuing my journey to Mersin, I return to the eastern part of Turkey which I reached by train from Istanbul in the spring of 1984.)

My decision to take the three-day train journey to Lake Van disconcerted the Turks who assured me it would be easier to fly. But I find no romance in air travel: few places on earth can be more hellish than airports where the passengers are punished as if they had done something wrong. Once you are airborne after the interminable delay you might be flying over Belgium or a Baked Alaska for all you see of the land below until you start that grisly descent and begin to identify, though hardly appreciate, such details as lakes and roads. A train journey offers a different perspective altogether, the longer the better with ample time to unpack and relax secure in the knowledge that you are travelling to the end of the line. Apart from all that, it is cheaper – only £18 for a journey which took me from one end of Turkey to another making me realise yet again that the contrast is that of a continent rather than a country.

The journey starts romantically. Instead of crossing the new bridge to Asia, take the Karakoy ferry from Galata and sail out of the Golden Horn and across the Bosphorus to Haydarpasa Gari on the other side, landing outside the steps to the station which you enter through vast domed entrances of decorated glass.

The take-off of an aircraft is fraught but the exhilaration as a ship sails out of harbour or a train slips from its station is one of the rewards of travel. The time of day was perfect, the hovering hour of dusk with light enough to see the villages as we raced along the Sea of Marmara with boys playing football in every available space and that unique opportunity to see the back door of a country which only a train provides.

Soon we left the built-up areas and headed for the open country as darkness fell. My compartment was comfortable with a washbasin and a bunk which became a bed. I only had to walk a few yards to the dining car in the next carriage which had two main tables for those who wanted to eat, one of them usually occupied by the staff of four who served themselves constant and delicious-looking meals throughout the next few days. The impassive waiter volunteered no menu so I struggled laboriously with my Berlitz and came up with 'What do you recommend?' He had the nous to take the book and responded with kadin budu translated as 'lady's thighs', cold croquettes of lamb and rice which proved surprisingly good, accompanied by a bottle of wine provided by the Pera Palas as I was leaving. My only criticism was an absence of ice, though they promised to put future bottles in the cooler. A youngish man with a friendly, humorous face looked into the carriage at one point and might have been British, but I was glad when he retreated for I wanted the chance to rest in silence over the next few days and settled in my bunk with contentment, falling asleep to that lovely clattering sound of the train underneath.

I woke with that dark brown taste of the morning after and looked under the blind at the large but nondescript station where we had stopped. The time was 6.30 and as we left I saw that the passing trains were crowded with commuters and realised we were leaving a massive city – Ankara.

There was no temptation to stop there now, but I stayed in Ankara on another occasion and find it much maligned as a town everyone has heard of but no one wants to go to. Admittedly it is a governmental pretext like Ottawa and Canberra, but I prefer Ankara to either of these capital cities even if it is less exotic than Istanbul. From all the disparaging accounts, I had been expecting an ugly, claustrophobic town and was pleasantly surprised by the wide, tree-lined boulevards, hills and parks, the first-rate hotels and restaurants. In contrast to the exotic turbulence of Istanbul, Ankara is closer in spirit to a modern city in Germany or Switzerland, an astonishing achievement when you consider that the Anatolian population was only 75,000 in 1925 and is now more than one and a half million. This is due to one man whose inspiration dominates the city today, Kemal Ataturk, who chose Ankara as the base for his new administration in 1923, determined to wrench his republic from the grasp of sultanate and Ottoman traditions – also it was less vulnerable to attack than Constantinople, where the forces of occupation were planning a carve-up among the Allies which would put an end to Turkey forever.

Inevitably, when every village boasts its monument to Ataturk, Ankara has the grandest shrine of all with the massive mausoleum of Anitkabir placed on a hill with superb views of the city. It was built on a colossal scale with a colonnaded square leading to the neo-classic mausoleum itself and the effect would be impersonal except for such human touches as the photographs and souvenirs and the splendid old Lincoln car used by Ataturk himself. Ruthless though he must have been, and had to be, it is easy to understand the reverence shown by the Turks who walk through the lion gates and surrounding gardens to pay their homage. 'Beyond all doubt, government belongs to the people' reads the inscription above his tomb. Some will argue that this condition has yet to be fulfilled, but not the majority of Turks who enjoy a greater freedom than they have ever known before.

Unlike the Soviets, the Turks have mastered the art of life. I had gone to Ankara to interview President Evren for the *Spectator*, but when I arrived I was told he could not see me after all, though it is likely that my message never reached him. The only time I saw the President was during his election in 1983 as I was leaving Dalaman airport for Istanbul and he flew in from Ankara on his way to the Holiday Village at Marmaris.

There was a certain irony as we waited that morning with all the pomp and preparation, the local people pouring in to provide the greeting crowds, schoolchildren brought by coach to decorate the foreground with their flags, the red carpet, the braid and all the trimmings and anticipation of a great *occasion*. At last a covey of helicopters preceded the plane, a distant figure alighted, the band played, the President made his speech and everyone cheered, and then he had gone in a storm of flags. It was surprisingly moving. The irony lay in the woman beside me whose expression was shrouded by the inevitable dark glasses but whose thoughts must have been poignant as she remembered similar occasions shared with her husband until the fatal day in Dallas.

As the train left Ankara this time, the city obscured in an early fog, I made my way to the dining car where the staff were consuming a large breakfast of boiled eggs, white cheese, black olives, cucumbers and tomatoes which they shared with me immediately. I felt relaxed at last, prepared to enjoy the constant stops, the views on either side, and the luxury of windows which open rather than the enforced air conditioning of British Rail set at just the wrong temperature. Above all, I relished the lack of intrusion, the total absence of an English voice. This was the reason for my taking the train in the first place with the chance to absorb every detail, such as the four soldiers who sat down opposite chatting agreeably though I noticed that one was linked by large handcuffs to another. The train stopped for a longer halt outside a village where a stork had built her nest on the top of a pole, rivalling the muezzin's balcony on a nearby minaret. I gained a childish pleasure when the stork rose up and stood in silhouette. As if they had received a radar signal that the stop would be a long one, flocks of passengers descended and crossed the tracks to gather wild flowers in the fields beyond. When we started off again, the waiter placed a vase of poppies and mignonette on my table, and walking down the train afterwards to see what the other carriages were like, and many were surprisingly empty, I found children clutching their bouquets of wild flowers too, staring at me with wide-eyed appraisal. Everyone stared: a white-bearded old man with bushy, black eyebrows and a stick; a peasant woman of great beauty though her eyes were tragic beneath the inevitable scarf; her husband, bluffer, heavily moustached, more confident and smiling.

The most welcome surprise of all was the greeting from children at every station, eager to learn my name as they told me theirs, anxious to be photographed though they would never see the result, devoid of self-consciousness and dressed as smartly as any child in Hampstead on a Sunday afternoon.

This is one of the startling aspects of Turkey – there is hardship and people are poor, but there is rarely a sense of poverty for the Turks are not a cringing nation.

Back in my bunk with *Greenmantle*, I was dismayed to realise what a silly book it is though entertained by Hannay's hazardous adventures along a similar route. The day lingered pleasantly until the evening when I found that I was not alone for dinner. The alert face which had peered into the buffet the night before reappeared and introduced itself: a young British photographer accompanied by a dark, attractive woman who scrutinised me sharply as they joined my table explaining that they had paid the difference to move to a sleeper too. Within moments I discovered that the woman was highly intelligent and everything I was fleeing from – an editor in a leading publishing firm. Soon we were having exactly the conversation I was used to in London, all the latest news about authors, books and the wiles of publishing, while the photographer listened with unconcealed impatience to our shop talk – a busman's holiday on board a train. My satisfaction in being the unique traveller was shattered. The sense of adventure diminished for I might have been in the French Pub in Dean Street. I could not have asked for brighter company had I been in England, but this was the very milieu I thought I had left behind and my dismay was mutual.

'For God's sake,' cried Jerry at last, unable to stand our chit chat any longer. 'Can't you speak of anything else but *books*?'

'Let's make a pact,' cried Joy gratefully. 'We won't talk shop until we meet again in London.'

'I couldn't agree more,' I confirmed. 'Let's talk about *Turkey*.'

But of course we were at it a few minutes later as I told her compulsively about the journals of the painter Benjamin Robert Haydon which I had started that afternoon after finishing *Green-mantle*. The evening dissolved in a literary haze, diluted by the bottles of raki which the waiter had bought at one of the stops.

The scenery on the last day expanded and I felt I had arrived in Asia at last. The rolling plains were infinite and virtually empty except for the occasional herds of sheep. We climbed higher through a mountain gorge and descended to Tatvan at the western end of the lake which is the largest in Turkey, allegedly six times the size of Lake Geneva. This statistic is repeated in various guide books and does not strike me as particularly helpful unless one happens to be intimate with Geneva, but there was a resemblance to Switzerland in Tatvan as the train drew into the station that afternoon, and the air was keen. The armed soldier, who patrolled the open platform with his gun, posed proudly for his photograph as Jerry alighted with his camera, and then the train shunted slowly backwards towards the lake where we had to wait for the ferry. Tatvan looked inviting and I was tempted to stay there overnight, though I have heard conflicting reports of the hotel since then and do not recommend it. The mountain of Nemrut Dagi (not to be confused with the famous mountain of the same name which I shall mention shortly) loomed above us, an extinct volcano with one of the largest craters in the world, 7 kilometres in diameter and a lake which is 2,400 metres above sea level. As I waited for the ferryboat to arrive, I watched the powerful steam engine shunted on to the rails which would take it on board before continuing the journey to Iran. A family might have been destined for Iran as well for their cart was piled high with possessions while a skeletal horse munched morosely from a skeletal nosebag. They looked unhappy and their anxiety became obvious when it was time to push the cart on board for I saw that the father's hand was bandaged, obviously a catas-trophe if his injury was serious. Ever optimistic, I had been imagin-ing a pleasant dinner with Joy and Jerry in a jolly dining room on board the boat, which would help to pass the five-hour passage across the lake. Instead there was no dining car, the bar was closed, and the atmosphere in the saloon was hardly enhanced by the most ferocious man I had seen in Turkey, who turned out to be a Scot. He staggered to a bench where he lay writhing, his head twisting and turning on his rucksack which was covered with the usual cooking utensils and gadgets. As I had discovered a tin of sardines buried in my luggage, but keyless, Jerry dared to ask him for an opener while Joy and I watched with some alarm as the Scot rose up and shook his fist apparently half-mad with anger. Returning, slightly shaken and without an opener, Jerry revealed that the Scot was not ferocious at all but suffering from malaria. Meanwhile the peasant family were crying as they surrounded the father who insisted on unrolling his bandages, finally displaying a bunch of crushed and crimson fingers. The family watched helplessly as he presented the gash like a patient in a surgery. What could we do? Jerry rose to the occasion and found some TCP which he poured over the open wound while Joy and I looked the other way.

'He didn't even wince,' Jerry informed us proudly, though I noticed that the man's eyes were glazed from pain. The only tablets I could find were some headache pills so I gave him these as a panacea and went in search of the man who had taken our tickets to demand a cognac which was the most effective contribution I could think of. Reluctantly, he went behind the counter to announce that there was no cognac, not even raki, only beer which the invalid refused. Presumably, he would have refused a cognac too because of his religion, so I ordered three beers for ourselves and five bottles of fruit juice for his unhappy family which seemed to please the wife who managed to smile.

It became colder and was so black outside with no moon and no fleck of light from the shore that we might have been at sea. There was no map or poster in the saloon to guide us, proving how few tourists take the ferry though it goes several times a week, and barely a dozen passengers this night apart from ourselves, the delirious Scot, and the injured man and his family. After Jerry managed to open the sardines with a knife, I tried to return to the artistic world of Benjamin Haydon but it was difficult. A man wandered up, stared at my book, picked up my spectacle case, snapped it shut and wandered off again. The Scot groaned. The injured man began to moan. And a jaunty *Hart to Hart* was shown on the snowy television set which seemed ludicrous in the circumstances. I might have been travelling in limbo, like one of those novels where a group of ill-assorted passengers are thrown together only to realise they are dead.

We arrived in Van at midnight and the first shock was the discovery that the town is inland and not on the lake at all. Instead of a crowded quayside with welcoming lights and bustling lokantas and bars, I looked down at a deserted dockyard with no more than half a dozen people standing forlornly under a solitary light near a single car which I prayed might be a taxi.

'Mister Farsons, Mister Farsons!' My name shivered across the water as the ferry inched her way towards the jetty where I saw a young man with a bushy moustache and a beaming smile waving excitedly: 'Mister Farsons! I come to welcome you to Won!'

The town of Van lies inland as I have mentioned, so there is no lakeside waterfront with the quaint cafés I was expecting, nor even a glimpse of water. This was evident during our drive in the car which belonged to a lady wrapped up in a grand fur coat, Van's director of tourism who was waiting to greet me with the young man, whose name was Raif, who would act as my guide. I felt a further disappointment when I drew my curtains the following morning in the Akdamar Hotel and looked out on a straggling, modern town with the letters COMMANDO emblazoned on the hill beyond to mark this as a military zone. Van cannot be described as pretty, but as I discovered later that day it is set in one of the most beautiful regions in Turkey and I began to warm to the busy unpretentiousness of the town itself.

Lake Van will be smartened soon enough. In years to come the shores will have scores of attractive restaurants and holiday villages for this is destined to become a popular resort with an international appeal. Until now, the elements which make it so beautiful have preserved its isolation for the level of the water shifts constantly, drowning a number of settlements in the nineteenth century which still remain below the surface. There are earthquakes too – the last, in 1976, killed 4,000 people – but given the odd flood or earthquake this shoreline is a natural pleasure ground for the developers and one can only pray that Turkish discretion will keep their buildings low. In the winter, these could well be used for winter sports, providing accommodation all the year round if transport problems can be overcome when the area freezes up.

Yet, when I looked out that first morning, I did feel a sense of anti-climax. Had this been *Tushpa* the capital of Urartu, a rocky fortress occupied by successive states for 3,000 years until the First World War when the battles between the Russians and the Turks devastated the population as the Armenians fled? That was the old town a few kilometres away and little is left of it today except for the great citadel with a mile of walled ramparts along a sheer rock face on one side and a steep climb on the other. The rock is a natural stronghold, dominating the surrounding countryside with spectacular views from the top which put the lake in perspective. Centuries ago the water reached the walls of the citadel below and it is possible to distinguish the outline of the ancient harbour and the shells of ruined Seljuk mosques. Inside the citadel you can see remains of temples carved into the rock, Ottoman mosques, and inscriptions which date as far back as King Sardur I of Urartu who built the citadel of Tushpa in 825 BC.

I knew little about the Urartians until I came to Van, except that they followed the Hurrians and I knew even less about them. According to John Freely, Urartu reached its peak in the reign of King Menua when it became 'the most powerful state in western Asia', continuing to flourish under the rule of his son Argistis I (c. 786–764 BC) when Urartian works of art were so fine they were prized in Greece and Italy.

Evidently Menua built on a grand scale, not only fortresses and palaces but the more utilitarian canals and aqueducts whose irrigation enriched the wheatfields and vineyards which made the district so famous that Freely claims it was known 'in ancient legend' as 'the site of the Garden of Eden'. Finally, the Assyrians, Urartu's foremost enemy, recovered their strength and defeated Sarduris II, the son of Argistis, in 743 BC. 'I shut up Sarduris of Urartu in Turushpa (Tushpa) his capital city,' the Assyrian leader boasted. 'I made a great slaughter in front of the gates of the town, and opposite the town I set up an image of my royalty.'

The impregnable fortress withstood the siege while the Assyrians occupied the surroundings, decimated the gardens and the town, but the battles weakened both sides to a fatal extent and the Assyrian Empire fell with Nineveh in 612 BC and Urartu to the Medes only twenty years later. As a capital city, Tushpa ruled for less than two hundred years but regained its importance as the capital of Armenia in the tenth century AD, becoming the centre of the Van Province under the Ottomans. The difference in the various building styles can be noticed today, starting with the Urartians who used no mortar but uniform blocks of stone weighing as much as thirty tons.

Undoubtedly the massive citadel is formidable, and perhaps it is better seen at dusk or dawn, but I found it bleak when I climbed there in the afternoon. By comparison, the small island of Akdamar is one of the loveliest I have seen with the curious shape of the old Armenian church framed against the snow caps of mountains on the mainland, and a wealth of wild flowers in the foreground in the spring. You can take a boat in summer directly from the jetty at Van, otherwise it is easier to drive along the south-eastern shore where women wash their clothes from the rocks in the water which is famous for the sulphur springs that make it exceptionally soft with a high salt content, like the Dead Sea except that this is 6,000 feet high. I have been assured that fishermen who catch the local *darekh*, known as 'the poor man's herring', tie their trousers or jackets on a line behind them which are cleaned by the time they pull them in. A wilder legend claims that notorious, yellow-eyed cats swim in the buoyant water of Lake Van, also in pursuit of the *darekh*. Surprisingly this has been confirmed by no less an institution than *The Times*, except that the cats in this case have one green eye and one blue and are small and fluffy. This sounds like a publicist's dream or a raki-ridden nightmare. Disappointingly there was not a cat in sight, neither sunbathing on shore nor stroking its predatory way across the salty surface, and Raif, my guide, had never heard of such a creature. 'Perhaps,' he volunteered, trying to be helpful, 'it is special cat who swims.'

'I am sure you are right,' I agreed, and he smiled with relief.

After 44 kilometres from Van, as you approach the village of Gevas, you can see the attractive Seljuk tomb called Halime Hatun Turbesi which was built in 1358 for a Karakoyunlu princess. A Seljuk tomb is a Seljuk tomb is a Seljuk tomb, and unless you are an expert one looks much the same as another. The conical shape is pleasing to the eye, but that is the extent of it as far as I am concerned. However, as this one lies no more than a few yards from the road, I suggest that you stop to examine it for the tomb is a fine example of the art and this will absolve you from making the trek to Ahlat as I did later.

At Gevas there is a restaurant with a balcony overlooking a small jetty where the boat takes you to the island which lies opposite, costing less than a pound for the return journey depending on the number of passengers who wish to take it, unless you prefer to hire it on your own.

This was a perfect day. The journey took twenty minutes with the details of the island growing more distinct, the colours refuting the photographs which make it look barren. It was the end of May and warm, without an English voice in earshot though I noticed several Turkish families having picnics among the trees as I walked up to the church, one with a samovar and another with a fire and barbecue.

The Church of the Holy Cross is all that remains of a settlement which included a palace and a monastery with orchards and gardens, but the church which was built by the Armenian King Gagik I in AD 915–921 remains as one of the finest examples of Armenian architecture though there are others at Ani near the Russian border.

All too often there is a sense of anti-climax when you climb to a mountain monastery like Sumela and find it in a state of disrepair; or enter a famous church where the frescoes have faded to the point of invisibility. This applies to the interior of the church on Akdamar, but the outside is a revelry of richly decorated reliefs, wonderfully intact due to the seclusion of the island which became an Armenian refuge. Only a corpulent Adam and Eve with the Tree of Life between them have suffered a facial battering.

Presumably the design of the church and the exterior carvings were conceived inseparably for the curious, many-sided geometrical shape provides a perfect backing for the decorations carved in the dark, pink sandstone with diagonals and niches to show them off. David is dwarfed by Goliath who stands 2 metres tall; Daniel was in shadow but I recognised my namesake from the two lions on either side who are licking his feet. Individual heads of animals, lions and antelope, jut out like gargoyles under a glorious frieze of figures and animals entwined with vines and bunches of grapes. The carvings are a celebration of life on earth and the emphasis on the animals is the more delightful when you remember the tradition that the kingdom of Armenia was founded in the region of Lake Van by Haik who was a descendant of Noah. The word Urartu is derived from Ararat, which is 'Armenia' in Latin. These carvings may not be unique but I had seen nothing like them before.

It needs time to identify the various scenes and absorb the atmosphere, but I had the good fortune in having Raif as my guide with the luxury of a car and driver which meant that I could set my own pace. I was determined to travel alone on this particular journey through Turkey though grateful to accept the assistance of the local tourist offices, especially in a place like Van where transport is vital. Equally, I am too contrary an individual to adapt to a group though I appreciate that a coach tour is an ideal way to cover long distances in a comparatively short time. Even so, I have to admit a slight resentment when I reached a distant point, priding myself on being the lone, intrepid traveller only to find that the hotel was full of people speaking English. Everyone goes everywhere today, even to the slopes of Kathmandu (by courtesy of Encounter Overland Ltd), but I was momentarily dismayed to find the Akdamar Hotel in Van occupied by twenty-four British art lovers on a Swan Hellenic coach tour who pitied me for not having gone to Kars and Ani. Armed with thermos flasks provided by their tour director Sybil Sassoon, to be filled whenever they passed spring water, swotting up their homework in advance from the talks given by their lecturer, Paul Gotch, who accompanied them throughout, they were determined to see as much as possible and declared it was 'excellent value'.

Like all groups, they sounded ghastly *en masse* and proved to be charming when I spoke to them individually. This should have been self-evident for they had the gumption to go to eastern Turkey in the first place, but though I admired their sense of adventure I deplored their constant boast: 'Everything is done for us, we don't have to lift a finger.' That is why a group is not for me, nor I – with my lack of punctuality – for them. To my mind, the more independence the better. When I return to Turkey in the future I hope to do so with no guide, no schedule, and no 'itinerary'. I want to drift at will, stopping longer when I like the place, finding myself lost in the wrong town altogether. Such wilfulness would shock the tourist guide. Not only is it his nature, but also his duty to show you *everything* in sight, and my heart sank when one guide announced, 'There are ninety-two antiquities in this region. Today we have seen only three. Tomorrow we go faster.'

On this occasion I was lucky in having a guide and driver with such long distances to cover. Joy and Jerry told me later that the closest they came to Akdamar Island was the view from the bus as they hurtled past.

Even so, I suggested to Raif that I should welcome an hour wandering about the island on my own. He nodded sympathetically and continued to guard me as if I was an unexpected prize drawn in a lottery, to be deposited after the weekend. Climbing a slippery hill to photograph the church, Raif kept right behind me: 'If you fall badly, you need help,' he warned, which made me lose my footing instantly.

His devotion was remarkable considering his shabby treatment when he arrived at Heathrow a few years ago. He saved his money to come to London in order to learn English and help his career, a young Turk whose very innocence raised suspicion but whose only crime was a low estimate of the British cost of living. In spite of his return ticket, he was accused of arriving with insufficient funds and after being held for three miserable days in Immigration he was deported back to Turkey. Such an experience would have embittered me against Britain for life, but Raif has a generous nature and shrugged off the incident with Turkish resignation, turning to textbooks instead in order to improve his English. Perhaps he was glad of the opportunity to practise it with me but I was shamed by the warmth of his welcome after my own country had dismissed him so cruelly.

Even so, I insisted he rejoin his friends who were preparing a picnic while I tested the famous water in the hope of glimpsing a yellow-eyed cat in search of a 'poor man's herring', and he retreated unhappily. The water justified its reputation: silky soft and refreshingly cold rather than freezing, even at that early time of year. I dried myself and sat contentedly in the sun for a few blissful seconds of idleness until an instinct made me turn round and I caught a glimpse of Raif half hidden behind some bushes on the hill above making sure I was safe. Disarmed, I conquered my lassitude and joined Raif and the driver for the picnic they had laid out on one of the tables under the trees.

The meal included a delicious local cheese, moist instead of the usual dry white slab, and mixed with 'grass' as Raif assured me, and it might well have been. Back on the mainland at the lokanta opposite the jetty, I reciprocated by ordering two beers, one Pepsi, one orange juice, and two plates of excellent yoghurt and honey – for just over £2.

Raif is one of those Turks whose faces look stern until they smile and then their humour is a revelation. This good-hearted young man was touchingly generous throughout my stay, even paying me the compliment of inviting me to his home the following day where his mother had prepared special local dishes though I was sorry that Turkish traditions meant that she had to stay in the background throughout.

As a guide, Raif came into his own that afternoon after Akdamar by taking me to a place I should not have seen otherwise. We drove off from Gevas to Gurpinar across a plain which became increasingly romantic in spite of a pack of dogs which raced from a settlement near the village of Mejingir and attacked the car while I wound up my window rapidly. I would not confront such animals unless I had to, for I have little doubt they would tear an arm off. And I could not blame them for this in a land where dogs are trained to kill though I am not certain that my attackers, rather jolly, woolly creatures like large, grey chows, were the kurt-kopegi referred to by Peter Hopkirk at Patnos to the north of Van where a contest had been staged by the villagers between a captured wolf, a sheepdog and a kurt-kopegi: the sheepdog fled, but the kurt-kopegi went straight for the wolf's throat and tore it out. Hopkirk was told that if a kurt-kopegi was released into a pack of wolves, one such animal would kill up to half a dozen.

Wolves are common in the province of Van in the winter, surrounding anyone rash enough to walk alone, blinding him with snow which they kick in his face with their hind legs before they go in for the kill. The only hope is to shoot one, for then its companions will turn away to devour it instead. Probably my pursuers were merely sheepdogs though they did not wear the usual spiked collars which protect them from wolf attack. We left them clamouring behind and came to a swiftly running river apparently coming from nowhere. This is one of the marvels of Van, the Semiran Suyu – the Waters of Semiramis – one of the irrigation canals built by Menua, a triumph of construction which stretched from here to the town of Van 55 kilometres away.

Seldom have I felt such purity. The water springs literally from the rocks at the foot of a mountain like a waterfall in reverse, and it was so blissful, so pastoral a scene with the hundreds of grazing sheep nearby that I could understand how people who live here might believe in the miracles recorded in the Bible. In such remoteness where the seasons are the only constancy, there would be a need to believe in miracles in order to explain the impossible. With water gushing forth from the mountain, the land rent by earthquakes, the lake of Van in frequent flood because there is no known outlet for the water, how logical the story of Noah would be, with the Ark which came to rest on the mountain of Ararat to the north.

It is one of the most attractive qualities of the Turks that they are fiercely proud of their country, and Raif was pleased by my obvious pleasure. Told that the spring water remains miraculously hot in winter though icy in summer, I purged myself with a second swim that day and lay in the bubbling shallows beneath the mountain in very cold water, a sharp contrast to the lake, but as it was May this was probably a half-way temperature between the two extremes.

The following morning we climbed into the mountains towards Hakkari near the Iran/Iraq border, a mountainous area I long to visit in the summer at my leisure when the roads would be more passable. Snow had fallen overnight which gave the countryside a wilder look than ever though it was melting fast as we passed a nomadic settlement of dark tents and dogs, skulking figures and strutting chickens with the snow peaks behind, another scene from the biblical past. The road is good but virtually deserted – few tracks are beaten in Turkey – though builders were clearing a fall of rock which had slipped overnight, and three children stood by the side with bunches of an asparagus-looking root below the ruins of *Gavustepe*, another ancient Urartian fortress in the process of excavation which has revealed the outline of a city with a temple and a palace.

After 57 kilometres we turned a corner near the village of Guzelsu and saw the magnificent fortress of Hosap Kale with the recent fall of snow around it. The citadel at Van is powerful but it had not thrilled me like this. The craggy outline here is the castle of childhood fantasy. Rebuilt on Urartian foundations in 1643 by Sari Suleyman Bey, Chief of the Mahmudis under the Ottoman regime, it lies above the Hosap river lined by rows of green birch, spanned by an elegant, double-arched bridge of black and white stone which dates back even earlier to 1500. Because of the melting snow it was a slippery process reaching the top, especially as the entrance below the great, decorated gateway was filled with water. When we finally edged our way inside, it was possible to guess the hierarchy of such an enclosed existence from the ruins of the former prison, the two mosques, the three baths, and the harem, but it was the view outside which was even more illuminating. From one of the open archways, I could make out the seven observation towers on the surrounding hills, and the crenellated walls protecting the fortress which was occupied by 8,000 people before the First World War.

The settlement is still a living community, much as it must have been. With the peasants going about their work below, and the walls with their jagged ramparts beyond, I was reminded of what life in medieval England must have been like with similar self-enclosed communities clustered beneath the baronial castle. This was something I had pictured from lessons at school, but here was the living reality with all the animals and activity within the fortress walls. Even more than the citadel of Van, it made me realise how such natural strongholds were fought for over the centuries.

The church of the Holy Cross on Akdamar Island, and the fortress of Hosap Kale, are the landmarks I shall remember, but the province of Van as a whole is unforgettable. If I am scrupulously honest with myself, I admit that I have seen parts of Scotland which are equally impressive except for the overwhelming disadvantage that they are usually obscured by rain; I celebrated the New Year in 1985 by walking with my dogs along the coastal path from Westward Ho! to Hartland Point with the limitless sea on one side only broken by the outline of Lundy Island, and the sleepy hills with grazing cattle and brown winter woods on the other, enhanced by patches of such a hard frost it looked like snow in the brilliant January sunlight. Every detail was radiant and I thought I had seldom seen anything so beautiful.

So why does the memory of eastern Turkey persist, encouraging me to agree with the nicely naive brochure of the Akdamar Hotel that 'it would tempt you to stay in this enchanted part of the country for a longer period than what you intended for'? The brochure attempts the answer with a romantic description of Van – 'where the green landscape meets the blue waters of the lake lip to lips' – and a reference to the longevity of the people – 'with the average age being above 75 years'. This is followed by the claim that Van 'invites you here to spend rest of your life. The whole atmosphere suggests the secrets of life is here.' There is some truth in that extravagant final phrase. As James Bryce recorded after climbing Mount Ararat in 1876, 'Below and around, included in this single view, seemed to lie the whole cradle of the human race. . . . No more imposing centre of the world could be imagined.'

Even today the visitor feels closer to the decencies of life in eastern Turkey. The land and lakes have not been tamed.

Information

Ankara

Hotels

There are several big, deluxe hotels of the highest quality: the *Grand Hotel* is part of the Emek group with an attractive bar and well-designed foyer and downstairs restaurant with plenty of space. Also a swimming pool, and these can be a blessing on hot days in big cities. There are 208 air-conditioned rooms and a roof-grill. But of course you pay for such luxury. Address: Ataturk Bulvari no.227, Kavaklidere, Ankara. Tel: 17 34 93.

Hotel Dedeman is another big, first-class hotel. I have stayed here and enjoyed the luxury in spite of the pretentiousness of 'Bell Captains' which was compensated for by the marvellous abandon of an end-of-high-school celebration which continued for two days with boys and girls cheering their friends who performed marvellous acrobatics of dancing until they were finally pushed in the pool outside. A glorious atmosphere of joy and youth, confounding anyone who thinks of the Turks as a dour people. Nightclub, American bar, and everything costs you accordingly but is worth it if you want and can afford such comfort. Address: Buklumsokak, Ankara. Tel: 17 11 00.

Hotel Bulvar Palas is the one I would recommend. More modest than those mentioned above, it gains in atmosphere and the lack of such pretension though it has many of the same facilities at a lower cost. Also, it is right in the heart of Ankara, situated on the main boulevard. Easy to walk from here and explore the city, which is underrated, with attractive beer gardens under the shade of chestnut trees, though a pink rubber glove floating in the lake beside my seat had a disconcerting resemblance to a swollen, severed hand. Address: 141 Ataturk Bulvari, Ankara. Tel: 17 50 20. Telex: 42613 blvd tr.

Restaurants
These were recommended to me: *Evren*, Cinnah Caddesi; *Ihtiyar Balikci*, Yuksel Caddesi; *Yakamoz*, Bayindir Sokak. Hotel reception desks may encourage you to go to the *Chinatown* restaurant. Excellent but too expensive and about as Turkish as Milwaukee.

Museum
The Museum of Anatolian Civilisation in Ankara, also referred to as the Hittite Museum, is set in splendid sloping gardens near the citadel, and the spacious building takes advantage of an old caravanserai. Exhibits range from massive sarcophagi to small objects like the vessel in the shape of a duck which has two heads, absolute perfection dating from 1600–1500 BC.

For an understanding of the different civilisations which have marched across Turkey's history, this is the most helpful place and an antidote to the modern mausoleum.

Lake Van

Accommodation
Hotel Akdamar, Kazimkarabekir Cad., Van. Tel: Van 30 36 2908. A new hotel was being constructed in 1984 but this was evidently the best when I was there, though unpretentious. There are 75 bedrooms with bath and phone, lift and lobby, a sympathetic bar on the first floor at one end with a spacious dining room at the other with better than average food.

The tourist office around the corner should be able to help you if you want to explore the area.

Transport
The train from Istanbul goes at least twice a week (check) and arrives at Tatvan where you take the ferry to Van or continue to Iran if you are desperate or insane.
Airport: check times – the flight from Ankara takes one hour forty minutes.
Road: if you are travelling south from Dogubayazit there is no direct route and you need to drive via Agri, Patnos and Ercis.

13 Losing a guide
in Diyarbakir

On my last day and at my insistence, we drove to Ahlat at the north-western end of the lake, a long but interesting drive along the peaceful shore where I had my obligatory, purging swim from a lonely beach, past the rows of huts at Muradiye erected since the last earthquake, until we reached the busy little town of Ercis on the route from Dogubayazit to the north. Ercis, also called Arjesh, was found by the Urartian king Argistis II (713–685 BC) which explains the similarity of the names, and was referred to by Marco Polo as one of the three greatest cities of Armenia though there is no hint of this today. After the flood when the water rose in 1838 and drowned the shoreline settlements, the town was rebuilt.

Ahlat must have been an exceptional place as well, fought over by every conqueror you can think of, a centre of culture and science in the thirteenth century when it was the capital of the Moslem state which governed the Van basin. My anticipation was as strong as my sense of disappointment, for as a typed local leaflet explained, 'Unfortunately, invasions, wars and earthquakes destroyed this centre and turned it into a small and dim town.' Exactly.

But though the city of Ahlat has been abandoned it remains famous for the extraordinary number of Seljuk tombs or *turbes*, described as the most impressive in Turkey, both the attractive mausoleums with their conical roofs, like that of the mausoleum built for the princess at Gevas, but also the vast number of decorated tombstones scattered in their hundreds over a forlorn stretch of treeless land, leaning in different directions, eerie relics of the past. John Freely has described this as 'surely one of the most romantically beautiful graveyards in the world'.

I wish I had felt the same. On another day I might have done, but the sky was overcast and so was I. I recognised the sombre distinction of the place, yet I found it depressing. I could not help thinking, as we drove interminably back to Van, that one perfect swim is worth a hundred Seljuk tombs. The loss, of course, was mine.

Instead of returning to Van I should have allowed time to

continue to Tatvan and Bitlis. Tatvan looked attractive but I suspect it is dull while Bitlis looked more exciting than its reputation, a lively town crowded with people situated on a hillside overlooking a green valley and a tributary of the Tigris. This was my impression the following day when I took the bus from Van to Diyarbakir at noon. Faithful unto the last second, Raif arranged for a bottle of water from the hotel for I had developed an insatiable thirst, a totally unnecessary precaution as Turkish buses give you free bottles of water anyhow. Unfortunately the hotel had used an empty bottle of raki with its label intact and when I settled in my seat and raised it to my lips I heard a furious tapping on the window, like one of the seagulls at home demanding their daily bread. Instead I saw an angry Turk gesturing outside, and this was several days before the start of Ramadan. I gestured back appropriately while Raif, who was standing awkwardly outside with the foolish grin of someone waiting for departure, explained to the man that the bottle was only filled with water – though even that would be an offence during Ramadan. Deciding it was none of the man's business anyhow, I took another slug, spluttered as if it was the strongest raki ever made, and tried to look drunk which was not too difficult. After this puny protest, the bus took off.

Bitlis lies 165 kilometres from Van, a glorious drive along the lake to begin with, past Akdamar Island and the little church, followed by wilder Tyrolean scenery with rivers racing beside the road, wild spring flowers, and stunted oak, an echo of the massive oak forests which used to cover the area. Centuries ago, the wildlife in the forests attracted the nomads with their supply of food. As the animals decreased, the permanent settlements began.

There was the usual friendliness on board the bus, and one of my last packets of Benson & Hedges helped to make immediate, smiling contact. At the small town where we stopped for half an hour, I bought some decorated tablecloths for fifty pence each and tea was forced on me by the coach driver who insisted I move to the front when the bus took off again, to enjoy a better view. Typical, furious-sounding arguments burst around me, instantly resolved, and the driver giggled lasciviously about the 'girl' singer on the radio, and then my privileged position up front was justified as we started to cross the great plain of Mesopotamia and approached the black, basalt walls of Diyarbakir as the sun began to set.

There was no one to meet me at the bus depot at Diyarbakir and I was delighted. This gave me the chance to absorb the atmosphere of the *garaj* as it is called, situated as usual on the outskirts of the city several kilometres from the heart of it, a vital point to remember if you are catching a bus which leaves at a specific time.

Because the bus is the main and cheapest transport in Turkey, the *garaj* is a microcosm of Turkish life, a living community in its own right. Some of the permanent inhabitants are the shoeblacks and vendors who never seem to leave the place so one suspects that when they snatch a moment's sleep they curl up in some corner.

A boy who might have been fifteen years old caught my attention after he sold me a Coca Cola and wandered off with his perpetual chant of 'Cola! Taksi! Taksi! Coca Cola!'

I was immersed in *Bleak House* at the time, revelling in every page, and though the comparison was absurdly sentimental I identified this boy with Joe 'the crossing sweeper', or, at least, a cheerful, Turkish version of that solitary youth.

In my rush to catch the train at Istanbul, I had been unable to collect my 'itinerary' which listed the hotels I was supposed to stay at, so I had asked Raif to phone the tourist office in Diyabakir to arrange for someone to meet me. Plainly there had been some confusion and as I sat there amongst my luggage, the Turkish crossing sweeper came back to help me. Discovering that I was English, he went in search of someone who could understand me and returned with a student who was studying French. My own smattering of that language was dredged from my memory bank and the student was kind enough to accompany me in a taxi to the Demir Hotel where I was not expected though the surly receptionist reluctantly provided a despondent room.

After a vodka and vishne at the deserted bar, I was glad to wander out on my own. I found Diyarbakir immediately sympathetic, it is a compact city of nearly 150,000 people enclosed by 3 miles of massive walls constructed by Emperor Constantius in AD 349 and still remarkably intact, a town I should like to stay in for a month with no particular purpose in mind except to know it better. The atmosphere is vigorous: I felt I was poised on the borders of Arabia yet the wide main streets resemble continental boulevards. Around the corner from the hotel were several kebab lokantas where I enjoyed one of the simplest but tastiest meals of my journey, kebab plus a donner kebab for I was hungry after the bus trip, served with rice, all for the price of that vodka. On my walk afterwards I passed a beer-only, men-only bar but was daunted by the sight of fifty motionless Turks mesmerised by a blaring television set showing some historical romance and wandered on disheartened, but when I returned the set was off and the atmosphere looked more human so I went inside. A poverty-stricken-looking Turk sent me over a plate of cucumber and cheese – a perfect combination of tastes – in return for a cigarette; two deaf and dumb men were deep in silent conversation; two soldiers walked out arm in arm which seems perfectly natural here. Inevitably the television set was switched on again, for this was a new and wondrous toy, and there were actually belly dancers beamed from a cabaret in Istanbul and a singer who seemed to be miming badly until I realised it was just the way he performed.

I blessed the fact that I had not been met for the strain of having to struggle through a conversation when neither side is fluent can be exhausting.

'I like n'actor,' one guide volunteered tentatively, when I was trying to write some notes.

'Mmm,' I replied indifferently, 'which actor do you have in mind?'

'N'actor,' he repeated, equally baffled. I put my notes away.

'Yes, but *who*? Olivier, Brando, Clint Eastwood? *Who*?'

The poor man flinched and it took five minutes before the n'actor became nactor and finally emerged as *nature*. 'Oh yes,' I agreed, feeling I had gone the verbal distance. 'Oh yes, I'm very keen on nactor too.'

However kind the guide there are moments when I have longed for silence, if only from myself.

The director of tourism found me the following morning: a charming, French-speaking man with the out-of-date good looks of a 1930s film star, a Robert Taylor or Don Ameche, who tracked me down in the Demir Hotel as I was having my ideal breakfast of cool yoghurt and local honey, served in the bar which had low tables and deep, comfortable armchairs. He told me I should have been in the Turistic Hotel around the corner.

I was grateful for his concern but dismayed to find myself chaperoned by one of his assistants afterwards, a man who smiled ceaselessly but did not understand a word of English though he spoke it so rapidly that the director assumed he was fluent. Yet, how arrogant on my part to complain that his English was largely meaningless when I could hardly speak a word of Turkish. The only difficulty I had with my various guides came from myself and it is time I revealed that I may be a travel writer but I am one of the worst travellers going, truculent, impatient, and easily rattled, and that morning I was at my most intolerant. Confronted by this dutiful but exasperating smiler, I tried to shake him off explaining that for once I had no wish to visit the obligatory mosques and tourist landmarks, preferring to see people rather than places. This met with no success whatsoever. The moment I raised my camera, he shooed the people away to ensure a nice empty view of the balat wall, though he frequently stood in front of it himself, beaming broadly, spoiling the spontaneous shot I had in mind. Marching ahead rapidly in the hope of establishing some distance between us, I turned into the *Ic kale*, an old fortress, and noticed a crowd of emotional women in the corner of a pleasant, shaded square with trees and grass. The women seemed to be shouting at some invisible object behind a wall, and I raised my rollei instinctively. Within seconds I was surrounded by soldiers and policemen for I had stumbled on a prison where the women were trying desperately to communicate with their men and hand them food. On such occasions it is difficult to know how to react: with abject submission, which indicates guilt; sheer insanity, which officials find so tiresome they are thankful to let you go; or loud indignation from a man who is plainly innocent and within his rights. The latter course is most unwise and this was the one I chose. Soon there was such a clamour of raised voices that it was heard by my pursuer who caught up with me, joined in the mêlée and was promptly arrested while I wandered off with an air of outraged innocence and photographed a boy with a tray of bread upon his head as if this had been my objective all along.

Guilt overwhelmed me a few minutes later when the guide reappeared and stammered 'my name, they have written my name'. With my own dislike of officialdom, I shared his concern but remained hard-hearted in my determination to wander on my own, losing him at last in the labyrinthine bazaar, probably the most interesting that I saw in Turkey with streets devoted to a single craft, such as copper or shoes, not only selling them but making them in front of you.

In a square leading from the markets to the town hall, lines of men waited for transport back to their villages, carrying the shining new blades of scythes as if they were going to war, presumably in readiness for the harvest. At that moment, from a considerable distance, I thought I saw my faithful guide dart into a doorway as I turned round, so I crossed the road and disappeared into a secluded courtyard with a fountain in the middle and a shop in the far corner which was draped with kilims and carpets.

14 Losing a kilim in Urfa

Buying a kilim to take back to England had become an obsession. The year before I had seen a kilim which I liked in a back street in Marmaris, but it was expensive and I was assured that I would find better and cheaper kilims in the grand bazaar in Istanbul. Far from it; this proved a lost opportunity aggravated by a tiring afternoon as scores of kilims were flung in front of me like pearls before swine while I felt increasingly guilty as I drank the cups of tea brought by a boy on a tray though this is a matter of courtesy rather than moral blackmail and should not be allowed to intimidate. The advantage of the rougher kilim over the grander carpet is a liveliness of colour, but none of the designs excited me as I had hoped on that afternoon in Istanbul. At last, partly from a sense of duty, I offered such a low price for one of the kilims that the owner took offence and lost interest. This is a mistake: sometimes you can beat the shopkeeper down by a quarter but this requires the utmost diplomacy and tact. Never run the product down by saying it is not worth the money, but shake your head sadly as you declare it is the most beautiful thing on earth and you would love to buy it if you had the money. At this you may be told 'No problem', cheques of any sort will be accepted.

In the end, I left the bazaar in Istanbul without a kilim though hardly empty-handed for I frittered most of the £90 I had put aside on trivial objects I neither needed nor particularly wanted. This is why I was determined to buy a kilim in the shop in Diyarbakir where I drank the obligatory cup of tea while carpets were spread gently before me as if we had all the time in the world, as indeed we had for the guide had not detected my escape route. I decided it was time to buy.

There was one kilim I liked especially because of its shade of blue and I beat the owner down from £60 to £40. Even then I was not decided and I crossed the road where I drank yet another tea in a small garden where some students joined me and insisted on paying for the tea when they saw my copy of *Bleak House* and realised I was English. They were so friendly and their generosity so much greater than the few lira involved, that my mind was made up and I returned to claim my kilim only to be confronted by another. This was extraordinary: an abstract design in vivid green, black, blue, white, orange and yellow, converging on a scarlet cross in the centre, which would not be out of place in the Tate Gallery though woven by peasants near Kars. Inevitably it was more expensive than the first, and larger too, but I had always vowed that if I fell in love with a kilim that was the moment to buy it, and after further bargaining I left triumphantly. I had bought my kilim at last! Back at the hotel I found the sophisticated director of tourism waiting with the disconsolate guide beside him. It was obvious that he had registered his complaint over my disappearance before I could make any criticism of my own, and the director brightened when I told him the truth, that my morning in Diyarbakir had been a total success. I am sure the guide was thankful to see the last of me as they arranged for a taxi to take me to the *garaj* on my way to Urfa in the south where I was staying the night. There was Joe, the Turkish crossing sweeper, with his familiar cry of 'Taksi! Cola!', who helped me put my luggage in the vast boot of the bus, including the precious kilim, refusing to accept a tip, shaking his head with a smile. Safe in my seat, happy with my kilim, I started to relax when a thought assailed me. How much was a 10,000-lira note? £10 or £20? It shows the state of my arithmetic that it needed several moments before I knew it was £20 pounds, and then in a moment of aberration I concluded that the carpet seller had cheated me. After all, and I remembered it distinctly, I had handed him four 10,000 lira notes assuming that each was worth £10 – yet he had accepted them and they were really worth £20! My reaction seems inexplicable now, for it was one of outrage rather than meanness. For some reason I was damned if I was going to be cheated.

Scrambling out of the bus, much to Turkish Joe's surprise, I asked him to remove my luggage and call me a 'taksi'. All this was bad and mad enough, but I had driven scarcely 300 yards before I realised my mistake: of course I had given the carpet seller four 10,000 lira notes, and of course they were worth £20 each. What I had overlooked was the elementary fact that the carpet had been sold to me for £80 and not for £40. The sum was right. Afraid that I was going to miss the bus, I told the bewildered driver to race back again and then – I must have been in a very odd state that day – decided he had charged me too much and I was mean with my tip. This is another point to bear in mind when you take a taxi, that the initial charge is steep if you only go a few yards, much the same as it is in London. The bus was still there and so was Joe who took my luggage out of the taxi with a puzzled air and put it back in the boot again. He waved with evident relief as the bus left the *garaj* with myself and the luggage secure inside it.

I gained a foolish satisfaction from the biblical names involved on this new journey, driving south across the plains of Mesopotamia, leaving the Tigris behind us as we headed for Urfa and the beehive villages of Harran near the Syrian border.

The land grew more barren with the plains stretching interminably, and the atmosphere inside the bus became wilder as we gathered speed. I had bought some strawberries in Diyarbakir and offered these to two small boys perched on either side of the aisle, so identical they must have been twins. They refused the strawberries with startled dismay which became understandable a few minutes later as they started to vomit into a brown paper bag which was handed from one brother to another as they took it in turns to be sick, the whites of their eyes rolling upwards with the wretchedness of piteous puppies.

The man in the seat beside me attempted a conversation, suddenly pointing through the window with the exclamation, 'Nanky!' I looked out at a bridge across a small river but noticed nothing remotely resembling a 'nanky'.

'Nanky?' I echoed.

'Mankey,' he corrected me.

'Ah, *monkey*!' I looked again with new curiosity, but neither a nanky, mankey, monkey or even a Peter Sellers *minkey* came in view and I sank back defeated, pretending to fall asleep. I wondered what Urfa would be like, one of the oldest cities in history. I had not intended going there until I was persuaded by Hasan Suzer of the Pera Pelas who was born in south-east Turkey and assured me that I would find it 'different'.

How different, I wondered, and still do for my visit proved short-lived.

Arriving at the *garaj*, I retrieved my luggage from the boot and realised something was missing – the kilim. I searched the bus in case the Turkish crossing sweeper had placed it in the rack above my seat, but I recognised the truth from the outset – I had left the kilim in the taxi. What should I do? I went straight to the tourist office where I found a set-up which was similar to that in Diyarbakir, with a sophisticated director and a guide only too eager to show me around. As patiently as I could, for I was infuriated by my own foolishness, I tried to explain my dilemma and, to my relief, they understood. A phone call was booked to the tourist office in Diyarbakir as soon as the lines were free, and I checked into the

Turban Urfa Hotel which looked excellent. When I returned, the director of tourism greeted me with a triumphant smile: 'It is all right. They have asked the driver and you leave *no* kilim in the taxi.' At this point I realised I had lost the game, set and match. 'No,' I explained with infinite forbearance, 'not the *first* taxi, the *second* taxi. I left it in the second taxi.'

'A *second* taxi!' exclaimed the director in the same tone of voice as I had echoed 'Nanky?'. The madness of trying to retrieve the lost kilim overwhelmed me. What chance would a truculent Turk have in Bootle if he tried to explain in a language he could not speak that he had left an Axminster carpet in a taxi in Chorlton-cum-Hardy? None whatsoever if he added that it was not the first taxi in Chorlton-cum-Hardy, but a second.

I turned to the waiting guide: 'All right, let's go and see the Sacred Carp.'

Mourning my missing kilim, my heart was not in tune with the ancient monuments of Urfa, especially as the guide seemed more concerned in showing *me* to his numerous friends and relatives. It was the the early evening by now when the walls of the city turn rose-pink, but it was also the moment when the light begins to fade and I was anxious to reach Abraham's Pool before it vanished altogether. Unperturbed, the jolly guide paused every few yards, dashing inside a shop to reappear with the owner and make a meticulous introduction before we moved on. In other circumstances I should have relished the Arabian atmosphere which really does make Urfa different, with boys offering sunflower seeds, pretzels and socks, and elderly beggars asking for money to be dropped into large metal plates. The lokantas looked as if they would be different too. I should have been flattered that the guide took such pride in my company that he wanted to show me off, and I should have appreciated his determination to explain everything in detail as we walked along the main street, though I could not understand a word he said. Convinced that I had an obsession for kilims, he even went to the trouble of wheeling me into a shop owned by a 'friend', but the gaudy objects thrown on the ground in front of me recalled those small scarlet carpets with a camel beside a pyramid brought back by sailors from Bombay bazaars as a souvenir of the voyage, with a piece of coral for the mantlepiece.

By the time we reached Abraham's alleged birthplace, the light had almost gone and it was just bad luck that the guide scared off the marvellous bird which was perched on the centre of a parapet as the focal point of my composition. It is a beautiful place, a rectangular pool 20 metres wide and 150 long, filled with the carp which were transformed into fish from the charred sticks of a fire in some ancient miracle. Tradition also claims that anyone who eats one of the fish will go blind, and two soldiers who had taken a couple of carp several months earlier apparently fell ill and died in consequence. Such stories have discouraged fishermen to such an extent that the pool today is bloated with carp who rise in furious shoals and thrash the water when you throw them bread or a sort of pea provided nearby. An attractive Turkish family with two small girls were doing that when I arrived, a pleasing photograph until the guide took over and ordered them to pose for me instead, which they did with the obedient rigidity of waxworks. The elegance of the walls of the seventeenth century *medrese* (a religious school), a series of graceful archways surrounding a mosque and minaret, is undeniable, enhanced by a sense of history for this is the legendary birthplace of Abraham who was called from Ur to go to Canaan, stopping at Harran on the way, the ancient city of Charan mentioned in Genesis.

Such names had thrilled me on the journey across the Mesopotamian plain, but the loss of the kilim had jaded my appetite for exploration. Suddenly, my hesitation was resolved. I was damned if I would accept failure so easily, I would go back to see if I could find the wretched kilim though I realised my chances of doing so were slight. To the consternation of the guide, I announced my decision, and checked out of the hotel, arriving at Urfa's *garaj* with a minute to spare. I need not have bothered to rush, for retribution now set in. The driver was an hour late, disappearing with his 'mate' for a further half hour, and when we took off at last he drove throughout the journey with one hand on the radio as he twiddled from one wavelength to another, with Turkish music interspersed with snatches of a news bulletin in English, cut short after several tantalising words, a chorus from Doris Day, and at one surprising moment a few bars from Malcolm Arnold. Due to the delay and the darkness, we arrived late in Diyarbakir where I ate a solitary meal in an empty lokanta and went to bed.

Going down to breakfast the next morning I was none too pleased to find the place occupied by the Swan Hellenic Tour, so my comfortable chair was denied me and I was shunted into a dark corner where I listened to the shrill early morning conversation, a dawn cackle of 'Good morning' – 'Good morning to *you*' – 'Did you sleep well?' – 'Not very' – 'Nor me. Why *can't* I have milk with my tea? I want milk with my tea. Such a *simple* request I'd have thought', louder and shriller until the woman achieved the impossible and was actually brought some milk for her tea. 'Oh, it's Mr

Farsons!' she cried when she trooped out, 'I thought you were in Urfa.' 'So did I,' I replied.

My message had reached the director of tourism who arrived at the Demir with the disgruntled guide from the day before, and the charade of my explanation was repeated: 'But *why* a second taxi?' he demanded. Why indeed? My mistake in confusing the price of the carpet was so preposterous that I made the excuse that I had left my camera in the hotel. 'Ah, yes,' he leant forward with a glimmer of understanding, 'and then?' 'Then I realised I had packed it after all.'

He shook his head pityingly and told the guide to accompany me to the *garaj*: 'You realise you have no chance of finding it,' he shrugged, 'But if you insist. . . .' I had the feeling that he doubted if the kilim had existed in the first place, and I cursed myself for my cruelty to the guide the day before, on whom I now depended. Unsmilingly, he accompanied me in the tourist jeep to the *garaj* though by now I was tempted to abandon my search. Arriving from Urfa the night before, I had looked for Joe, the Turkish crossing sweeper, but even he was absent from his post. Everything seemed against me until I caught sight of him. There he was, still walking up and down with his cheerful cry of 'Coca Cola! Taksi taksi! Cola!' – smiling as wistfully as ever. Quickly, I pointed him out to the guide who shook his head pessimistically but approached the boy. I watched without much hope, though curious to see the two of them in animated conversation. They walked off without a word to the far end of the *garaj* about a hundred yards away where I saw them climb into a solitary taxi which sped towards me. I hardly recognised the man, but this was the driver of the second taxi. There must be a thousand taxis in Diyarbakir and the odds against finding the right one at that moment in the *garaj* were incalculable. We drove to the man's home where he had kept the kilim overnight and when he handed it back I felt I was recovering a lost dog. It jumped into my arms with relief.

I took photographs of the tourist guide who was now his former, smiling self. I took a photo of the grinning driver leaning against his taxi, and gave him a reward of 5,000 lira. For a second I was slightly disappointed that he accepted this without a murmur of protest, then I was shocked by my reaction. It would have been so easy for the driver to deny all knowledge of the kilim. Also, the achievement in finding it went far beyond money – it marked the crucial difference between failure and success and was further proof of Turkish honesty. I offered Joe the Turkish crossing sweeper some money too, but he refused and only accepted a packet of Benson & Hedges with reluctance. There was a pleasing postscript to come. I returned to the hotel but this time when I left for the *garaj* on my way to Adiyaman, the director of tourism insisted on going with me. 'I wish to see you safely inside the bus,' he explained, '*with* your kilim.' He did not actually say 'your damned kilim', but this is what he meant. When we arrived at the *garaj* he asked to see the boy who had been responsible for its recovery. Joe was produced in front of him, looking bashful as if suspected of doing something wrong.

'So *this* is the boy!' the director exclaimed, rising to the occasion with a voice of benevolent authority. 'He is good boy. He must be helped.'

The bus arrived for Adiyaman, and the luggage *and* the kilim were put inside. By now a crowd had gathered hearing of the mad visitor and his foolishness which had a happy ending he did not deserve. When the bus drew away a small cheer went up as people waved goodbye, and I waved back to Joe, the Turkish crossing sweeper, in particular.

Information

Diyarbakir

Hotel

Demir Hotel, Izzet Pasa Cad. 14. Tel: 23 15 16 17. The manager is Osman Tan, and extremely helpful. There are 76 beds, a garage, and apart from the Lobby Bar there is a Roof Restaurant with oriental dishes, and the Amida Terrace Bar for dancing and music. In spite of all these 'facilities', I found the Demir comfortable, friendly and unpretentious.

Urfa

Hotel

Turban Urfa Oteli (part of the Turban hotel and holiday village chain). Though I checked into my room, and smartly out again, it looked first-class and the hotel seemed sympathetic as a whole. Anyhow, I doubt if there is much choice unless you have time to look around and want somewhere cheaper. This is the newest hotel, opened as recently as 1981, with 55 rooms all with bath or shower, and some even air-conditioned. If you have been travelling hard, this is a luxury to be indulged in. The brochure suggests that 'Another way of cooling at the end of a tiresome day is sipping a cold drink at the terrace and watching the evening set on the Harran Plain.' I am sure it is. Due to my pursuit of the missing kilim, I denied myself this pleasure.

15 Climbing to the vainest man on Earth

It looked as if it was going to be easy after all, which seemed a pity.

The going is best when it's hardest, and from all the warnings I had received it was going to take a considerable effort to climb to the top of Mount Nemrut (also spelt Nimrud) to witness one of the strangest man-made follies on earth, created by Antiochus I (62–32 BC), the son of Mithradates who founded the kingdom of Commagene in the region between the Euphrates (Firat today) and the Taurus Mountains known as Kummuhu by the Hittites. At a height of 8,205 feet, at the top of one of the highest peaks of the south-east Taurus, Antiochus built his colossal statues of the gods 25 to 35 feet tall – or rather an amalgamation of Greek and Persian gods considered worthy enough to be recognised as the divine, heroic ancestors of Antiochus himself. They stood on the eastern terrace before a sacrificial altar: the first represented Hercules, the son of Zeus and symbol of strength in Greek mythology combined with Artagenes, a Persian deity; and there was Ares, the Graecian god of war. Zeus-Ahuramazda sat in the centre, probably the largest head in the world apart from Easter Island, symbolising the greatest deity in the Greek and Persian religions; then the Goddess of Fortune, her head-dress adorned with fruit; and Apollo, Mithras, Helios and Hermes, the apotheosis of the sun god. And between Hercules and Zeus, Antiochus had erected his own god, *himself*, the King of Commagene, Antiochus I, descended from Darius I of Persia on his father's side, and Alexander the Great on his mother's. 'I, Antiochus,' he proclaimed, 'caused this monument to be erected in commemoration of my own glory and that of the gods.' It was an act of megalomania comparable to the building of the pyramids. He must have been the vainest man on earth, yet is scarcely known outside of Turkey.

I was eager to see this folly for myself. But, as I have mentioned, the actual process of 'Getting there' by sunrise promised to be easier than I expected. At Adiyaman, I made my way to the Antiochos Hotel where a local schoolteacher was waiting to help me. Explaining the arrangement for the night ahead, he asked if I would mind sharing the transport with two Australians, and he gestured to a couple in the corner of the outside restaurant.

'I should be delighted,' I said, and went over to introduce myself. I thought the couple looked rather old to be Australian, until I realised the absurdity of assuming that Australians are always young. Without actually assuming a strine accent, I tried to be matey: 'Hi. Good to see yer!'

'*Bitte*?' The *Austrians* looked at me suspiciously. It was plain that they preferred to eat on their own, and the schoolteacher had finished his own dinner though he watched me while I ate my kebab, washed down with a glass of *lav*, a local and rather moving little wine presumably named after the lava which poured from a volcano on the label.

Afterwards, though I was anxious to seize some sleep before our early start, the teacher led me across some wasteland to his school to introduce me to his headmaster, but came back shaking his head – 'Eric is sleeping.' Lucky Eric, I thought, as I was taken to the annual, end-of-term exhibition of embroidery, from doilys to a wedding tent which encloses the couple when they are at last alone in bed. I was introduced to every schoolgirl in sight, and though they were delightfully shy I appreciated the hell such occasions must be for royalty whose reactions are watched so hopefully. I put my arms round my back, scrutinised the smallest hankie with amazement, and congratulated everyone on such a first-rate turn-out.

I was woken at one and stumbled downstairs by 1.30 to find the others waiting as bright as babies while I felt, and probably looked, like a warmed-up sausage. Annoyingly, all the glasses of tea had been drunk and before I could ask what had happened to mine we were taken to the dolmus which I shared with the Austrian/ Australians, the teacher, and Eric his headmaster who looked seventeen and was still yawning from the depth of sleep.

Hardly a hardship in any respect. Even the dolmus was not the bone-shaking landrover I expected but a Ford station waggon. It was then that I experienced this absurd Anglo-puritanical sense of disappointment that it was going to proceed too smoothly. Soon after this the discomfort began.

You can reach the village of Kahta from the north, and even stay the night there to be closer to Nemrut, but if you go from the Antiochus Hotel the distance is roughly 80 kilometres. Leaving the main road, the track became as bone-shaking as even I could wish with wildlife caught fleetingly in the headlights: three rabbits, a fox, and several elegant deer-like dogs which pursued us growling like lions. Reaching Kahta we turned left for Gerger and if you are driving you keep on past the army post at Narince after which the direction to Mount Nemrut is signposted. If you love your car I advise you to share a dolmus as I did. I have known worse tracks, no more than dried-up river beds, but this went on interminably.

Warned that it would be cold I had seized the chance to wear an expensive safari jacket, full of useful pockets, which buttoned up at the neck. I bought this grotesquerie from a fashionable shop in London in the vain belief that I would lose weight and it would fit me better. On Mount Nemrut, at least, this tight-fitting garment came into its own and I was thankful for such protection when I saw Eric shuddering from the blast, a blanket from the car draped across his shoulders. Surprisingly, he had not been to Nemrut before, but few people had until ten years ago when it became possible to drive as far as this. Beforehand, people made their way by mule or foot, and visitors were rare. For 2,000 years the ruins lay dormant until the local shepherds and hunters described them to Helmut von Moltke when he came on a military expedition 150 years ago. Even now, the road is covered by snow for most of the year and you are advised to go in July and August though this was the end of May.

It is not so much the cold that knocks you out as the wind, and I was not prepared for that. And though the climb is no more than a few hundred yards, there is no track visible in the darkness or by daylight for that matter – so I was grateful for the beam of the teacher's torch which guided us forward. This was a slow progress due to the slippery shale which made it hard to secure a foothold. Good, I thought as the wind almost pushed me over, it is not so easy after all!

When I reached the top, nothing was quite as I expected it. To begin with it is not the top because a tumulus rises like a pyramid 50 yards higher, a sepulchral mound which may contain the tomb of Antiochus himself. It defies every attempt to trace the entrance due to the risk of causing a landslide of stones which tremble at the first thrust of excavation. Doubtless they will find the tomb one day, if it is there.

As for the statues at the base, they sit there in a headless row. Time, earthquakes, erosion, storm, all the elements have taken their revenge for the human insolence that dared to claim equality with the gods. The last head to fall was that of the Goddess of Fortune which came tumbling down in a violent thunderstorm as recently as 1962.

Curiously, it may be even more impressive as we see them now in a state of upheaval, uncovered, an astonishing feat in itself, with the heads hoisted upright, another extraordinary achievement for they look as if they have stood there since the start of time. These heads are tremendous, higher than a man, the bearded Zeus near the beardless Antiochus with their eagles and lions nearby. One magnificent, open-mouthed lion seems to be roaring his defiance, the first outline to emerge that morning. Another head lay sprawled on the ground, yet to be straightened, with several strange conical shapes and the steps of the sacrificial altar beyond.

The wind was so violent that I sheltered behind a wall and noticed half a dozen figures who had joined us. We waited; there was little point in talking against the din, and I thought, as I have done so often, that the hour before dawn is the most dismal of all. Gradually it began to lighten and I made out the endless view below us by the faint, serpentine ribbon of the Euphrates meandering into the distance.

The scale was eerie. How could Antiochus have built here? An army must have been needed, a generation of ants to build his monument to himself, dragging the huge blocks of marble for his statues, eight for each god, to be placed on top of each other, white marble carried from Gerger 30 kilometres away, black marble used for the reliefs at the bottom of the tumulus from the eastern quarry of Karabelen. How had they achieved this 2,000 years ago? Yet it was easy to understand why he had chosen such a prominence as the landscape unfolded before me in the light for this was Ancient Mesopotamia, once so fruitful and so rich, now a barren plain soon to be transformed by another man-made wonder even greater, if less romantic. An immense irrigation scheme is planned for the next ten years, diverting the Euphrates and the Tigris, constructing a damn which will be the third or fourth largest in the world, creating a lake as big as Van, even changing the climate in doing so – Mesopotamia revived!

By now I could see the plains below for it was daylight, yet, curiously, there was no sun. How long it took to rise! I moved behind the head of a god to be ready to photograph the sun the moment it appeared though I feared it must prove a disappointment.

And then the sun came up.

It was neither black as someone had told me, nor green as another had insisted, but a molten explosion which gave the impression of a raw-red force bubbling from the earth as if the core had been shattered – more blood than fire.

The power was so overwhelming that I knew why Antiochus had faced his gods in this direction for it was a form of blessing. If a man had never seen the sun rise before he would fall on his knees in front of it here in terror of what might follow. The molten shape pulsated; I could see it throb and thought it strange I could not hear it, and suddenly the ball of the sun was torn from the earth and resumed its natural shape. The whole ascent cannot have lasted for more than fifteen seconds.

Hail to Antiochus for boasting that 'no living human being shall be able to build anything higher than this shrine'.

Though the heads of the gods have fallen, his own among them, this is a glorious affirmation of the inevitability of life and death. 'What I have done,' he proclaimed, 'is proof of my belief in the presence of the gods.'

Hail to Antiochus and his final command: 'At the end of my fortunate life my body will plunge into eternal sleep here, and my spirit will be in the heavenly paradise of Zeus Ahuramazda.'

Hail Antiochus. You deserve no less for this is beyond vanity.

The sun was rising rapidly now, paler in the sky, and I was left below for a few ecstatic moments more, shaking with excitement in the howling wind.

16 Driving back from Nemrut

As soon as we descended, the wind dropped and the air grew hot though it was barely seven in the morning. The first hint that something was wrong came with our stop at a pleasant, open-air lokanta at the foot of the mountain, plainly there for the benefit of travellers like myself. Ravenous by now, I asked the teacher to order yoghurt and honey and tea. The owner shook his head mournfully and the teacher translated his reply: 'The yoghurt has not arrived.' Used to such excuses in England, I settled for tea. The man shook his head again, the tea had not arrived either. In a country where tea is forced on one at the slightest excuse, this was baffling.

Tea was forgotten as we stopped at two memorable landmarks. The first was the ancient castle of Eski Kale with a massive relief, 34 yards high, erected by Antiochus in memory of his father, Mithradates I, shaking hands with Hercules, stout and strong but considerably shorter. Beside it is a long inscription in Greek, as much a testimonial to Antiochus himself as to his father: 'built by the Great King Antiochus, God, the Righteous, Epiphanes, the Romanphile and Hellenophile, son of King Mithradates the Queen Laodike, daughter of Antiochus Epiphanes'. The excellent condition of this relief is startling in such wild surroundings, a museum piece left for once in its natural setting, but no less remarkable than the preservation of the Roman bridge of Cendere nearby, built by the people of Commagene as a tribute to the Roman Emperor Septimius Severus. The proportions are so perfect that the ninety-two carved blocks of stone still support a single arch which is 92 yards long, withstanding the traffic above and the powerful River Nympheos below. The only flaw is a missing column from the pair at either end: two to Severus and his wife, the Empress Julia Domna, the other to his son Caracalla who ordered the destruction of the adjacent column to his brother, Geta, after he killed him on becoming emperor himself.

Thirstier than ever, I walked to the lokanta a few yards away and asked for tea. Why they went through the charade I cannot imagine, but it was totally confusing: first a smiling response, but no tea; then the promise, translated by the teacher, who had joined me, of hot water. When no hot water arrived, the truth struck me at last – this was the first day of Ramadan when absolute fasting is demanded throughout the hours of daylight. This is taken so seriously in remoter parts of eastern Turkey that people are stoned if they are seen chewing nuts or drinking from a fountain in the daytime.

The effect on the Austrians was startling, for they had kept to themselves until now. 'This is not bloody good enough!' shouted the husband at the schoolteacher. 'Ramadan for you, but why for us? Very good, we declare our own Ramadan – we pay half price for dolmus because there is no tea.' As he sat back triumphantly, his wife turned to me reassuringly. She had made no comment on Mount Nemrut having stayed in the station waggon until the sun was safely in the sky, but now her face brightened for the first time. 'Be sure, when we come back to Adiyaman, to go the lysée. They have there this exhibition of embroideries. Now, *that* is *lovely*!'

I spent the night in *Malatya* to the north, one of those towns where it depends on luck and your frame of mind if you enjoy yourself. I liked the 'feel' of it, the attractive park in the centre, an excellent downstairs restaurant called Dogu and that lively cheerfulness which has gone from so many of our northern cities in England, deprived of their own peculiar personality by the soullessness of 'planners'. However, I met a group of English workers who hated the place. I found them in the bar of the Kent Hotel, fed up with the conditions and the Turkish food. 'We phoned up base this morning,' one of them told me, 'to complain about the lack of protein in our diet. As luck would have it, base understood, describing this place as one of the nastiest little towns base ever stayed in.' I found their whining tiresome, especially as they looked as strong as oxen, yet, disconcertingly, they were charming to talk to.

Then I met an Englishman of another type. He worked for the British Embassy in Ankara and I recognised him as one of the few companions at Mount Nemrut that morning. He had left his wife, mother-in-law and youngest son in Ankara and driven his father-in-law and his oldest boy, who was six, to see Mount Nemrut. He was still in a state of euphoria, like myself. 'I want my son to see everything he can of Turkey before I'm posted back home.'

Having shared the sunrise, there was a bond between us: 'Wasn't it marvellous!' he exclaimed.

When I went to bed the construction workers remained at the bar, still complaining about their stomachs. The contrast between the two types of Englishmen was disquieting, for it showed me once again that travel depends on your point of view: a lace doily for the Austrian, protein for the blasé Englishmen, Nemrut for the man from the Embassy, and all of the reactions true in their different ways.

Information

Adiyaman

Hotel
Antiochus Motel, Menderes Cad. Tel: 1240 1184 2685. Approximately £12 (when I was there in 1984) for two people, half pension. I found this perfectly all right in every way.

Kahta (on the way to Nemrut)

Hotel
Merhaba Hotel, tel: 98 139, or the *Komegan*. I cannot vouch for either.

Malatya

Hotel
Kent Hotel, Ataturk Cad. 151. Tel: 2175 28 13. 51 rooms. This is where I stayed and I found it excellent. There is also the *Sinan*, Kisla Cad. 14. Tel: 2907 3007. 55 rooms.

Do not cause ill-feeling, as I did, by overtipping the driver who takes you to Nemrut and certainly not in front of the guide unless you are going to give him more. Because the guide has become a friend, it is wrong to assume that he is above reimbursement – though of course he might refuse.

17 Tarsus – but what's in a name?

(Continuing the journey south from Urgup, to Tarsus and Mersin on the Mediterranean)

If you thought I had abandoned my search for a paradise in Turkey, I should explain that I am obsessed by the need to live beside water. Even in London I made a home on the bend of the river at Limehouse before that untamed stretch of the Thames was patronised and became as fashionable as it is today. In Devon I lived above one of the finest beaches in England, Putsborough Sands, in one of half a dozen houses on the dunes near Baggy Point, and when I had to leave I moved to a fishing village on an estuary where I can climb from my backyard into the rowboat moored below.

Though there is a solace in the constantly changing face of water wherever it is, the combination of sun, whitewashed houses, unfamiliar smells and tastes, and semi-tropical plants add a sensuality which makes the Mediterranean incomparable. This is why and where my search for a new home now began in earnest and my highest hopes were confirmed: of all the coastlines I have seen around the world, I believe that the Turkish shoreline which stretches from Alanya in the south to Bodrum in the north, with a thousand inlets in between, is the most exciting.

I am not an archaeologist, though I often wish I was, but I enjoy a sense of history even if my knowledge is meagre and I find it enthralling to climb above a beach like that at Patara, walk across a Roman theatre half-covered by sand, and look down on walls and a massive gateway with the realisation that this was a city, one of the great chain of ports before the water receded occupied by a succession of conquering armies as they marched south. Far from being remote military outposts, as dull as Aldershot today, they represented the height of Hellenic and Roman culture with temples and theatres, gymnasiums and markets, and elaborate baths which were used as meeting places too.

This is the unique advantage in going on holiday to Turkey today for many of these ancient cities are only being excavated *now*. In addition to the sun and sea, you have the excitement of finding places which are still unspoilt, with no fences to keep you out, no signposts to direct you, no guides or souvenirs. There are some you can only reach by sea and others which you stumble on more or less by accident.

Their names sound like poetry to me: Alanya and Antalya, Kas and Kekova, Olympos and Patara, but that is being romantic. What's in a name? It would be as daft to go to a place because it sounds attractive as to choose an island because the shape looks nice on the map, though I have done that too.

What name could be more tempting than Tarsus – the legendary birthplace of St Paul set among cedar groves, banana, date and fig trees? In 41 BC Cleopatra's galley sailed into town when it was still a port, across a lake that has long since disappeared, up the Cydnus River:

> The Queen in the dress and character of Aphrodite, lay on a couch of gold brocade, as though in a picture, while about her were pretty boys, adorned like cupids, who fanned her, and maidens bedecked as nereids and graces, and some made as if they were rowing, while others busied themselves about the sails. All manner of sweet perfumes were wafted ashore from the ship, and on the shore thousands were gathered to behold her.

Could anything sound more voluptuous than Plutarch's description of Cleopatra's arrival in Tarsus for her tryst with Marc Antony? Yet Cleopatra's Gate, also called the Gate of the Bitch, is surrounded by traffic and seemed nondescript after such anticipation. I have never agreed with Stevenson's dictum that 'to travel hopefully is a better thing than to arrive,' written before the ordeal of flying which makes any arrival, even in the most godforsaken spot on earth, a blessed relief. If you travel too hopefully, you are courting disappointment.

I did not know what to expect from Mersin, apart from the satisfaction of knowing that we had crossed from the Black Sea coast to the Mediterranean, but it proved a vast, modern port to stay in briefly rather than to savour.

I had been booked into the best hotel, the Mersin, which was almost too luxurious with the tiresome paraphernalia of a yashmakked girl behind a gilt trolley taking an interminable time in serving one a tiny cup of coffee, and a fierce-looking Arab in full regalia who stalked the foyer until he decided to use the lift, whereupon the hall porter kicked out the occupants who were just about to go up, waving them into the lobby so that the towering Arab could rise in solitary splendour. The people who had been evicted included an elderly man with a stick and did not seem to mind, but I did.

Such places are for those who do not calculate the bill. Dinner for one with a single raki cost £10, but dinner for the three of us with five raki at a restaurant round the corner cost £2. Inevitably, the bars in the best hotels are expensive, but I am not complaining for the measures are huge and the prices still cheap by English standards. I am simply indicating that prices vary wildly.

It is wise to check your extravagances beforehand. In search of a livelier atmosphere I walked to the fish market nearby, enclosed by the formidable walls of an old building, possibly a caravanserai though the wooden roof has gone, and ordered a dish of large though not gigantic prawns which came from Iskenderum (formerly Alexandretta) further down the coast. I reckoned that they cost 100 Turkish lira for five which explains my dismay when I was charged 100 each. It shows how easily one is spoiled by the low prices in Turkey that I considered this exhorbitant and ate them disconsolately while I watched a barefoot urchin holding the beak of a tied-up pelican.

If I sound critical of Mersin, that is unfair. There is no logic in warming to a town like Malatya but not to Mersin simply because it is modern. The only real objection concerned the view from my balcony at eight in the morning overlooking the long waterfront park laid out with the Turkish devotion to trees and palms, red hibiscus and eucalyptus, watered and cared for by the gardeners below. A smouldering ball of sun hung from the top of a ship's crane in the artificial harbour beyond and the whole panorama should have been delightful. Instead it was marred by a bilious streak which stretched across the sky expanding as it went, a monstrous man-made poison of industrial waste from the tall, spindly chimney from an oil refinery in the docks.

Conversely, the disadvantages of a new, industrial port are balanced by the swimming pools and restaurants just outside the city after a couple of miles of high apartment blocks. How much I enjoyed their luxury then, for I write this now with the benefit of knowing the greater beauty which lies beyond. Though I am not a 'pool person', I revelled in the self-indulgence at Ligos with a first-class restaurant on a terraced balcony, the spacious pool below and the sea just a few yards away with a score of cargo ships lined on the horizon. The gardens were rich with bougainvillaea and dark blue morning glory and there was a pleasing holiday atmosphere inside with a father playing with his three small daughters, ecstatic in their waterwings, attractive Turkish women, one with a barking poodle, and the inevitable Adonis showing off on the diving board. Only too easy to idle the hours away with a bottle of beer beside me, sunbathing to the voice of Elvis on the pool's loudspeaker. Fine in its place, but should that place be Turkey? The pools with their nightly cabarets on the terraces above are not really for me, nor the vast hotel at Silifke, our next stop. This sounds ungrateful, for the building was new, the rooms spotless, and the deep pool above the sea was invigorating, but I found it impersonal, made all the emptier by the whistling wind that pursued me down the corridors and the chilling bluster of the muzak in the dining room. Yet such hotels with all their facilities are meant for the invasion of holiday package tours and as such they could not be bettered. Because tourism is such a new development in Turkey, there is less choice for the independent traveller. There is no tradition resembling an inn or a Greek taverna and it is rare that you find a modest house by the sea where you can have a simple meal and spend the night. This will come. On the way to Silifke, after the astonishing fortress which stands in the sea – the Maiden's Castle or Kiz Kalesi – we stopped at Narlikuyu to see the mosaics which adorn the floor of a Roman bath, showing the three graces beside the inscription, 'He who drinks from this water will become wise and long-living, and, if ugly, fair.' It was the wrong time of day to linger, but the cluster of houses and restaurants looked ideal for the independent traveller. So did the low-lying hotel and restaurant at Bogsak a few miles on the other side of Silifke along the coastal road to Alanya, which is set in its own bay. These places signal the promise of more intimate and cheaper places to stay at, combining atmosphere with basic comfort, a combination that seems so elementary yet is always hard to find.

Meanwhile, in the new hotel in Silifke, there was little to suggest that I was in Turkey. I was marking time and felt relieved the moment we moved away and drove into the mountains in search of the Tomb of the Fearless King.

18 The Tomb of the Fearless King

What's in a name? The title of the Tomb of the Fearless King was so resounding that I was determined to see it for myself, which is why I had stopped at Silifke. All I had to go on was a typed sheet of paper which someone had given me about the 'Mausoleum where you can see the relief of the phallus, symbol of Priape', in other words, the tomb of a king who was not only fearless but well-endowed.

For a moment I was confused, assuming that a genuine king had been buried here, or that it was a temple erected to Priape, the God of fertility and illegitimate son of Zeus and Aphrodite. Legend claims that Hera, the wife of Zeus, was so jealous of Aphrodite that she deformed the child giving him a phallus nearly equal to his height, the subject of postcards sold throughout Turkey today, but when he became a man this deformity was so attractive to the women of Lapeski, his home town, that their husbands drove him out. The sheet of paper informed me that 'Priape infected his incurable illness to the men to take revenge on them,' suggesting that he had the pox as well.

Consequently, in much the same way as the Medusa's head protects the grave from robbers, the phallus of Priape carved on a gravestone indicates that the man who was buried there had exceptional courage and such potency that young brides would visit his tomb before 'going to the nuptial bed'. Unlike the Medusa heads, the symbol of the phallus is rare, though I have seen one in the ancient city of Thera on the island of Santorini: a bold carving above the generous inscription, 'I offer this to my best friend.' And there is another on Delos, surmounting two gigantic balls.

I had not heard of such a symbol in Turkey, nor could I find any reference to the Tomb of the Fearless King in my various guide-books. How marvellous, I thought, to go to a place which was that unknown. The problem lay in getting there: the piece of paper warned of a 'difficult road' for 10 kilometres, 'and the last 2 km will have to be covered by foot.' To start with, people shook their heads humorously when we asked them the way, denying all such knowledge. One man thought he knew but refused to give the directions though he was delighted to warn us, 'You'll need a tractor.' To my surprise we found it easily, clearly visible from the main road which goes to Demurcili. Far from a long and arduous trek, it was just a gentle stroll up several terraced fields and over a low stone wall.

The description of a 'temple-tomb' is exact. Of all the mausoleums I have seen, this style has the most graceful proportions: two levels supported by four columns on each, with those on the top in the finest Corinthian tradition. An arch encloses the sarcophagus, with a perpendicular roof above decorated by a frieze, though only the corners remain on this particular Tomb today. Inevitably, time had corroded the stone but the pale colours glow in the sunlight and the whole effect is peaceful, though a second tomb nearby was less impressive.

With the help of a pile of stones, I managed to haul myself on to the top level where I was saddened to find that the two great lions guarding the tomb were virtually beheaded and the frieze at the top had been vandalised by treasure seekers over the years. Inevitably, the sarcophagus was open and empty.

Yet it was undeniably beautiful and the visit seemed complete when I picked up a fossilised seashell which seemed a sensational find at such a height, dropped perhaps by a Roman soldier, or a bird, or simply thrown up in some unheaval a million years ago? Knowing nothing about fossils I had no idea, accepting it simply as a symbol of good luck. It lies on my window ledge as I write this now.

In spite of this omen, I felt that something was wrong. The sheet of paper had not referred to a second tomb, and I had not seen the cistern let alone the giant oak tree which it did mention. Above all, where was the famous phallus? Far from being rampant, there was no sign of its enormity and I began to wonder if it existed.

'Let's drive a bit further,' I suggested, 'we might see something else,' and indeed we did, a *third* temple-tomb which prompted the nagging suspicion that the Tomb of the Fearless King still lay ahead of us. So we drove on and this is how we came to Uzuncaburc, just a peculiar name on the map until then, 30 kilometres from the coast and 1,200 metres high. Having travelled hopefully to the anti-climax of Tarsus, this took me completely by surprise. Even more than the chain of ports along the coast, the ruins at Uzuncaburc confirmed that this part of Asia Minor was the key to civilisation, the route for the armies from the east on their way to conquer Europe, and equally for the Greeks and Romans in their colonisation. Unprepared for a city set so far inland, I was astonished by the colossal scale but in particular by its magnificence. Inscriptions on the Temple of Zeus reveal that the area was known as Olba in Hellenistic times, while the discovery of Roman coins shows that this was Diocaesarea in the reign of the Emperor Vespasian (AD 9–79), the founder of the Flavian dynasty who was proclaimed emperor by his soldiers, indicating how important this headquarters must have been. There is no clue to this today apart from the splendid ruins, with the Romans enhancing the genius laid down by the Greeks. A massive gateway with a lion's head protruding high up leads to a colonnaded street, once the main road to the city; a Hellenistic tower, 22 metres high with five storeys, explains the name of Uzuncaburc today, for it means 'high tower'; and the finest monument of all is the Temple of Zeus with rows of headless columns, probably built by Seleucus I, one of Alexander the Great's generals and a king of ancient Syria, who founded the Seleucid dynasty. It dates from the third century BC, and reminds me of Baalbek in the Lebanon. The low-lying tombs nearby were exceptionally fine, many with the carved heads of bulls, and because this was the golden hour before dusk I had arrived at the perfect moment, without another person in sight.

Uzuncaburc was an unexpected reward, but as I drove back the doubt about the Fearless King persisted and I stopped at the tourist office at Silifke, as I should have done from the outset. My doubt was confirmed – we had gone to the wrong temple-tomb. The one to Priape was more remote and difficult to reach and though the director had no photographs he showed me a detailed drawing which proved that the phallus was indeed as immense as its reputation, carved on one side of the tomb.

Back in the vast hotel on the outskirts of Silifke, I wondered if I should wake at six the next morning to see the tomb before we continued our journey to Alanya, but Osman had left with his taxi and for all I knew he might have raced back to Mersin to see his friends. So I rationalised my failure by deciding that a photograph of the phallus would be too offensive for this book. Anyhow, some things should be left to the imagination and surely a gigantic phallus is one of them?

Rather than compete with the muzak in the dining room, I walked into the village, the ferryport to Cyprus for the traffic which pours south from Ankara and Konya to Silifke, once the most important city in Cilicia, now little more than a junction on the coast. I found Osman sitting outside one of the lokantas, smiling as broadly as ever, so the taxi would have been available after all. My sense of regret increased when I wandered idly into a souvenir shop opposite and noticed some postcards showing extraordinary carvings in the cliffs nearby, known as Adam Kayalar – 'the Rock Men' – evidently a hundred times the size of life, compelling images unlike anything I had seen before.

Ah well, I rationalised again, one cannot see everything; better to leave something for another visit, but I did not deceive myself for a moment.

We set off at nine the next morning and drove in silence while I tormented myself with the vainest of human pastimes – the thought of what I had missed.

'No!' I exclaimed suddenly. 'This is not good enough. We must go back. I have to see the tomb for myself.'

By now we were well on our way to Alanya, but to his credit, Koksal, the guide, understood me at once and we set out in search of the Rock Men first. Unless you have a jeep, a mule, or an obsession with rock men which passeth all normality, I cannot advise you to do the same. To begin with we had to retrace our steps towards the Maiden's Castle, the fortress in the sea, near the village of Susanoglu whose lively-looking restaurants would have tempted me to pause on another occasion, turning left at the Geler lokanta opposite the Nobel Hotel, past some houses where a young hunchback, probably the village idiot, bared his behind in our direction though his family around him seemed indifferent to such an exhibition, doubtless having seen it countless times before.

The track petered out though Osman continued valiantly, until I insisted on walking up an ancient, deeply indented road which gave the impression that I was stepping over history and certainly seemed to have no purpose now. At last I saw the Rock Men far, far away across a valley on a distant ridge, just discernible due to the paler cliff face where they had been carved – a man reclining above a massive sort of bed, another standing, and a group, each enclosed by a frame resembling the Lycian tombs carved into the cliffs further up the coast but still too vague to be photographed from where I stood, especially as the light was behind them.

Even with the whole day to spare, it would have been a hellish expedition. For once I should have welcomed a road to bring us within range, for the Rock Men are a phenomenon to observe rather than explore. So we made our way back to the car and headed for the Tomb of the Fearless King which was my main objective, armed with the instructions given me by the tourist director in Silifke.

The drive to Turkmenusagi is a constant pleasure, climbing through pine forests, glimpsing a clearing where a girl led a camel laden with firewood following by a donkey and a cheerful dog, until we took the turning to the village of Dracek. The landmark to look for after roughly 5 kilometres, is a modern house with a flight of stone steps on the outside leading to the roof. We made our first mistake by carrying straight on, but you should turn right and start going downhill, or so we were informed by a small girl on our return. The road looked as if it had been recently bulldozed in places through there was little indication why, raising clouds of reddish dust, and at times the underbelly of the car screeched so painfully as it scraped the stones that I could bear it no longer and preferred to walk.

With grim determination we continued, Osman sweating in sympathy for his taxi, until it became obvious that we had gone further than we should have done. Chancing to look back, I glimpsed a monument half-hidden in the trees about 5 kilometres away – damn that little girl! We must have taken the wrong road after all. It was too disheartening, as if the fates were resolved to prevent us. By now we had been driving for five hours and it was the middle of the afternoon. I was hot, dishevelled, thirsty and fed-up. Petulantly, I said, 'Shall we call it a day?' hoping that no one would agree. Koksal did not even bother to call my bluff; 'Of course not,' he replied severely, 'Having gone so far, we cannot give up now.'

So we drove back to the top of the hill though it was more of a crawl than a drive, where we found the young girl again, this time with her family who foiled us completely with their assurance that it had been the right road all the time, so down we went once more prepared to venture even further for by now it had become a point of honour. Then we had our first stroke of luck when we saw the welcome though surprising figure of a young man walking along the side of the road with the natural elegance and certainty of an Oxford undergraduate, dressed in dark pantaloons, a blue shirt, and a wide straw hat as if he had strayed from a country house party in Wiltshire. I was only surprised that he was not carrying a volume of nineteenth century poems.

Smiling with bemused tolerance at our distraught condition, revealing perfectly white teeth which is a rarity in itself in Turkey, he squeezed into the taxi beside me to show the way, pointing to the side of the road a few minutes later where there was no sign whatsoever nor the slightest indication of a gap, let alone a turning. No wonder we had missed it. The track roughly resembled the top of one of the stone walls that line this area and after a kilometre we could drive no further and had to walk, opening a gate which led to a peasant's hut where an elderly man bowed to us politely.

If the Tomb of the Fearless King had been a disappointment, my imagination would have transformed it into the Taj Mahal after the difficulty of getting there, but no enhancement was needed. The temple-tomb is marvellous, dwarfing the others we had gone to by mistake. Not only is it twice the size but virtually intact. And there was the phallus carved on the side, handsome, delightful and proud but wholly without offence. Nearby was the giant oak, big enough for eight people to hide in when they needed a refuge, and the deep cistern 5 metres wide and 20 long, though so overgrown that it had to be pointed out to us by the old man who joined us with two wide-eyed boys. I photographed the young man who had shown us the way, and he posed instinctively with his innate grace as if for Cecil Beaton though he refused the Turkish lira I tried to give him afterwards in gratitude for all his help, shaking his head with a courtesy which put me to shame.

The elderly man with a grizzled white beard and close-fitting, knitted cap, stepped forward as we started to leave, inviting us into his home. Though we were hours late by now, there was no thought of refusing: courtesy demanded that we accept and, more selfishly, the thought of something to drink was irresistible.

The peasant's hut was a stone block with rough, wooden steps leading to the flat roof, surrounded by an encampment of outhouses covered by a black material which made them look like nomadic tents. Inside, the room was cool and carpeted with a tier of beds in the background where the family slept above each other at night, now concealed behind a curtain of kilims. I took off my shoes and sat on the broad pillows laid out on the floor for our benefit; everything was spotlessly clean, and presumably it has to be with no water or electricity or modern 'conveniences'. Though we had been invited to drink *chai*, a banquet gradually appeared instead: first, initially the most welcome sight of all, a gleaming jug filled with cold water, then, apples, bread as thin as tissue paper to enfold the shirred eggs, and bowls of yoghurt, all served on immense, circular, silvery-looking trays. And, finally, the tea.

The women – the old man's wife and his daughter-in-law – served us but stayed respectfully in the background without uttering a word, apart from whispered consultations among themselves, and though the elder sons joined us and sat beside their father they refused to smoke in front of him.

How many children did he have? He smiled as he told us he had no idea. Nor did he know how old he was though he remembered the cistern when it was covered by the stone roof which has since fallen in.

How many visitors came to see the Tomb of the Fearless King? About ten managed to find the mausoleum each year, invariably losing their way. Once he had to let some travellers stay the night because they had taken so long in getting there that it was dark. Now the family were looking forward to the arrival of a new road approaching from the other direction which will bring the blessing of electricity and transform their lives. The family own their land and they will be sitting beside a tourist landmark once the road comes through and the track is beaten. They are waiting for this bonanza which will end the hardship of their life as it is today, and how could I begrudge them such good fortune? I was grateful that I had arrived when the going was difficult and the visitors few, and their hospitality spontaneous. Tourists alighting from their coaches in years to come would adore such a rustic meal as we had enjoyed if laid on for them especially, but the peasant family could never be so devious. Instead they will sell them Pepsi and fizzy drinks from their new electric cooler, they will have people to talk to, and the children can act as guides while the women sell souvenirs and postcards. The phallus will provoke shrieks of consternation, the cameras will click furiously and the family will smile but not really understand. How odiously condescending this must sound, especially as I am blazing the way. Perhaps that is the reason, the guilt of the travel writer who helps to kill the place he loves.

When we left there was a moment of embarrassment when Koksal offered the two little girls some money rather than insult the father's dignity by offering it to him, but even this was rejected until Koksal protested that the money was 'for books for school, for education', and then it was accepted reluctantly as the old man accompanied us back to the car.

We drove straight off to Alanya along a noble coastline of low mountains or high hills (I wish there was a word for the in-between) with bays and stretches of empty sand. Darkness began to fall and we had reached that hour of driving when distances seem longer than expected, when there is always another hill beyond the hill beyond.

We passed three wild, snarling dogs and I have wondered since if they were wolves for we came across men with guns soon afterwards, and caught the outline of the great Crusader castle of Anamur on the edge of the sea, the largest medieval fortress on the Mediterranean coast of Turkey, with huge walls and thirty-six towers, though these were little more than a ghostly silhouette in the dying light. By the time we reached Alanya it was too dark to see the fortress of the Red Tower which dominates the hill above. I

came back to earth as I booked into the modern complex of the
Alantur motel which boasts three swimming pools beside the
perfectly good sea.

'Are you two persons?' asked the supercilious clerk at the reception desk as he pushed the inevitable form in front of me.

'No, I just look like that,' I replied and asked for the bar, to be
informed that it was closed.

Information from Mersin to Alanya

Mersin

Hotel
The *Mersin Hotel* is the best with three bars and a roof restaurant for
dancing and dining, but is not particularly Turkish. Tel: 2200.

Hotel Toros is half the price and though it is far less grand than the
Mersin, the bar is decorated with Turkish carpets and gilt mirrors
and has greater atmosphere.

Korikos

On your way to Silifke 83 kilometres away, stop at Korikos – this is a
splendid sight with the Maiden's Castle apparently rising out of the
sea opposite the town it was built to defend. Built on a low island,
this was once a fortress and defied attack. Two kilometres to the
north of Korikos are the gorges known as The Pits of Heaven and
Hell. Heaven is a natural chasm formed by the erosion of underground streams, and is 90 yards deep. Hell is even deeper, as it
should be, and tradition claims that the giant Typhon was impris-
oned here. Hell is difficult to reach and I should not bother to
attempt it. If hell beckons, you will get there soon enough. Frankly,
Heaven and Hell are hardly worth the detour unless you have ample
time to spare.

Narlikuyu

Narlikuyu, however, is well worth stopping at to see the Roman
bath with the famous mosaic of the Three Graces, decorated with a
frieze of red partridges and turtle doves. Apart from the mosaic,
the group of restaurants off the main road looks promising and the
water in the bay has two levels of temperature, so that you can swim
from hot to cold. It is alleged to have miraculous healing powers
too.

Restaurant
Ali Baba Fish Restaurant, Narlikuyu.

Silifke

The port for Cyprus lies just outside at Tasucu, with ferryboats every day in summer.

Hotel
I stayed at the massive new *Tastur* hotel at Tasucu which I have referred to, but I would recommend the simpler *Bogsak* motel a few kilometres further on. Set in its own bay, near the village of Bogsak, this was the sort of place I was hoping to find, without the oppression of a vast, organised complex. There are 22 bedrooms, a restaurant, and a friendly atmosphere. Also, extremely cheap compared to the larger and less sympathetic tourist hotel, though this does have a touristic licence too.

19 My second guide to Turkey

(Resuming my first journey through Turkey, after leaving Yusuf at the airport in Istanbul as I flew south to Antalya where I was met by Ibrahim)

Ibrahim Buyukbenli is a gentle man. He met me at the airport in Antalya advancing with the waddle of a jovial penguin. His limp was caused when his foot crumpled beneath him as he fell from his horse at the age of seven, and there is a terrible irony in Ibrahim's fondness for animals as I discovered over dinner that first night on the prow-like balcony of the Talya Hotel.

Several months earlier he had been told of an abandoned dog whose neck was twisted horribly by a coil of wire. Presumably this had been used to tie it up when it was a puppy, but now the wire was strangling the animal as it grew larger. Ibrahim hired a car, fetched the local vet, and set out for the village where the dog had been seen. Everyone denied its existence until a boy whispered that Ibrahim might find it hiding in a ruined house on the outskirts.

Sure enough he glimpsed a flash of frightened eyes in a corner. As the dog made a dash to escape, Ibrahim managed to seize it by the ears while the vet moved in quickly and gave it an injection. They cut the wire, cleaned the dog up, and when it recovered it was free. Before they left the village, Ibrahim gave some money to the boy's family so that he could feed the dog, but the vet refused his fee exclaiming. 'If you're mad enough to do all this for a strange dog, then I haven't got the heart to charge you.'

Ibrahim is self-taught but speaks English perfectly, doing so at his own pace which compelled me to listen to him closely. Anyhow, I was just as delighted by the story as he was. Ibrahim had a special reason for feeling pleased. Only that morning a man from the village had called at his office to tell him some good news: 'The dog has had five puppies and all are well.'

'I am rewarded,' said Ibrahim.

A pleasing story, but there was more to it than that. Ibrahim's courage in seizing a wild a dog was beyond the natural reaction of someone who is fond of dogs – Ibrahim is *allergic* to them.

It started with that fall from his horse when he was a boy for it left him with his upturned foot which convinces every dog that it is about to be kicked and had better act first. Consequently, when they see him advancing with outstretched hand, dogs recoil or run away. This has been a penalty of Ibrahim's life ever since. Even so, when he noticed a stray mongrel the year before, sleeping in front of the wheels of a car near the tourist office in Antalya, he did not hesitate to lift it out of harm's way. In the panic of being woken, the dog scratched his hand accidentally but deeply enough for Ibrahim to visit the doctor who told him flatly that unless he traced the dog within four days and found it free from disease, he would have to be injected for rabies.

For the next four days Ibrahim and his friends searched every corner of Antalya but the strange dog had disappeared. No one had seen it, no one had heard of it, so Ibrahim started his course of injections. After the fourteenth his body became paralysed while another man died from the same drug. Ibrahim recovered but he had to spend the next five months at home convalescing, looked after by his sisters. At last the long-awaited day arrived when he was able to return to work and as he approached the office he saw the same stray mongrel trotting along the edge of the pavement, healthy and happy. His year of pain had been pointless. Now a reaction has set in for though he remains as fond of dogs as ever, he cannot even bring himself to stroke them, even touching his sister's cat brings him out in a rash, so he wears a glove to do so.

His action in seizing the wild dog by the ears was courageous.

If this makes Ibrahim sound too sentimental for his own good, I should mention his sly sense of humour – he was the first Turk to make me laugh – and his sudden, unexpected passions. When we stopped at the lagoon of Olu-Deniz, I noticed an attractive young woman with a much older man and wondered about their relationship.

'Eighty-five!' cried Ibrahim in my ear, reading my thoughts, or so I thought.

'What?' The man did not look that old.

'You stare at her breasts?'

'Well, as a matter of fact. . . .'

He interrupted me proudly. 'I can always tell measurements of ladies' breasts – I am expert.' For a moment it could have been Yusuf.

Ibrahim's knowledge proved remarkable, for his education came

to an end with the fall from his horse when he was sent by boat to a
hospital in Istanbul and never resumed his studies when he came
back to Antalya. When he was nineteen he had the luck to work for
an American firm which was laying pipelines for diesel oil across the
country, and Ibrahim proved so efficient at working a crane that one
evening his boss presented him with the gift of a splendid sleeping
bag.

'Where did you get that?' his mother demanded when he showed
it to her proudly.

'The American manager gave it to me,' he explained.

'Is he the owner?'

'No, mother.'

'Then you do not ever enter my house again if you accept it.'

Ibrahim pointed out that this would be embarrassing for him, but
his mother was adamant. The next morning Ibrahim returned the
sleeping bag and the manager listened with surprise to his explanation.

'Hmm,' he said, 'your mother may have a point.'

A few weeks later he presented Ibrahim with a handsome radio
complete with the receipt to prove that the manager had paid for it
with his own money.

'All right,' said Ibrahim's mother severely. 'This time you may
keep it.'

Word spread through the company of Ibrahim's honesty and he
was made paymaster, and when their work was finished and they
started to move on to Egypt the manager asked Ibrahim to join
them. Turkish mothers may stay in the background, but their word
is inviolate and in this case it was 'No!' She refused her permission,
and this was how Ibrahim became an English-speaking guide
though his lack of a formal education had kept him in a low grade
with a monthly salary which never exceeded £60. Yet Ibrahim
became the doyen of guides, a master of his art, advising ten
presidents and the Aga Khan over the years. Taking his work as
seriously as that of an ambassador, he regards the rapport with his
clients as vital: 'People are like envelopes. Until you open them up
you cannot understand them.' He refuses to be rushed but proceeds
at his own leisurely, waddling pace: 'I do not like to be robotic
guide.' When a party asked him to 'squeeze' a particular ruin into
their schedule, he declined: 'I have some feeling. I do not accept
their programme.'

When Princess Grace of Monaco and Prince Rainier came to
Antalya for Jacques Cousteau's conference on pollution in the
Mediterranean, it was Ibrahim who was sent for. Top officials and

first-grade guides had flown in from Ankara especially, but when they proved unable to answer the persistent questions from Princess Grace the whisper went out to fetch the lowly Ibrahim who had been banished from this glamorous occasion.

'But I am nothing,' he protested when they called at this home. 'I am eighth-grade guide.'

'That doesn't matter,' the official told him impatiently, 'We need you. Today you will be promoted to first-grade guide.'

When Princess Grace listened to his information and realised the extent of his knowledge, she insisted on Ibrahim as her personal guide for the rest of the visit, refusing to start her cocktail party on the final evening without him. Due to protocol, Ibrahim's invitation had been 'overlooked', so they hurried to his home again.

'Princess Grace wants *me*?' he asked with surprised, and I daresay mock humility. 'Are you sure you have the right man?'

'We are certain,' they told him coldly. And when he arrived Princess Grace waved to him to join her at the top table so he waddled through the 500 glittering guests and sat beside her. With her particular interest in the mythology of his coastline, they were engrossed for an hour until Ibrahim sensed the glares and irritation of the top officials denied their opportunity of hobnobbing with the beautiful Princess, so Ibrahim made his excuses: 'Princess, you are very important person and I do not like to prevent others from seeing you. It is time I go back to my home.'

Before he did so, Prince Rainier presented him with a medal, a family album of photographs, and the final compliment: 'If you should come to Monaco, *we* shall be your guide.'

Ibrahim in Monaco! It is not an image that springs trippingly to the mind. He told me this shortly before the death of Princess Grace, but if he had presented himself at the castle gates while she was alive, mopping his brow and wiping his spectacles, to be turned away by the Monacan guards, I like to think that the Princess would have spied him from her window in the best tradition of fairy tales as he limped down the road, and would have called him back, running down to greet him as she remembered his wisdom and his courtesy. This is how I felt about him myself. It was due to Ibrahim that I fell in love with Turkey for the first time, when we climbed together to the mountain city of Termessos.

20 A city in silence

Antalya provides the perfect base for exploring Termessos which lies 20 miles inland. You drive most of the way along the excellent road to Korkuteli before you turn up a rougher track which climbs into the mountains until it comes to a stop at a clearing where you have to get out and walk. Depending on your urgency, the final climb can take as little as half an hour, but it would be sad to turn this visit into a slog when every footstep should be a pleasure.

My first surprise, echoed so often on subsequent journeys, was the freshness of the pine trees, the wild roses and banks of yellow broom beside the gorge as the car drove up the last zigzag miles, and an alpine atmosphere with the keen zest of mountain air. Only one determined tortoise marked the difference.

Anyone can wander up the footpath, though few people do. This is the magic of Termessos. There is no souvenir stall, no ticket collector, no serried ranks of coaches disgorging a clatter of tourists that you would find at Ephesus, but the rarest of all qualities – solitude and silence. Conversely there is no refreshment kiosk and I urge you to take a flask of water at least, or preferably a picnic with fruit and bottles of beer especially if you have the decency to bring the litter back.

The flowers beside the footpath become more delicate – wild orchid, forget-me-not and lady's slipper – and then the ramparts of the old city walls loom above you, set in a fold of the mountain range near the peak of Gulluk Dag, also known as Mount Solymus which explains why the Termessians described themselves as Solymians in their inscriptions.

I call it a city rather than a town because 45,000 people lived here until the earthquakes shattered Termessos in the fifth century, scattering the ruins over the mountainside much as they are today, remaining undisturbed until they were discovered by a German archaeologist in 1885.

My first reaction was one of confusion: what audacity induced the Termessians to choose such an eyrie for their home? But that, of course, was the strength of it – Termessos was impregnable from attack, as Alexander the Great discovered to his cost. 'The site is very high,' wrote Arrian, 'and precipitous on all sides, and the passage by the road is difficult. The mountain descends from the city right to the road, and opposite to it is another hill equally abrupt. These hills form a kind of gate in the road, so that a small defence force can easily render the passage impossible.'

The Termessians were notorious for their attacks as well as their defence. Originally from Asia, though their primitive laws were tempered by Hellenistic and Roman influences once they had settled, they were feared for their courage in swooping from their mountain lair to raid the coastal villages and seize any woman who caught their fancy, racing back to the mountains with their loot and beauty.

When Alexander made his winter headquarters at Phaselis further up the coast, a raiding party of Termessians was rash enough to attack the town while he was there, or so the people of Phaselis told their conqueror having organised the raid themselves in order to insult his honour and provoke him into pursuing their detested enemy.

Alexander fell for the ruse and rode into the horseshoe valley below, where the hills form the 'kind of gate'. As he approached the Termessians waited on the slopes, but Alexander did not make the mistake of trying to force his way through but pitched his tents for the night with the expectation that the Termessians would retire to their city leaving a token guard which he could disperse the next morning. This, according to the legend told me by Ibrahim, was exactly what happened, but when Alexander came below the city the Termessians released gigantic nets filled with boulders, creating an avalanche which cascaded on the men below, injuring Alexander's horse, killing a number of his men. Defeated for once in his life, Alexander turned back with the scornful remark that he could not be bothered with any protracted siege of such an insignificant eagle's nest, but as he rode out of the horseshoe valley he set fire to the precious olive groves which brought the Termessians their prosperity. This is supposed to have taken place in 333 BC. Fourteen years later, Alcetas, who was one of Alexander's generals, settled in Termessos when he was defeated by Antigonus who was trying to rebuild Alexander's empire and establish himself as the ruler of Asia, but the elders of the city betrayed Alcetas and after he killed himself they offered his body to Antigonus who allowed it to be mutilated and subjected to physical abuse. When the young men in Termessos heard of this, they recovered the body of their hero and gave him a triumphant burial, probably beneath the tomb which you can find high up on the hillside today, handsomely decorated with a relief of a warrior on horseback wearing a foot soldier's armour which is how Alcetas, an infantry general, had appeared in his final, unsuccessful battle against Antigonus.

Finally, a treaty with the Romans in 70 BC brought peace to both sides while allowing the Termessians their own laws and a degree of independence, not even obliged to portray the heads of the Roman emperors on their coins. It was a fruitful arrangement judging by the scale of the ruins today, which are still being excavated. The courage of these wild mountain men cannot be denied, yet they created a culture we should envy. Their most exciting achievement is the open-air, Grecian theatre which hangs on a mountain face 3,500 feet high like a great curved nest. One way to estimate a population is to multiply the potential audience by ten, and the theatre here could seat 4,500 people, with plays performed into the night lit by oil lamps. There was a low back wall and you can see one of the arches in the far corner which led to a lower level with five doors, 3 feet high, to release the wild animals into the orchestra, the semicircular space in front of the stage.

With the rows of seats, the fallen stones across the orchestra, the range of mountains beyond and the Pamphylian plain below, this is one of the most exhilarating sights in Turkey.

Fragments hint at former splendour: nearby there is a smaller theatre, an odeum for musical performances once covered with a roof of red and black marble; there are twenty temples, a shopping centre, and a gymnasium with hot baths where the athletes relaxed and washed off the oil and sand. Another extraordinary feature are three containers the size of small houses where the Termessians stored their olive oil, connected by stone steps and passages. Ibrahim believes that the oil was channelled down to Antalya on the coast, the first oil pipelines in the world. Less romantically, I have heard these containers described as water cisterns, enabling the Termessians to withstand any siege however protracted, but as there was a spring supplying perpetual fresh water inside the city, I prefer Ibrahim's assurance that they were 'oil wells'.

These landmarks seemed astonishing to me on my first visit to Turkey, but it is the nature of Termessos as a whole which makes it unique. Acropolis means a city on a hill, while Necropolis is a city for the dead which is usually found on the outskirts, but the most dramatic feature of Termessos is the necropolis in the heart of it. The extraordinary extent can be guessed from the 10,000 tombs which tumble down the mountainside though it takes time for the eyes to spot them among the trees and boulders. The few signposts are so discreet that many visitors fail to realise there is a second necropolis higher up, but Ibrahim insisted on taking me there, leading the way with the agility of a mountain goat in spite of his upturned foot. The undergrowth is dense, the paths disappear, the droppings of a wild boar are fresh, and the climb becomes a painful scramble over rocks with a sudden, frozen halt as a long, grey snake slithers harmlessly away though Ibrahim assures me I would only die if bitten in the neck. The reward is finding the tombs much as the earthquakes left them, decorated with disc-like shields, apparently a symbol of Termessos, lions and gryphons, and the glaring, open-mouthed Medusa heads which threaten robbers that they will be turned to stone themselves if they dare disturb the graves – a warning disregarded by time.

Far from being oppressive, the atmosphere is invigorating. When someone died, the Termessians adopted the Roman rituals of grief for a limited period. A tear-glass was used, rather like an eye-bath, to pour their grief-stricken tears into a thin glass phial which was sealed with wax and placed beside the corpse who was able to produce it as he stepped into the next world as proof of his goodness: 'See how they wept for me!' If his family were so indifferent they found it hard to shed their tears, they went to the market place where professional weepers filled the bottles for them, like the ribboned mutes hired by the Victorians to stand in attitudes of grief outside the house on the day of the funeral. When the bottles were full it was time to stop weeping and the Termessians returned to the necropolis which was laid out like a park to celebrate the dead with music and dancing. How civilised compared to our twentieth century neurosis which has made the inevitable unmentionable.

If you visit the museum at Side, you can see examples of the tear-glasses and also the tombs of two children. No fierce Medusa heads for them, for they had nothing worth stealing, but decorations of the sweetest poignancy. One tomb has the favourite dog peeping wistfully through an open door, the other has symbols which Ibrahim had to explain: flowers, to show that the child was mourned, a swallow, to indicate that the family had moved away, a butterfly, to suggest the reincarnation they were hoping for, and a basket of cotton, enough to last a lifetime but with only two notches on the bobbin to explain that the girl was two years old when she died. On the carved steps of the doorway lay the mother's bleeding heart.

There were no watchmen when I went to Termessos, apart from

the Medusa heads. Restoration had hardly started. How satisfying
if the city could remain undisturbed, for the Termessians were too
rare a race for their homes to be dug up and labelled and put on neat
display for the benefit of people like us.

21 Luxury in Antalya – at the Talya Hotel

The climb to Termessos was one of the most rewarding days I have known, thanks to the gentle guidance of Ibrahim. After that I knew I wanted to live in Turkey, a decision enhanced by the shameless luxury of the Talya Hotel as I relaxed by the pool in the late afternoon.

There are various types of hotel in Turkey, veering from one extreme to the other. At their worst they are primitive with the bloodstains of crushed mosquitoes on the bedroom walls. To counter this impression the Turks are building the immense complexes or holiday villages for the benefit of tourists, which are hugely popular. Most people welcome a degree of discipline with 'pearls' as a substitute for money, like the coloured beads used by explorers, and instructions in their cabins telling them what they should not do – 'Don't take the hotel towels to the pool' – 'Don't hang your thing on the railings.'

This has the effect of making me hang whatever 'thing' I have on the nearest railing in sight, but the Germans in particular with their curious mixture of sadism and masochism relish such regimentation. After their disappointment in the last world war, they are invading these shores with a vengeance, talking in deafening tones on a tiny raft as if they were shouting to each other from opposite ends of an Austrian valley, strutting across the sand with a glistening oiled arrogance, the women walking topless oblivious to Turkish tradition which frowns on nudity. When Osman saw the German topless women parading on the beach at Alantur, he was goggle-eyed.

If the Germans take full advantage of a currency exchange absurdly in their favour, who can blame them, except for this determination to make the country conform to them, rather than adapt themselves. It means also that the corruption of tourism kills the natural hospitality of the Turks, tainting the staff with such familiarity that indifference smacks you in the face. Food has an international blandness in order not to offend anyone, and the dining room might equally be in Bromley, Bergen or Baden-Baden.

Conversely, with my own brand of snobbery, I relish the luxury of a really first-class hotel, exemplified for me by the *Talya* in Antalya. In my experience this is the most sophisticated Turkish hotel outside of Istanbul. I ate my first, superbly cooked dinner with Ibrahim in the open air on the prow-like balcony, followed by a breakfast which revealed the sensational view of the sea stretching to the snow-capped range of Taurus mountains fading into a hazy distance.

Ibrahim told me that plans are in preparation for a ski lift to the highest mountain which is covered by snow all the year round, so it will be possible to winter sport in the morning and swim in the Mediterannean in the afternoon. This reminded me of Yusuf in Istanbul who told me that he was a champion skiier, the captain of the Turkish team which competed in the Dolomites where he taught the Italian band the Turkish national anthem when he won. Like many of his far-fetched claims, this was probably true.

As for swimming, few hotels surpass the Talya. You can take the lift from your bedroom floor to the poolside level where they serve an imaginative lunchtime buffet. Better still, take a second lift down the cliff face to a landing stage by the sea below. Designed with echoes of Frank Lloyd Wright, the white hotel hangs on the cliff above contrasting with the pumice which resembles a pale, gnarled wood. Arches covered in bamboo lead to a Vitamin Bar, a splendid slab of marble where you can order fresh fruit juice for your health or raki to undermine it; with ample space by the water's edge to sunbathe or read in the shade of one of the straw-covered, umbrella-like awnings.

The view across the sea changes with the light. To begin with the water is completely calm and the mountains are indistinct, a smoky smear as if they were painted, but soon they start to separate and you realise they stretch for hundreds of miles. The two rafts begin to sway precariously in the wind from the west known as the *Imbat* and by the late afternoon they are bucking like broncos and you have to hold on while the silvery water lurches around you and the sun beats down – wonderfully invigorating.

Back on land at the Vitamin Bar I joined two Americans who were drinking vodka-fizz. Like so many Americans abroad, they looked like loveable caricatures: extremely old and as creased as peanuts with a disconcerting resemblance to Hollywood stars of the 1930s: Eugene Palette and Eric Blore. They were on a bible tour.

'I'm Paul,' chortled the fatter man, proffering his hand, 'but I'm no saint!' He laughed resoundingly and I suspected he had cracked this joke a thousand times before. His companion was introduced as the tour leader, too self-effacing to do this himself though a Master of Sacred Theology with a degree in New Testament Studies. 'We all have a lot of fun,' he volunteered, ordering another round of vodka-fizz, 'but we *argue!*' He giggled mischievously. He looked around him appreciatively: 'I find it very scenic around here, don't you?'

Paul described himself mysteriously as 'an apologist for the faith', no saint perhaps but a Lutheran minister. They were on a three-week tour and had driven from Damascus and Iskenderum comparing their coach to a steam bath – 'That's our biggest problem,' said the tour leader, 'the air conditioning.'

'I've just been through the Holy Land,' Paul declared proudly, 'and never went into a single antique shop. In Europe I live on $5 a day.' The tour was costing him $200 a day, but he ignored that, and the price of the vodka-fizzes. He was eight-three, happy and indomitable.

Information from Alanya to Antalya

Alanya

If you like the modern type of complex where you have to buy 'pearls' to use as money in the bar, the *Alantur* is certainly efficient and highly organised. There are three swimming pools which seems excessive as there is marvellous swimming in the sea just a few yards beyond, the best feature of the Alantur as far as I was concerned, with the bay sweeping towards the red towers of the Seljuk fortress of Alanya.

Beyond Alanya

After Alanya the coastline becomes flatter and the absence of hillside forts explains why cities like Perge were situated several miles from the sea, taking advantage of rivers instead. There is much of interest to see.

Manavgat lies inland, a natural series of waterfalls where you can rest and have a cool drink as the water swirls around you.

Aspendos also lies inland, but this is a man-made phenomenon and should not be missed, probably the best preserved Roman theatre in the world. This was built in the second century when Aspendos was a port on the river Eurymedon, and the bridge built across it is still in use today. With seats for 20,000 spectators, and extraordinary acoustics, the theatre is in such a good condition that plays are performed here today as part of the annual Antalya Festival. The ornate statues posed in elaborate alcoves above the narrow stage, supported by columns, have vanished but this dramatic backing can be seen in photographic reconstructions. There is a curious optical illusion, suggesting that the sky is curved above you like a dome. The whole effect is most impressive. To the north of the city walls are the remnants of the aqueduct which carried water to Aspendos over a distance of 32 kilometres. A signpost directs you off the main road to Antalya: 5 kilometres.

Side, which lies on the coast between Manavgat and Aspendos, is one of the most popular holiday resorts in Turkey. I find it a bizarre mixture of excavated ruins and rows of gaudy souvenir shops, but there is no denying the vigour of the place. There are a large number of hotels and restaurants, some of which, like the *Agora*, overlook the sea which is so shallow you can walk for 100 yards or so before you are out of your depth. The beach is ideal for those who like to display their bronzed bodies as they pretend to bounce a ball. If I sound unenthusiastic, I should stress that I have always arrived here in the middle of the day which is not a proper time to test a place. Most people who have stayed in Side cannot praise it too highly.

Perge, closer to Antalya, was a formidable city once, an independent city-republic, principle city of Pamphylia, and the base of Alexander the Great, prospering under the Romans until the Byzantines superseded them. It is a vast sprawl of ruins today, scattered across the plain, but the sophistication of the past is conveyed by the thoroughfare divided by a channel which brought running water to cool the city, with covered shops on either side, and trees, gateways and mosaic floors to alleviate the heat of mid-summer. The ruins include one of the largest stadiums in the world, with seats for 12,000 spectators. The Greco-Roman theatre seated 15,000.

Antalya

Antalya provides an excellent base for Aspendos and Side, Termessos, and Phaselis. Antalya is an attractive town well worth exploring, with wide, palm-lined boulevards which give it a French atmosphere, and narrow winding streets with old wooden houses which lead to the harbour where the Turks are making a first-rate job of restoring the old houses into accommodation for visitors, preserving the traditional façades while modernising inside with showers and air conditioning. The harbour is busy with cheerful tea gardens above.

Hotel

Talya Hotel: manager Gunac Gurkaynak. Address: Fevzi Cakmak Cad. Tel: 5900. Reservations: 5609. Telex: 56111 Tata. 150 bedrooms with baths and air conditioning, tennis court, pool. The Talya is 14 kilometres from the airport which has flights from Istanbul even in the winter when the climate is so mild that a Christmas holiday is one I should like to try myself. And of course it is cheaper out of season. This is the drawback of the Talya in the summer when it is undeniably expensive by Turkish standards though far less so by our own, around £20 a day per person, with board, but of course you must check. When you consider how welcome a few days of comfort are if you are travelling hard, this does not seem exorbitant. Indulge yourself and economise later at hotels which cost £5 or less.

Restaurant

The *Develi* is outstanding. The full name and address is: Develi Restaurant, Bahcelievler Konyaati Cad. Tel: 2979. I enjoyed an excellent Turkish version of Boeuf Stroganoff and the meal for two came to under £10. I found the service sympathetic too, but there is seldom any sense of rush in Turkey.

22 From Antalya to Marmaris – the new Riviera

'In Turkey particularly, a journey without history is like the portrait of an old face without its wrinkles.' *Dame Freya Stark*

For me, the Lycian coast from Antalya to Marmaris is the most rewarding in the world. Go there while it remains unspoilt, for this will become the new Riviera. Meanwhile, it *is* what other European coastlines *were*: friendly, uncorrupted and inexpensive. It remains fresh for several reasons, among which are the difficulty of getting there, though this becomes easier as the roads encroach, and the sheer length of the coastline which may look compressed on the map but has so many crenellated inlets and peninsulas it would stretch a thousand fold if laid out in a single line. It will take years to spoil it.

It can be argued that Turkey is more suited to the discerning traveller than to the mass invasion of the package tour, but there is room for both and this is another reason to savour the innocence while it lasts with the Turks wistfully anxious to please the visitor. They were so dismayed by the shadow cast by *Midnight Express* that they can barely speak of it today, yet this distorted film was one of those proverbial blessings which come in heavy disguise. Hardly a drug-taking hippie has set foot in Turkey since, scared off by the terrors of a Turkish jail though the prospect of keeping pets and cooking one's own food seems preferable to the banged-up isolation of a prison like Strangeways. Instead, the hippies and the cheapies clog the Greek islands, and their only equivalent in Turkey are the Australian nomads, that amazing generation of young people who have saved enough money to visit Europe before they settle down. They explore with their possessions on their backs and all the zest of youth. Turkey proves the favourite for many and not just because it is cheap. 'It's the most interesting,' one girl told me. 'But I'd hate to come back in ten years' time.' Her young husband shook his head sadly, 'I give it four.'

They are too pessimistic.

Meanwhile, this remains the ideal coast for a traveller of any age if he comes here with a sense of history. It is still one of the best-kept holiday secrets in Europe.

A first-rate road takes you along the coast from Antalya, though you have to plunge down riverbed tracks to abandoned cities like Olympos and Patara or reach them by sea. First we came to Kemer, the romantic setting for the Club Méditeranée with a crystal-coloured sea and snow mountains in the distance. Trees and foliage disguise the low-lying buildings, the welcome antidote in Turkey to the towers which have scarred the Costa Brava. The space is used generously with lavish flower beds, tumbling mesembrianthemum and clumps of oleander. The materials are wisely chosen with marble floors and bamboo coverings, and the chalets which climb along the bay can house 750 members if they sleep several to a cabin as I expect they do for the club has a reputation for sun, sea and sex and it would be a crime *not* to double up in such surroundings.

One does not have to be a member to stay here, nor is there an age limit. 'Even you,' said the wiry man in charge who looked North African, 'even you could be admitted.' I fear that my moment has passed, but this would be the perfect place for a sensuous holiday if you are young with a group of friends and want to burn the days and nights away in a state of semi-nudity. 'Not many English come here,' I was told, 'they do not know about it.'

The club was due to open in a few days' time on 17th May but the staff were busy getting everything ready and I joined them for lunch at a table already strewn with empty bottles of wine. Food and drink are one of the boasts of the Club Méditerranée with a hundred different dishes for each meal, twenty of them seafood, and all the wine you care to drink. The tennis courts are excellent, the water sports prolific, and if you want to snatch a moment on your own you can bicycle along the coast.

We had reached the Lycian shore and drove through pine forests with occasional clearings for picnics and camping before we took the turning to Phaselis at the end of a small peninsula. This was Alexander's winter headquarters when he stopped in Pamphylia, with three harbours serving as a port for his boats which were celebrated for their speed; in the summer it became unhealthy to stay there due to the surrounding marshes which spread disease. The excavations are recent and you are not supposed to wander about when the archaeologists are working, but there was no one there when I arrived which added to the sense of solitude with the light filtering through the tall pine trees and the wind suddenly coming alive with a joyous murmur as the clouds descended on the mountains behind.

Freya Stark in her noble book, *The Lycian Shore*, describes 'two mausoleums or perhaps little private temples for the dead. They are slipping into the sea that eats them slowly. One sarcophagus lies lidless in the waves; and another, with lion snout of marble and a headless, toga'd figure, is slanting on its way.' I could not find them; perhaps they have been saved from the ravages of sea water and lie in some museum now, but the paved street has been restored since her visit in the early 1950s though the haunting quality remains. As we walked down the road, it was possible to conceive Phaselis as a city as far back as 690 BC when it was founded by settlers from Rhodes as a base against attack from fleets which could be spotted easily if they approached from east or south. It was vital as a port, and Alexander landed here and marched along this same road while the harbours were crowded with his ships.

In 167 BC the Roman Senate allowed Phaselis and other Lycian cities their independence and the city continued to be lived in during Christian times until it was abandoned.

On that first journey it proved impossible to drive down to Olympos further on, but I have done so since and found it even more mysterious than Phaselis. These are the places which thrill me most in Turkey, with visual echoes from the past. Looking across a wide but shallow stream, with a quantity of tiny frogs on the edges, I realised gradually that I was standing on the quayside of an ancient city where thousands of people had walked up and down the pavings and mosaic floors in the cool of the evening. The remnants of a bridge stood in the water which swirled around them, and behind the overgrowth and oleander on the opposite bank, half hidden by pine and oak, I could make out the outlines of walls and arches rising steeply above the stream which runs to a sandbar and the sea.

The city has been enveloped by a jungle of creepers and I never found the doorway of the temple carved for Marcus Aurelius in marble hidden somewhere in the trees, with the Roman inscription lying among the roots.

A few kilometres behind, you can climb to Mount Phoenix, also known as Mount Olympos. Twenty mountains bore the name of Olympos in ancient times but this is famous for a freak of nature at 800 feet with a hole only 2 or 3 feet deep which holds a flame that never goes out.

Frankly the flame is invisible by day though it can be seen far out at sea by night, and was recorded by Captain Beaufort in 1811. Probably a form of gas, it cannot be extinguished by water and is certainly a phenomenon of fact if not in appearance. Dull in itself, time has magnified the modest flame into the legend of the Chimera, the fire-breathing monster slain by Bellerophon, described by Homer as a creature with the body of a goat, the head of a lion and the tail of a snake. 'Chimera the unconquerable,' he recorded in the Iliad, 'of divine birth was she and not of men . . . and she breathed dread fierceness of blazing fire.' But the Chimera was conquered by Bellerophon, the hero of Corinth and son of Poseidon, who was given the task of killing the monster. Slipping a golden bridle over the winged horse, Pegasus, he rode into the sky above the monster and pelted it with arrows. Then he fixed a lump of lead on the tip of his lance and thrust it straight into the monster's mouth where it melted from the heat of the Chimera's breath, ran down the creature's stomach and burnt it to death.

It is a splendid legend, but the flame on the hill today is closer to the definition of a chimera given in the dictionary as a 'fanciful conception'.

Dame Freya Stark climbed the hillside in order to see the flame for herself, but she has always been indomitable and in this case had a pony to take her to the top, a ride of one and a quarter hours. It ended disappointingly, for the Chimera proved 'small and very sooty, like a hearth. . . .' Dame Freya found half-buried fragments on the ground including a pedestal with an inscription dedicated to the Emperor Hadrian by the town council of Olympos, and the ruins of a small Byzantine church in an enclosure nearby. But as for the Chimera, Dame Freya conceded that 'Her fierce days are over.' Even so, I should have welcomed the chance to walk beside Dame Freya as she rode through the shrubland, for her wit and observation if not for the Chimera itself.

The association of the Chimera with such a place seems unlikely yet it was described by Seneca and Pliny. It has been suggested that the combination of animals which made up the creature was derived from the lions, goats and snakes which lived in these mountains near the eternal flame. Turkish shepherds cook their meat over the fire which is little bigger than an oven, but the legend remains sufficiently strong to prevent them from doing so if the meat has been stolen for this cannot be roasted and remains raw however long it is cooked. A fanciful conception indeed.

In the afternoon we descended to some fields beside the sea on the way to Finike and stopped to investigate an open-air event. It was the first day of the annual wrestling contests, an unpretentious affair with the gaiety of a mid-west rodeo, a mixture of small-town pride and bravado. A massive hoarding with the outline of

Ataturk's head dominated a cordoned stage where I was led to the platform as the only tourist present to be introduced to the governor of the district, a large, handsome young man with dark, glistening hair, dressed in a sleek cream suit. He presided behind a table with a sign marked 'Protocol' and a bust of Ataturk, and gestured that I should sit down beside him on a seat that was pushed forward. I bowed with all the dignity I could muster and he produced one of the oranges for which Finike is famous, proceeding to carve it with a sharp penknife as ceremoniously as if it were another bust of Ataturk himself. I accepted one of the perfect segments gratefully and he fed me the rest while we turned to the wrestling.

It was Ataturk who stressed the importance of 'clever minds on strong bodies', and though the event had all the fun of the fair, it was taken seriously too. As this was the first day the youngest contestants were wrestling, boys aged from fifteen to eighteen, their dark bodies glistening with olive oil poured from nearby barrels, many wearing the traditional black leather trousers inscribed with the lettering *masallah* – 'what wonders God hath willed!' – to ward off the evil eye. After a strident burst of music from horns and drums, the boys ran forward, danced a few, crazy steps, and became locked in interminable combat lasting for minutes on end. The victors, who had trained for this occasion for the last two years, received prizes which were most impressive: money, adding up to a total of £500, handsome medals with the symbol of the Finike orange awarded to the winner in every group, and a magnificent cup presented to the best *sportsman* rather than the best wrestler – a contrast to the mercenary Olympics.

It was here that I saw the disconcerting presence of soldiers patrolling the enclosure with guns apparently at the ready, only to learn that their function was to stop anyone crawling under the ropes instead of paying the entrance fee which was going towards a new maternity wing in the hospital at Finike. Innocence personified! Yet a passer-by who snapped a photograph might have gained a different impression altogether.

The atmosphere was so enjoyable it was hard to break away and by the time we reached the town of Demre it was late afternoon and the air was dense with flies and flying insects, a reminder that the villagers used to escape from the epidemic of mosquitoes in the summer by moving into the mountains. Today the mosquitoes have gone, or so they say, and the waters have receded since Myra was a port and the capital city of Lycia. It is worth seeing today for the Lycian tombs carved in the cliffs a couple of kilometres inland, and the church of St Nicholas who was Bishop of Myra in the third century, though the church which is named after him was rebuilt in 1042. We know of him today as Father Christmas.

St Nicholas, who was born at Patara further up the coast, died on 6th December 343 and was buried in a marble tomb which was ransacked in the eleventh century when Christians are supposed to have stolen his bones carrying them off to Bari in Italy though they dropped a couple on the way which are now in the museum at Antalya. In the Netherlands his feast day is still 6th December rather than 25th.

I was anxious to reach Kas while it was light and glad I did so for the approach reveals one of the loveliest villages on this Lycian shore. It was hard to believe that the road had only come through five years earlier, bringing electricity and water. Until then there had been the excitement of arriving by boat; now there are five buses a day. The jauntiness remains and the village is so modest you feel you have discovered it by chance, away from the tourist route which demands the big hotels which have yet to come. I ate my first dinner at the Mercan restaurant at the corner of the bay, my chair so close to the edge that I had to be careful not to lean back and fall into the water scattering a flotilla of deliriously happy ducks. Incongruous on the sea, they seemed more at home the next morning as they primped and preened in the fresh water from a running stream, after which they folded up on the rock for a blissful sleep in the sun though several perched motionless on one leg.

Again, I wondered if I had found my paradise in Turkey, attracted by the cheerfulness of the place rather than an abundance of ancient stones which can become oppressive. Though Kas was the ancient Antiphellus, a Roman port which exported sponges and timber, the monuments blend in casually, like the small theatre on the hill which looks out to sea, and the Lycian tomb with the heads of lions which lies at the top of a street behind the harbour, unfenced and unrestricted, under a leaning tree.

My imagination had been caught by that first breathless view in the evening light of the bay shaped like a crescent with the mole of the harbour curving round protectively to the lighthouse at the end which tilts tipsily like a miniature Pisa, battered by the force of the waves over the years.

On the horizon the Greek island of Casterllorizon looked so close I could make out the houses.

23 A Grecian plot in Turkish waters

The island is such an embarrassment that many maps omit it altogether. There are various spellings when you do find the name, some starting with *K* and ending without the *n*, but I have settled on Castellorizon which seems the most frequent today.

My voyage to Castellorizon produced elements of comic opera, but that is in tune with the nature of the place, the smallest of the Dodecanese Islands yet within the Turkish waters. The Turks shrug the discrepancy off but the Greeks are so obsessed by their proximity to Turkish territory that when a woman had a heart attack on Castellorizon and the priest went to the mainland to fetch a doctor, he was tried in Rhodes for offending the Greek state. The charge was officially one of 'leaving the country without travel documents' and the priest was acquitted, but the incident reveals the paranoia which surrounds this island, and it happened only two years ago.

At breakfast that first morning, I watched the Greek fishermen who landed for supplies though Turks are forbidden on their island. The owner of the restaurant studied them indifferently: 'If they want to spend their money in Kas,' he told me, 'why should we try to stop them?'

The history of Castellorizon is far from comic. It was glorious once. Homer referred to the island's ships at Troy and the fleets which sheltered in the harbour traded with Lycia bringing timber to Africa and the Middle East. The island was ruled by Rhodes from 350 to 300 BC, then it was used as a lair by Roman pirates until it was converted to Christianity in the time of St Paul who preached at Myra on the mainland opposite.

In the thirteenth century the Knights of St John gave the island its name, after the rose-coloured castle where they held their prisoners if they misbehaved on Rhodes.

With such a key position, it is not surprising that Castellorizon has been occupied so often: by the Sultan of Egypt who took the island in 1440 and the King of Naples ten years later, by the Ottomans and by the Venetians. But the Turks have been their foremost enemy.

Today it is a wounded place. After an abortive revolt against the Turks in 1913, which was not supported by the Greeks, Castellorizon was occupied first by the French and then by the Italians after the First World War, provoking a mass emigration to Australia and America, some of the islanders so desperate that they exchanged their houses for a one-way ticket. The remaining islanders proved so independent that the Italians refused to help them after an earthquake in 1927, accusing them of having failed to cooperate, but when the King of Italy landed there he found the quay covered with priceless carpets. Accused of sycophancy, the islanders explained that they wanted to make certain that no Italian king would set foot on Grecian soil.

A panoramic photograph taken in the 1930s is a poignant revelation today, showing a large, working port. What happened? Partly it was the drift away, reducing the population from 14,000 when the island controlled much of the trade along the eastern Mediterranean, to 1,500 in 1941.

Then came the worst of the island's misfortunes, and one that the British should be ashamed of though we have conveniently forgotten it. In the Second World War, recognising the strategic importance of the island and fearing an insurrection on the part of the independent islanders, the Allies shipped them to the Middle East for their 'safety'. They were not allowed to take their possessions and the pillaging, allegedly by British troops, was so uncontrolled that the soldiers set fire to the town afterwards to conceal the crime they left behind them, burning most of the houses.

There was a final tragedy after the war. When the islanders were brought home from their exile, the ship sank on the way and most of them were drowned. The survivors returned to discover that they had lost everything.

'I can never think of Castelorizo,' wrote Freya Stark in *The Lycian Shore*, 'without a stab as if someone had hit me.'

Today the population hovers around 200, with the danger that if it falls lower the island should revert to Turkey. The wounded island is dying.

Anxious to see it for myself, the tragedy was forgotten in the comedy of hiring a boat to take me there. Hoping to make an early start, I sought the help of Celal, the director of tourism who introduced me to Kaptan Kembal Gokcul, a grizzled, wiry man, who looked fierce enough to sail to hell and back if necessary on his boat called the Ozcan, and we agreed on a price of 10,000 Turkish lira, which was nearly £30 by the rate of exchange at the time, but I knew there was little alternative.

'We leave at ten,' said the Kaptan.

'That's perfect,' I confirmed.

Then he looked doubtful and shook his head, muttering words I could not understand. Celal translated them: 'He says they are funny people on the island. They could say welcome or refuse you permission to land.'

'No problem!' I declared bravely. 'If we are going, let us go quickly. I am prepared to take the risk.'

At ten o'clock the Kaptan returned to collect our passports and departure forms which we had filled in with all the necessary information, and he showed us various documents in return with photographs of himself at different ages. Producing the last with a flourish, the balding Kaptan with grey eyebrows pointed with pride at the youth he had been, black-haired, confident and twenty.

Realising this was going to take longer than I expected, I sat on a bench outside a shop that seemed to act as a café too, and drank endless cups of coffee while the 'formalities' were completed. The lethargy of such places is infinite, for their whole purpose is to while away the day. Under a mauve cloud of bougainvillaea and a yellow Schweppes advertisement nailed to the whitewashed wall, one man read a newspaper, two played a game of backgammon, and three did nothing but scrutinise the road in front as if they were waiting for something extraordinary to happen.

Two Germans sat down, bearded and dressed in the filthiest of shorts, as if they were making a virtue of dirt, and ate their own tomatoes; then a young Turk joined us, dressed in tiny, pristine-white shorts and a T-shirt, with the inappropriate name of Guernsey. Learning that I was going to Castellorizon, he asked me in a whisper if we could bring him Marlborough cigarettes and a bottle of whisky from Greece; I offered him a raki instead. This was refused: 'I only drink raki three times in life,' he said. 'I give you size for shoes and shorts,' he continued 'and you buy them for me in Castellorizon?'

'I greatly doubt it,' I replied.

By eleven o'clock I was becoming impatient. Celal stopped to let me know that the mayor who had to stamp our departure permits had been away for the night but had just returned, so everything was now all right. I started to rise but he waved me down again: 'Now we need the signatures of the customs officer.'

At twelve I saw the Kaptan walking past escorted by a policeman. He looked at me strangely, struck his face loudly with his right hand and his body with the left, and carried on.

'The Kaptan has gone to hospital,' Celal informed me later. 'He has nervous breakdown.' The idea of this tough old seadog indulging in a nervous breakdown would have been funny except for the possibility of arriving on the island when everything would be closed for the Greek siesta.

'Yes, the Kaptan is in hospital,' Celal confirmed. 'The delay has made him ill.' But the mate, a massive man who seemed totally unconcerned, implied that the Kaptan had struck the customs officer and was under arrest. Hence the police escort.

'They say the Kaptan is mad.'

At one o'clock I was summoned to the customs office where the official looked at me dubiously, apparently blaming Celal who was sweating beside him for having encouraged me to go to a Greek island in the first place. The Kaptan had returned from the hospital and waited trembling in the corner but I could not tell if this was from fear, rage, or his nervous breakdown. I thought it was time to lose my temper and did so to everyone's delight. New forms were produced, signed and handed back, and at two o'clock we climbed on board the *Ozcan* and shoved off from the quay.

Was it worth it, I wondered? Only a few weeks earlier an Englishman had been arrested by the Greeks in these waters and his equipment impounded, resulting in an official protest from the Turks for he had been staying at Kas and they felt themselves insulted too. Tempers were strained on both sides and it seemed increasingly unlikely that I would be allowed to land.

Then the Kaptan advanced, waving a piece of paper which I have had translated since: 'All the formalities have been taken care of by the customs official who has slapped and also hit Kaptan Gokcul. The district officer has the case in his hands and justice will be done.' Apparently the Kaptan had gone to the hospital with the policeman in order to register his bruise and substantiate his charge against the customs officer of physical assault.

It was early in the afternoon when we entered the harbour of Castellorizon and by now I was certain we would be turned away. My relief when I saw two men on the quayside was dashed when one of them gestured angrily at the Kaptan to turn back, with gestures which were all too plain. The worried Kaptan looked at me despairingly and raised his arms in submission, but having got so far after such a fuss I was damned if I was going to give up so easily.

The Greek who had spoken was the harbour master or the immigration officer, or both, and scowled at me unpleasantly. He was one of the most beautiful young men I have seen, far too beautiful for his own good for he knew it. His golden body was adorned by a tiny pair of swimming trunks and he wielded, of all unlikely weapons, a ping-pong bat. Obviously he had been playing ping-pong with the other man, though there was no table tennis table in sight. A domed building with a Greek flag stood behind him shaped like a mosque and might have been one once for a minaret rose above, an unusual sight on Greek soil. Luckily, the current had taken the boat closer to the quay and the beautiful barefoot harbour master scowled even more unattractively as our Kaptan struggled to prevent his boat from striking Greek territory. I seized the opportunity to jump on to it instead, to the harbour master's indignation. Suspecting that he did not understand a word of English, I smiled with the innocence of a mad milord: 'I have come to your beautiful island in order to eat *taramoslata – moussaka –* and to drink *retsina.*' I enunciated each word like the poems they are, three of the most miraculous tastes of the Aegean.

'Ah!' the sulky petulance vanished in the instant. *This* he understood. He pointed to his watch, the only other adornment apart from the briefs and the ping-pong bat, indicating that I should leave at three. As it was ten to three I started to protest until I realised there was an hour's difference in time, so I bowed graciously and went ashore.

With the wonderful resilience of man, the scars do not show on the wounded town, though so close to Turkey it is instantly Greek with the whitewashed houses with their blue archways and brown doors, the incomparable use of flagstones, and a profusion of kittens. The houses which circle the harbour are brightly painted, apparently without a care in the world but when you look closer you find a façade for they are virtually a single row presenting a bold face to visitors, with a few quiet back streets and wooden houses dripping with vines.

The shop was shutting but a couple of restaurants were open, and a cheerful group of Greeks and an attractive American woman from a visiting yacht devoured giant prawns. There was no taramosalata, nor moussaka, though plenty of retsina.

Afterwards I walked to the church which is disproportionately magnificent with such a tiny congregation but it signifies the past. There is a splendid view of Kas from the top of the fortress, but this must be an uneasy reminder for the islanders themselves. What is their future? According to Mario Modiano in his 'Letter from Kastellorizo' published in *The Times*, it may be saved by a new generation of would-be islanders who are starting to return to the home of their fathers and grandfathers and fall in love with it on sight. There is a nice irony that the Castellorizon Society in Sydney has more members than all the population of the island today, and they may help towards its survival and prevent the population from falling below the fatal point when it has to revert to Turkey. The Greek government are taking drastic measures to prevent this too: spending £5 million on a new airport, converting a former barracks into a museum, subsidising a new hotel, even offering a free third-class passage on the twice-weekly ferry from Rhodes though this has attracted the wandering hippie with the least money to spend. Until recently, a shepherdess lived on the adjacent islet of Ro simply to hoist the Greek flag every morning, but if the islanders are going to remain Greek the help will have to come from outside. Mario Modiano reached this conclusion: 'If there is any prospect for this island, it lies in the passionate love affair between it and the expatriates.'

This would be a nice justice, that the sons and grandsons of the islanders who were forced to leave Castellorizon should return to save it.

24 Kekova – history in the water

Unless you go there from Greek waters with the chance of staying overnight, which is the only way to judge a place properly, I cannot advise you to hire a boat to Castellorizon with the risk of losing your money if you are turned back.

I urge you to do so to Kekova at any cost, for this is one of the most mysterious sailings along the Lycian shores. It should be easy to join a boat which goes there for the day unless there are enough people to justify hiring one on your own, and I suggest that you take a lavish picnic. This is a day to savour slowly; it would be madness to rush.

On that first visit to Kas, I was taken by Celal, the director of tourism, and his wife, while Ibrahim seized the opportunity for a day's rest and stayed behind.

History is redolent along this entire coast, indeed there is no escaping the ruins of the past and there have been moments when my heart sank as I started the climb to yet another Seljuk or Lycian tomb. But the atmosphere is imperceptibly different at Kekova where the past hangs over the water as if it is still there, which in a way it is without the intrusion of roads and all the progress they will bring. The past can be seen hanging underneath the water too: Lycian sarcophagi, dating back to Alexander the Great, stand in the water like stranded creatures from another age, forlorn in the absolute stillness. The outlines of a Byzantine harbour can be glimpsed below the surface beside the island of Kekova and I yearned to swim above them for a further look.

We sailed into the Kekova Roadstead, a confusing maze of mainland, islands and inlets, anchoring in Xera Cove with the ruins of a church and a farmer's hut at the far end surrounded by goats where the present trespassed abominably with gouts of oil at the water's edge.

Celal, who had worked in Australia and spoke English, arrived at the small village of Ucagiz-Theimesa like Gogol's 'Government Inspector', bristling with authority as he examined a house whose owner had applied for a grant to turn it into a pansyon. The place needed improvement yet there was no evidence of the slightest effort on the part of the owner, nor any sign of the owner himself. Cows wandered aimlessly through the four doors at each end of a small courtyard which might have been charming except for the pats they left behind them. A friendly, yellow-eyed mongrel with fleas came up inquisitively but was shooed away, and I did not object remembering Ibrahim and his injections.

Our next approach was formidable: the cluster of houses known as Kale from the citadel which crowns the summit of the hill. It is a steep climb to the Seljuk fortress and the small Lycian theatre inside which dates from 300 BC but I was rewarded by the sight of an old peasant woman dressed in different patterned colours seated on a stool at a vast, harp-shaped loom as she wove her kilim with all the waters of Kekova seen in perspective far below her.

Time stood motionless in Kekova as if it had caught its breath. The few houses for the twenty or thirty families who live there straggled up the hill and one of them close to the jetty caught my fancy to such an extent that I asked Celal to introduce me to the owner though I was presented to his son instead. I have forgotten the exact price we agreed on, with my intention to return in the autumn to make the deal final, but it was around £13,000 though the house offered nothing except four walls and that extraordinary position on the hill which reminded me of Lindos when I first went to Rhodes many years ago, with that enchanted image of the white village, the darker, medieval castle above, and the graceful Akropolis higher still, open to the sky. Yet Kale *is* different. Lindos elates, or did so until the tourists killed it with coaches, but there is something about Kale that is threatening, and I met someone a year later who had this impression too. Perhaps it was the overcast sky which warned me of the storm which overtook us on the way back to Kas, but the threat seemed to emanate from the hillside itself as if it had endured too much to welcome new intruders. Yet, what an investment such a place would have been, a small taverna or a bar above the jetty to greet the swell of visitors in the forthcoming years. Of that I had no doubt, but as the boat moved away and I took a final look at Kale and the receding house that might be mine, my confidence evaporated. Madness, I thought, to contemplate such a place with no electricity, no water, no shade, and hardly a tree in sight. Apart from the heat in the summer, I would go mad with boredom after a week for what would I do in the evening? There is a limit to reading and writing, the visitors would have gone, for there is nowhere to stay, and I pictured myself alone in my discomfort.

My sense of adventure deserted me, but there was a warning instinct too. The wind was getting up and I shivered as Kale slipped out of view, finding it overpowering. Perhaps I was right.

Information: Antalya to Marmaris

Kemer

The *Club Méditerranée* is in one of the most beautiful situations imaginable. Twin-bedded bungalows with shower and WC. Children from the age of six. To get there you fly from Heathrow to Antalya, and drive from there – a journey of approximately fifty minutes. The cheapest out of season cost for an adult is £430, with a supplement of £204 if you wish to stay a further week. Prices could well have risen by the time you read this.
Club Méditerranée: 106 Brompton Road, London SW3 IJJ. Tel: 01 581 1161.

Kas

Hotels
The *Ali Baba* was simple but fun. A grander hotel had been built on the seafront nearby but for some reason this had offended the locals – and Kas is a village which seemed to thrive on feuds – and I was steered away from it firmly though it looked most promising. By now, it might be in favour.

Kalkan

This is a striking contrast to Kas: a modern village apparently created in order to become a holiday resort, full of restaurants and places to stay, with an artificial harbour of boulders protecting an intended marina. I am not sure why Kalkan should be so popular, but it is. There is a lively atmosphere and visitors are encouraged to enjoy themselves. A large lady from Istanbul has built a splendid, small hotel/restaurant called *Balikci Han* on the front, but my preference is the simpler and cheaper *Pasha's Inn*, also with a restaurant, run by Erkut Tackin who cannot do enough to help if you ask his assistance. There is an attractive rooftop balcony where you can sip your drinks. Mr Tackin speaks English and his knowledge of the area is useful for Kalkan is an excellent base to explore the area. Open from 1st April to 30th November. Breakfast is free and served until 10.30. His wife, Figen, is extremely sympathetic.

There seems to be an arrangement with the *Korsan* restaurant which specialises in lobster.

Though there is little trace of the settlement which existed here thousands of years ago, Kalkan has a certain charm and individuality. Herodotus claimed that this was the place where the moon and stars are closest in the world. With a nice lack of pretension, Pasha's Inn is not so extravagant: 'Dear Guests, we don't claim much but you can rest assured that we'll do our utmost to please you.'

Reservations: Bankalar Cad. 24–26, Karakoy, Istanbul.

Pasha's Inn, 10 Sokak, no. 8, Kalkan/Antalya. Tel: 77.

Korsan Restaurant: Tel: 76 (also has the *Patara Pension*).

Patara

For me, this is the loveliest beach in all of Turkey, so unspoilt that I hesitate to mention its existence. Like a desert beside the sea, the sand stretches for miles without a single person in view.

The surf is invigorating but the currents are strong so I advise you not to venture out too far. Osman, the driver from Trabzon, exulted in his first swim in the Mediterranean, dashing in and out of the waves like a dog, rolling in the sand afterwards.

There is one simple lokanta with a primitive trellis of eucalyptus leaves, burnt brown, supported on poles stretched from four olive trees. The manager of the lokanta wants to extend it, but permission – even for a concrete floor – has been refused. However, I relished my meal of small pieces of lamb mixed with tomatoes and peppers, followed by grapes.

Of course it is the terrible track, which resembles a dried up river bed, and the very lack of facilities once you get here, that has kept Patara so pure.

In addition, there is the reward of the ruined city. The magnificent archway inland is proof that this was another, extensive Roman port, but there are no signs of excavation.

It was worth the climb, even in the heat of the midday sun, to the theatre on the top of the hill which overlooks the sea, the curved stone seats half-covered in sand. There is also a gigantic well, presumably constructed by the Romans.

Once again, in Turkey, I had the deep satisfaction of feeling I had beaten time, that I had stepped back towards the past. No signposts, no souvenirs – Patara is breathtaking once the extent of it is realised.

Xanthos

Xanthos, to the north, is more famous but less rewarding. Once the main city of Lycia, its history is remarkable with the famous battle against the Persians in 545 BC when the men locked up their women and children, setting them on fire, and sallied out to attack their besiegers only to be killed to the last man. Certainly heroic, but hardly a victory.

The sense of disappointment today, unless you are an expert, has an irony if you are British, for the ruins would be more impressive if Charles Fellows had not stolen the best of them in 1838, bringing them back to the British Museum. The Greeks go on about their marbles; the Turks are remarkably restrained by comparison in not demanding the return of the antiquities which should belong to them.

Olu-Deniz

Around the corner from the famous 'dead sea' lagoon is a long shingle beach with superb swimming and several camping sites. Though not particularly glamorous to look at, they are cheap, unpretentious and friendly.

Camping

Deniz Camping is run by an English woman, Anthea Gurkan, who married in 1968. She found the site by accident, for there was no road, no development, and the sand dune was so high you could not see the sea. 'It didn't strike us that tourism would grow so big, but we acted against our philosophy by telling ourselves that if we didn't do it, someone else would.' She has three sons who help her and the atmosphere is happy. There are 57 beds and the cost for two people with full board was 4,700 lira in 1984.

Their brochure makes the familiar promise, 'We are at the gates of Paradise,' but the photograph beside it proves that the claim is justified for once, with the sweep of the beach reaching to the lagoon and shoals of basking hills beyond. Also, I like their list of 'What we cannot offer you': waiters in bow ties; five-star hotel formality; baked beans on toast; and gambling casinos. Surprisingly, the camping site is open all year round. Reservations: Tel: 01 937 6439, or, in Turkey, 6151 1668.

The *Cetin Motel* beside it (pronounced 'chet-in') seems equally efficient and friendly with an enthusiastic young Turkish staff.

Fethiye

Half an hour from Olu-Deniz, and one of the largest cities along this coast. Dating back to the fourth century BC, this was known as Telmessos and is still referred to as that today, not to be confused with the mountain city of Termessos further on.

Today the main attraction is the Lycian tombs carved in the rocks on the outskirts of the city, which you can go right up to. The largest is most impressive.

Personally, I have never felt as happy in Fethiye as I have in Marmaris or Bodrum – but, again, I have not stayed there overnight and might have been persuaded to like it more if I had done. There are several excellent restaurants on the way to the *Hotel Likya* which is outstanding though usually occupied by the Cricketers Tours, which can be infuriating if you turn up on your own. The Hotel Likya has a first-rate restaurant with different dishes every day and a special cold buffet with 25 varieties of mezes including my favourite chicken and walnut. Fatin and Ayser Ergen are the managers. Tel: 1690 1169.

The *Hotel Dedeoglu* provides the alternative if the Likya is full.

Gocek

As yet, a comparatively unspoilt bay on the other side of Fethiye. A boat can be hired from the village to take you out to Gonzo's nose at the end of the bay and the famous sunken Cleopatra's Baths. I have not been there yet myself, but have heard mixed reports of the two restaurants, and gather the Baths are a bit of an anti-climax too. But the atmosphere of Gocek itself sounds rare indeed and well worth exploring.

25 An avenue of eucalyptus

On the main road from Fethiye to Izmir, you turn left for Marmaris down an avenue lined by eucalyptus, one of the loveliest of trees with their silvery bark and cascades of leaves, curving together above the road like a long triumphal arch.

The trees are old, planted fifty or sixty years ago, and as they have grown the traffic has too, until the order went out from the civil authorities in Mugla that they had become a danger and it was time to tear them down.

The outcome was heartening, and Ibrahim assured me this is true. The young men ordered to carry out the execution refused to do so. Many of the eucalyptus trees had been planted by their grandfathers and they could not bring themselves to destroy them. So the avenue of graceful eucalyptus stands today delighting anyone who comes to Marmaris.

You reach the town along a twisting road through the mountains ahead, with regiments of beehives assembled in the clearings in the forests, and plunge down towards Marmaris after that first view of the sea which never fails to excite.

The Turks had booked me into the place they were proudest of, the Holiday Village just outside, but I decided to move into the heart of the town itself when I said goodbye to Ibrahim the following morning. I could not have had a wiser guide and when we parted on the quayside I embraced him suddenly in the Turkish style, kissing him on both cheeks, for I knew I was leaving a valued friend as well.

26 The Greek shadow

Sailing through these waters should be an unalloyed pleasure without the slightest hindrance, yet there is a shadow which makes it difficult.

From Kas to Kusadasi there is the constant presence of another coastline looming opposite. At times it is hard to tell if this is a twist of the Turkish mainland or an island like Kekova, but frequently the land which lies closest of all is Greek. This offers the opportunity to take the ferry from Marmaris to Rhodes, Bodrum to Cos, or Kusadasi to Samos. Nothing could be simpler yet the squabbles between the enemy countries make it difficult. On my first visit I was told it would prove impossible to take the ferry from Marmaris to Rhodes, yet the moment I reached the quayside I saw a sign advertising a 'daily ferry to Rhodes'. Since then, Dogan Tugay has invested in a new ferry which has room for cars as well as passengers and today there is a choice of several sailings which leave each morning except for Sunday, for most of the year. After three or four hours the ferries slip into the harbour of Rhodes as surreptitiously as possible, almost under cover as if the passengers are contraband, though you have to go through a vigorous immigration control.

This atmosphere echoes the incident a few years ago when a large, government-sponsored Turkish ferryboat arrived in Rhodes to establish a precedent and created a small war in which several people were injured. A thousand Rhodians stormed the ferry, cut the ropes and stoned the crew – that was just the initial welcome. The reception became so violent that the authorities in Athens flew in several thousand troops with tear gas to subdue the Rhodians rather than the Turkish crew. 'It could have been Vietnam,' an eye witness told me. In the end the shopkeepers were responsible for calling a truce when they realised that the riots were losing them business, for few people are so venal as the Rhodians.

Parts of the island of Rhodes remain unspoilt but the town has been corrupted by tourists whose invasion has become so intoler-able that the only solution is to fleece them. It is difficult even to buy retsina in the smart open-air cafés along the front because the profit margin is so small. There is no denying the splendour of the old walled city or the fun of the markets, but Rhodes has always been ripe for exploitation and this has come about with a vengeance, complete with lines of topless housewives spreadeagled on the tar-stained beach below the phalanx of new hotels – a Greek Benidorm, with arrogance.

The best reason for going to Rhodes is to carry on to somewhere else. This is unavoidable anyhow for you cannot sail directly from Marmaris to a Greek island without being cleared in Rhodes beforehand. Fair enough: such formalities are tiresome but universal. Annoyingly, the Greeks do not play the game and invent their own rules. While barely tolerating the tourists who come from Turkey, they actively discourage those who want to go to Marmaris in spite of the return ferry. Never be discouraged by shakes of the head and the assurance that such a journey is impossible.

Unsuspecting British tourists have landed on a Greek island to be turned back because their passports showed an entry for Turkish Cyprus several years earlier, and though such an instance is isolated, and causes such bad publicity that it should not happen again, the risk remains for those who fly direct to Rhodes on a package tour if they continue to Turkey for the rest of their holiday instead of just for the day. They might get the shock of being informed that their return ticket is no longer valid and they must buy a new one.

There should be no problem if you take a scheduled flight, nor if you fly to Athens and take an *internal* flight to Rhodes or Cos or whatever island you wish to go to, and proceed from there. I have been assured that the immigration officials in Athens are too busy to worry over a Turkish stamp in your passport, and are more worldly too, for such acts of spite are unworthy of Greece. Also, they are self-defeating. The Greek government have made it so difficult for yachting flotilla groups to operate around the islands that they have created a drift towards Turkey where there are few restrictions. Consequently, the Turkish coastline is the new alternative sailing area and the Greeks have been hoist by their own pettiness in attempting to punish those who visit their Turkish enemy.

I find it sad that I am expected to choose between the two nations. I regard myself as a friend of Turkey but I should hate to turn my back on Greece forever if I am forced to declare an allegiance. Meanwhile, the political obstacles can be ignored if you plan carefully or have the luck, as I did, to be given a lift to the Greek island of Symi.

27 The Greek island of Symi

I went to Symi on that first journey which started at Thassos in the north. It would be hard to imagine a greater contrast: Thassos so lush and Symi so barren. Far from the poster image of a rock with a windmill and a cluster of dazzling white cubes, the considerable nineteenth century town of Symi rises steeply up the hills which enclose the harbour with houses built in a neo-classical style though every one is different. This is one of the most pleasing harbours in the Aegean.

The first impression as you sail past the clock tower at the entrance is one of surprising elegance, reflecting the prosperity of the merchants who made fortunes from the sponge diving for which the islanders were famous and built their mansions with a ground floor for storage while the cool, spacious rooms above were reached by steps outside. Though many of these homes became derelict, the façade has remained with wrought iron balconies and windows shielded from the glare by decorative, wooden shutters. It is the colouring which enhances the whole effect, the roofs of reddish tiles which form a low triangle and the plastered walls ranging from yellow and terracotta to scarlet, changing in the light throughout the day. Open the shutters at dawn and the effect is as golden as it is at dusk and the water in the harbour so clear you can make out every detail including shoals of tiny, silvery fish.

Unlike many Greek ports, such as Mytilene where I found it hard to sleep in the Lesbian Hotel due to the deafening din of cars and the clatter of carts propelled by motorbikes, Symi was blessedly free of transport when I was there for the road across the island was still being built though plans were threatening to widen the quayside for transport to come.

It is easy to understand why Symi is becoming so popular with the English, and hard to begrudge the island its new prosperity. Like Castellorizon, Symi knew grander days when the population was 20,000 compared to 2,500 now, and the Symiots owed their allegiance to Turkey. When Suleyman the Magnificent prepared his invasion of Greece, the Symiots were among the first to submit of their own accord which seems logical when you see the Turkish coastline across the water only 4 miles away. Their submission was rewarded with the privileges of a free port and access to all the sponge fishing in Turkish waters.

Other nationalities, especially the Turks, might dive for sponges but the Greeks had the monopoly of selling them and the island grew rich on the industry. This started to decline with the Italian occupation in 1912 which ended the association with Turkey though it brought little else, apart from the typical, Italianate police headquarters beside the clock tower, the first buildings you notice as you sail into harbour today. In the German occupation in the last war, British incendiary bombs left many of the houses in ruins though we turned the port into a distribution centre for food afterwards. A plaque can be seen outside Les Katerinettes, an excellent taverna on the harbour, which marks the transfer of the twelve islands of the Dodecanese to the Allies in 1945. Symi returned to Greece three years later, yet there is a sense of permanence as if there had been no interruption whatsoever.

The permanence and peacefulness give Symi its unique charm: there are few tourist 'facilities'; there was a disco but the owner extended it without permission and it was closed down, so the music which sometimes echoes around the harbour at midnight comes from the musicians at the Cretan restaurant. There are no beaches, though swimming off the rocks is superb.

Tourists arrive on the ferryboat from Rhodes which is two hours away, but they have gone by the evening and then you have the numerous tavernas to choose from. My favourite was the simplest, at the end of an alley at the base of the harbour run single-handed by a large, smiling Greek with a big moustache, who serves bowls of small shrimps in the spring. Another, grander taverna astounded me one afternoon when the owner, who was celebrating with friends, started to knock down the bottles from the shelves behind him until the floor was covered with broken glass and sticky, coloured liqueur. No one protested and the owner was happy, though I thought of England where someone would have called the police and wondered, cynically, if the bottles were just for show, filled with coloured liquid.

Though the life centres around the harbour, with the old part of the town at the very top, it is worth climbing into the hills for one of the religious festivals held throughout the year in remote little chapels built by the wealthier families to perpetuate their names, for namedays are more important than birthdays. On 21st May in that first idyllic spring, I went to the feast for Constantine in the chapel of Ayios Konstantinos.

The 500 hard stone steps to the old town proved tougher going than the mountain track afterwards, and then I had the luck half an hour later to hitch a jolting lift in one of the trucks used by men who are building the road from Symi to the monastery of Panormitis on the other side. After they dropped me off in the midday sun, I was grateful for the shade of the vast oak tree in the cool, whitewashed courtyard of the chapel where the service had just taken place. There must have been a hundred people altogether, lighting the candles as the silver icons were blessed by the priests who wore white and yellow robes instead of the usual black, and then the feasting began. A large, cheerful woman carried a gigantic basket of doughnuts seized on by the children. Most of the 'Constantines' had brought their contributions of food which were now prepared in style, with souvlaki, the small pieces of lamb, grilled on wooden skewers over charcoal fires. The smells of meat, oil and herbs became irresistible and though I was an outsider and a 'Daniel' I was treated like a Constantine. A priest gave me a vine leaf stuffed with rice; someone else handed me a tiny, red fish and waved towards the bowls of salad.

Families were reunited for the day, laughing and chattering; one father nuzzled his daughter pretending to bite her ear; children ran everywhere; and though I could not understand a word, as I watched from a ledge with the mountains beyond, the well-being needed no translation.

A man started to play bazouki on an accordion and people began to dance, the women in patterned dresses, an army officer with hand on hips as he performed the delicate, ritual steps, a handkerchief stretched from his other hand to that of his companion. Bottles of ouzo were emptied and replaced and the hand clapping grew as an elderly man burst into vigorous song which seemed to be spontaneous though the others chanted a familiar chorus. And so the afternoon drifted on with the lure of the Greek islands summed up in that combination of ecstatic sound, the smell of herbs and charcoaled meat, with the sunlight filtering down through the oak tree which they say is 200 years old.

I walked back to the town of Symi with a cheerful girl from Manchester who had been on the island before and had just returned on a sudden impulse, taking a 'bucket shop' flight to Rhodes. She was chaperoned by a stern, unsmiling Greek, a member of the family she was staying with, who never allowed her out of his sight and never spoke a word. The girl has written to me

since and so have several others whom I met on that visit. Rarely
have I made friends with so many sympathetic English people
abroad: the lady civil servant in Whitehall who has sent me absorbing letters and information on the next island she visited, too
unspoilt to mention here, the sexy girl in the tiny skirt who was
designing the definitive costume for girl croupiers on the liners, and
had snared the local doctor, the distinguished couple fleeing from
two monstrous, teenage daughters in order to save their marriage
with a second honeymoon, and the young man who had taken his
wife to Symi because his father landed here in the last war in an
ill-fated Special Boat Service Raid in September 1943 led by Major
Lapriak, which included Anders Lassen, awarded a posthumous
VC two years later. They persuaded the Italian garrison of 150 men
to come over to the British and Major Lapriak enjoyed his reign as
'King of Symi' for a month, entertained by the Abbot of Panormitis
on Italian food and wine, until the Germans counter-attacked a
month later. The SBS had to evacuate the island and the Abbot
Chrysanthos, who had befriended them, was shot. A plaque exists
in his memory and this was one reason for the young man's
pilgrimage. Ironically, he had struck up a friendship with a young
German couple who had come to Symi for much the same reason,
though they took the opposite point of view. Then there was Hugo,
looking like a priest himself with his grisly, greyish beard though the
first impression was quickly belied by his shorts and the green
carrier bag which bore the Harrod's label.

Hugo is a man who has found his paradise. He works in England
in the winter but his home is on Symi in a house by the edge of the
harbour which he bought when property was still amazingly cheap,
the familiar story when you get there a few years later. At that time
he had to register the house in the name of a Greek friend but in the
summer of 1981 he married the Greek girl he introduced me to
when I came to Symi. Not only is Sylvana young and beautiful, she
brought him a dowry with a penthouse in Athens and he was able to
register his house on Symi in their own name. When we sailed out of
the harbour he pointed to a tiny chapel on a promontory and
explained why he had chosen such an inaccessible place for his
wedding. He had attended a ceremony in Symi which was wrecked
by a group of French tourists who elbowed their way into the
church, pushing the guests aside as they took their flashlight photographs, and gatecrashed the festivities afterwards. The Greek
family were too hospitable to refuse them, but one of their guests
was a Belgian girl who was so enraged by their cries of 'free food!'
that she went down the table tipping their brimming plates on to
their laps.

'Is that nice:' they screamed.

'What you're doing,' she yelled back in the uproar, 'is that nice?'

Remembering the débâcle, Hugo was taking no chances and ferried his twenty-five guests to the distant chapel where they could repel boarders while welcoming the vast barrel of wine from the nearby island of Cos, seven lambs roasted in the baker's oven in the town, and a three-storeyed wedding cake from Rhodes.

Apart from his winter job in England, Hugo profits from his half-share of a caique called the *Trident* which he bought with his partner Sotiris, a grizzled, weather-beaten fisherman. It has proved a profitable collaboration for Hugo can cope with the English tourists in the summer and do the accounts, while Sotiris takes them round the island with quantities of brandy and ouzo passed around as soon as you step on board.

It was on the *Trident* that I went to Panormitis.

28 The woman who kicked a tortoise

Like many of the Greek islands, Symi has a monastery which can only be reached by boat. I sailed to Panormitis one morning in May with a number of other tourists who had seized the opportunity to travel around the island. The caique, or 'cakey' as some of them called it, was so crowded with people speaking my own language that I wondered if I could stay the night at the monastery on my own.

Two hours later we entered a bay which was invisible from the sea and approached the low-lying monastery with a watchtower in between. Far from the resemblance to Mount Athos I had been expecting, it might have been a modern hotel on the shore of some Italian lake, and the wings do provide accommodation for pilgrims who flock here several times a year. The monastery in between is reached through a cool inner courtyard shaded by trees, with pebbles laid out in black and white patterns stretching to a small church which is overcrowded with frescoes and the life-size icon of a saint, brashly bedecked in silver.

I discovered too late that there is a taverna inside the monastery itself, and followed the others to a solitary restaurant at the end of the bay which looked enticing until I climbed the steps and found an atmosphere of panic as the harassed staff struggled with the orders from the invasion of tourists. Far from being pleased to see us, they were dismayed. Evidently the owner was somewhere in the background and the onus fell on a humorous-looking waiter with the air of a jovial goat and tufts of coarse, brown hair sprouting over his T-shirt. He was assisted, though that is hardly the word, by a sharp-faced waitress with the swivelling eyes of a hen who regarded us all with unconcealed dislike, accepting our orders with an outraged scowl. It became obvious that the only phrase she understood was 'Greek salad' until someone marched into the kitchen and pointed directly to a pot of stew, whereupon everyone ordered 'Greek salad and stew' to make things easier. Even this was fraught.

'Fred Karno's!' exclaimed a northern man at the table next me.

'My wife doesn't take oil with her salad, but I bet you they give it her.'

A Greek salad *without* oil was so unthinkable that I might have taken the side of the waitress, except for the disgraceful incident with the tortoise.

I recognised the nice young couple who joined my table because they had taken their baby son everywhere they went on Symi. Now he was sprawled asleep in his pushcart, shaded by a pink parasol which was strapped to one of the handles. His gentle, bearded father had a particular interest in the wildlife of the island and was also a keen photographer, so he produced his camera enthusiastically when he spotted a tortoise advancing interminably towards some scrubland at the back. Having too much heart to wake his son, he asked a peculiar-looking boy with a petulant mouth, wearing a red cap which was far too large for his head, if he would hold the tortoise instead. The boy regarded the tortoise balefully as if it had done him wrong, and was about to drop it when the bearded father retrieved it in time and returned the woebegone creature to its home in a shoe box under a eucalyptus tree. I realised the alarming vulnerability of tortoises in spite of that shell and wondered how they reach the age of forty.

Ruminating on the longevity of tortoises, I was distracted by a curious sound – 'thud, thud, THUD!' – and looked up to see the boy in the red cap kicking the cardboard box across the terrace in an apparent fit of sadism. I winced as I thought of the tortoise inside.

'THUD!' This time the tortoise was ejected from its home, landing on its shell with its little legs waving indignantly.

'Oh no!' I muttered, 'this is too much.' It was hard to guess what the tortoise was thinking, but it must have been frantic. The bearded man looked unhappy too, but it was his wife who left our table and spoke to the boy sharply, telling him to stop. At this moment the waiter arrived with our meal which was such a miracle in itself that I forgot about the tortoise as I scrutinised the food and repeated my order for wine.

'Well done!' I exclaimed, when the wife returned. I looked round: 'But where is the tortoise now?' I noticed that the woman was trembling. 'Didn't you see?' she asked.

'Didn't you see what happened? The waitress kicked the tortoise over the ledge.'

'But that's a drop of . . . 20 feet, on to concrete! Is it still alive?' Her husband hurried down the steps to find out, and this time he returned the tortoise to the scrubland where it had been heading in the first place. He looked shaken too. 'The shell's a bit scratched,' he told us gravely, 'but it's hard to tell how a tortoise *feels*.'

'How could the waitress do such a thing?' I asked, and tried to find an excuse. 'Perhaps she thought the tortoise was a customer.' The humour was misplaced: people do not kick tortoises.

My appetite for the Greek salad and stew was blunted, and the bill proved ludicrously expensive in the circumstances, but I had discovered it was possible to sleep in one of the dormitories in the monastery and decided to stay the night with the hope of hitching a lift on a fishing boat the next day.

I waved to the young married couple and their baby from the jetty as the caique sailed out to Symi and walked back to Panormitis where Father Constantine, a heavily whiskered man, signed my name meticulously in a large book and accepted 200 drachmas, approximately £2, for my room. Then he gave me a tour of the museum with rough models of ships and messages in bottles sent to St Michael by sailors at sea in the hope of his protection.

A grim-faced woman, possibly the mother of the boy in the red cap, led me to a spartan but spacious room with five empty beds though I was the only pilgrim in the vast modern block.

Irrationally, now that the caique had gone, I felt myself abandoned and time stretched heavily before me in the heat of the afternoon. What on earth was I doing here? I walked to the furthest corner which looked idyllic with grazing goats until I found it littered with bottles, cans and plastic containers. Garbage dumped in paradise, a deplorable habit on Symi. Looking up, I noticed a hut on the hill, plainly a military outpost, with several soldiers staring at me suspiciously. There was no beach but I swam from the rocks and emerged unrefreshed.

After scraping the tar off my feet with a piece of wood, I returned to my monastic room, read for an hour, and as I was thirsty I took my book and walked back to the taverna. Father Constantine had warned me not to drink the water; also there was little else to do.

The taverna was quiet now, empty of customers apart from two soldiers in shorts sipping Pepsi Cola, one of whom was manicuring his nails meticulously. The hateful waitress had gone but the jovial waiter with the nice, squashed face was sweeping the floor in his bare feet, a pen stuck in his mouth like a cigarette. His trousers were so long they flapped beneath him and constantly tripped him up, making me wonder if he had no one who could shorten them. I took my ouzo outside and watched the miraculous change of scene: the light which had been so harsh at six o'clock had lost its glare, and the sky softened, shimmered and glowed until the darkness slid down the mountains and enveloped us. I went back inside where the waiter had reappeared in a different pair of trousers. To my delight he placed a small but unopened bottle of ouzo on the table and sat down to help me drink it.

Not only did the ouzo loosen our tongues, it made linguists of us both.

With a semaphore of sign language, we forged an instant friendship fortified by alcohol. I told him the story of my life and he revealed that he had been born in Panormitis and grew up there, working around the monastery for a pound a week until he joined the Greek Merchant Navy and started to save money for the first time in his life.

Six months earlier in the Argentine he had received a telegram from his father informing him that the taverna was up for sale. So the waiter was not just the waiter but the new owner. The taverna, now *his* taverna, had been open for a month and he blurted out his fear that he was going to fail. With a confidence born of ouzo I promised him success, why, I was so certain of it that I would even go into partnership myself if that were possible – and suddenly that seemed the answer to everything. I would cope with the daily invasion of tourists off the caiques and cruise ships because I could understand their orders. The fact that I could not speak Greek seemed irrelevant for I was plainly fluent now. The owner listened gravely to my plans for a self-service counter, nodding and shaking his head by turns, though not necessarily at the right moment, but that seemed as irrelevant as the news that his eight brothers were arriving to help him out in the summer.

The taverna filled up gradually with most of the population of Panormitis: a few fishermen, and a tiny old man with no teeth but a raucous laugh who wore a cap with a jaunty red and white ribbon. He drank profusely and the others patted his head fondly as if he were a dog.

A shrivelled man and a woman whose wrinkled face was beautiful in repose were introduced by the waiter as his father and mother. Retsina replaced the ouzo and I congratulated the father on his wisdom in sending the telegram to Argentina and he smiled back benignly. Curiously, I had no difficulty in speaking Greek by now, nor, apparently, had anyone in understanding me. I smiled at the woman, thinking what a marvellous face she had, such repose. More retsina and then a baby was produced, cradled by the old woman, the grandmother, who had twelve children of her own including the waiter who was now the owner.

The baby was the waiter's son and suddenly, in the flourish of our friendship, I gathered that he was asking me to be the godfather and return to Panormitis for the christening in September. Tremendously flattered, I accepted the honour tearfully, ordered retsina for everyone, and vowed to return.

When I woke at six in the morning in my monastic cell, the sounds were unfamiliar: the distant yelping of a dog in pain; and the agonised shrieks of peacocks answered by anguished 'meows' which came from the peahens or some gigantic demented cat. I had noticed the geese the night before, with pale, grief-stricken eyes, but the screams of the peacocks were a nasty shock. So were my memories of the night before as I lay there in a torpor, wondering why a hangover makes one so susceptible to every hurt in the universe.

I moaned as I remembered my role as godfather to baby Nikos. I was vaguely aware that the godfather is expected to pay for the christening feast as well as provide a gold crucifix, also that I would be liable for the child's welfare should any misfortune befall his parents, but it was not the cost or the responsibility which troubled me.

How could I be godfather to a boy whose mother kicked a tortoise?

The waitress, of course, was the waiter's wife.

Information

Marmaris

Hotels
The *Kaptan Hotel* on the quayside is nice and cheerful, though the garbage vans at dawn are a punishment. Inexpensive and recommended. The *Halici* is set a few hundred yards inland further down the road which runs beside the sea. I have stayed here and found it excellent, a compromise between the simpler hotel and the massive *Lidya* which sports a hundred fruit machines. For some reason, the Halici is a favourite of the Finns and I take this as a recommendation. There is an attractive use of Turkish carpets everywhere (the owner has a shop in town) and a balcony for breakfast, surrounded by shrubs and flowers. The swimming pool is another advantage. Some hotels inside Marmaris claim they are a minute from the beach but the swimming there is not as clean as I would wish.

If you want a hotel beside the sea, try the 'Holiday Village'. The *Turban Vacation Village*, Marmaris, is a clever manipulation of buildings among the pine trees of a forest further along the bay from the Lidya. Swimming is excellent, the bars are shaded, but the food could be improved. However, this would be ideal if you are travelling in a family with children for there are games rooms, table tennis, playgrounds and other sporting facilities laid on. Tel: Marmaris 200. Very reasonably priced by our standards.

The *Marti Hotel*, roughly a quarter of an hour's drive from Marmaris, is more de luxe and expensive, though obviously cheaper if you are part of a tour. Set in its own grounds with attractive gardens, the building is an agreeable fantasy with echoes of a madman's Bavarian castle and scores of chimneys. An agreeable place to swim and sunbathe, and drink in the shade afterwards.

Restaurants
The *Birtat* in the centre of the quay, with the tourist office just around the corner, is by far my favourite. This is largely due to the friendly service and the chance to eat indoors or outside as you please, lingering for hours if you wish. Also, the food is outstanding. The *Liman* on the main road towards the Pammukale bus office is more modest but the food is superb, chosen by going inside the kitchen and pointing.

Kulubuku Yacht Club is just outside Marmaris Bay, reached by one of the many boats which go there throughout the day, taking an hour to get there. This is a 'chic' restaurant run by a Dutchman and the Turkish owner Ahmed Ozkal, both of whom provide a warm welcome. It is the sort of restaurant one hopes for, with a stone floor, cool and airy, and a wooden roof above. I had an excellent fish salad followed by barbecued swordfish. Opens 15th April and closes at the end of October. Obviously ideal if you are travelling by yacht.

Symi

Getting there
Ferries go daily from Rhodes, the last in the early evening, an agreeable journey of two hours.

Accommodation
The *Aliki Hotel*, just around the harbour from the clock tower, is deceptively simple from the outside but is listed as a 'first-class' hotel which makes it far more expensive than you would expect. Elegant inside with a bar and roof garden, and rooms with baths and shower.

The Nireus Hotel (B-class) nearby is less posh and cheaper.

Villas etc.: If you want to get away from the scrutiny of reception desks and find a place on your own where you can do what you like, I suggest you contact *Nikos Sikalos* who looks after fifty villas for the various tours and could recommend you where to stay. Obviously this works out cheaper if you are a large family. Avoid those in the upper town unless you are inveterate climbers. I stayed in a private villa on the harbour front, lent to me by Lina Voyantzis of Seagull Tours, and relished my sense of privacy though it seemed a shame to waste such space on a single person. Anyhow, Nikos Sikalos is the vital contact – the Dogan Tugay of Symi.

29 The man who blazed the trail – Eric Richardson of the YCA

Though I hardly know port from starboard, unless it's Cockburns, even I can appreciate the exhilaration of sailing your own yacht in these unparalleled waters. Once this would have been the prerogative of adventurers or millionaires, but due to Eric Richardson who blazed the way with the YCA, thousands of people enjoy such a holiday today at a tenth of the cost of chartering your own boat. The Yacht Cruising Association started flotilla sailing eleven years ago and remains the biggest and the best, offering extraordinary value.

Eric Richardson is a courteous man who reveals a passionate enthusiasm when he talks of the yachting types of holiday he pioneered. He is very English, highly intelligent and takes pride in stressing that the YCA is frequently the first tourist development the area would have seen, and the least destructive: 'Our sails enhance the look of the place without being too conspicuous. In some bays forty yachts could sail in and you'd hardly notice them. We borrow a fisherman's jetty and when we sail away the only thing we leave behind is our money. The place in unchanged, unscarred. I care desperately about these places – it's a shame when they're wrecked.'

His claim for the YCA is undeniable. Compared to the towers which cast their daily shadows on the beach on the Spanish coast, the passing yachts leave without trace. Conversely, it can be argued that they infiltrate *everywhere*.

While rival firms have foundered, Richardson's discreet but absolute control has kept the YCA afloat with constant expansion. He has a knack for employing young, rather robotic crews, many from the antipodes, who revere him. They are right for the job for he needs a disciplined staff to guide the members on their yachts, some of whom may be retired admirals but include amateurs with only a few hours' sailing behind them in practice for their holiday. The combined operation in Greek and Turkish waters is big business with a large sum of money involved, more than 150 yachts at a cost of £18,500–£25,000, built especially at Eastbourne, transported overland to Brindisi where they sail to join their separate fleets.

Originally, the YCA operated exclusively from Rhodes until the Greeks presented so many obstacles that Richardson turned towards Turkey and a new base in Marmaris. Though the Greeks have penalised the YCA for such desertion with an extra flurry of formalities, the move was a lucky and a shrewd decision. The opening of the new Dalaman airport has transformed tourism along this part of the Turkish coastline. Now the YCA have direct flights from Gatwick to Dalaman.

In 1982 at Olu-Deniz, I met some of the yachtsmen who had flown in on the first charter flight to Dalaman airport and were still dazed by their reception with gifts of honey and raki, songs from schoolchildren in national costume, and wild Turkish dances in which they took part: 'We couldn't have been made more welcome anywhere.' The only flaw was their distress at seeing soldiers patrolling the airport armed with guns, precautions taken for their own protection. The British know that guns are there; it is just that we dislike *seeing* them.

After their arrival, the YCA members are driven either to Datca, three and a half hours away, or to Fethiye nearby, and then sail from one destination to the other. A pilot yacht guides them for the first few days, but then they can break free if they wish to and sail along the route for nine days on their own. The couples I spoke to were typical YCA members: Maureen and Alan Groombridge, a retired police superintendent from Sutton Coldfield, and his wife; and Maureen and Bill Summerton, a Sainsbury's supervisor from Redhill. They met for the first time on a cruise around the Greek islands two years earlier, sharing a yacht on their next holiday. This time they had taken two yachts and had chosen Turkey.

On that spring morning, Olu-Deniz was one of the loveliest places I have seen, a calm lagoon which is landlocked apart from a narrow channel, with the clear water changing to an astonishing azure blue as it reaches the sea. A picture of tranquillity.

Today, like so many posters, the image is lovelier than the reality. 'Olu-Deniz' means 'the dead sea', a name that is used for part of Kekova too, but this one is deader. The water which looks so tempting offers a lacklustre swim compared to the vigorous surf on the beach outside and though this might seem ideal for children there have been reports of impetigo though I should not take them too seriously.

The owner of the restaurant on the shore had an endearing innocence as he prepared a special meal of sauté of octopus for Ibrahim and myself and besought me to encourage tourists to come to Olu-Deniz. He has no need for such promotion now. His complex occupies a hillside and you could do with an alpenstock and St Bernard dog if assigned to the highest chalet at the top. The food is plain but bad and none too popular judging by the rash concession of a visitor's book in reception. The setting is romantic: a terrace with music and lanterns reflected in the still water, but like the baronial halls in Britain where impoverished aristocrats serve inferior food, this is inadequate compensation.

Surrounded by pine forests, Olu-Deniz is still a photographer's dream. It is wrong to judge a place by an atmosphere that has gone, but I find it ironical that the famous dead sea of Olu-Deniz has proved so moribund that the slightest pollution lingers interminably and the yachts which helped to make the place so popular are no longer welcome today.

30 A first look at Dalyan

Today there is a new YCA flotilla which sails from Marmaris to Kas, which I should have thought was the best of all, but in 1982 there were just the two sailings between Fethiye and Datca with Marmaris as the halfway point which is where I joined the pilot boat *Merlin*.

Marmaris provides the perfect pause. The quayside is lined with small boats and Dogan Tugay's ferry docking opposite the Kaptan Hotel run by his father, and his office for Yesil Marmaris Travel. Then you have the grander yachts like the *Moana Vahine*, with the smaller, sardine flotilla of YCA around the corner.

Marmaris has a constant air of being *en fête* and pleased to see you. In the summer the quayside is crowded with tables and chairs and a promenade of people passing to and fro, with a magic moment as the sun sinks behind the surrounding hills and a crescent moon ascends to complement the Turkish flags at the top of the masts.

I doubt if Marmaris will lose this smiling countenance even though the population explodes from a mere 8,000 in the winter to 80,000 in the summer and will keep on increasing. This sounds alarming but the bay is big enough to absorb the visitors and the Ministry of Tourism prohibits the construction of tall buildings close to the water, encouraging the architects to build around the existing trees so that the Holiday Village is invisible when you sail out, apart from a single white plinth.

To help me see how the YCA works, Eric Richardson had arranged that I should travel on the pilot boat, *Merlin*, from Marmaris to Dalyan, crewed by Fiona from the Isle of Arran, as hostess, Colin from Uxbridge, skipper, and John from New Zealand, the engineer. At the start of each sailing they act as nanny to the flotilla of twelve yachts but at this stage I was the new boy, awkward as I clambered on board in the wrong school clothes, grossly out of condition compared to the lithe bodies of the crew who were tanned to a pristine perfection. They must have resented my intrusion into their world but they concealed it as we motored out of the bay on a warm, windless afternoon and I helped them chop the garlic, cucumber and tomatoes for the salads to go with the flotilla's special barbecue that night.

They told me why they had chosen this life: 'The pay's not that brilliant, but with no house, no food, no gas or telephone we're able to save a lot. If you look at it cynically, all we're doing is motoring 200 miles up and down the coastline but we're away from the crowded metropolis and we're our own bosses.'

The drawbacks are the repetition and the heat in mid-summer when it reaches 120° – 'It knocks you out. All you wish to do is swim and read in the shade.' None of them missed television but Fiona longed for 'a proper meal of roast beef' and John missed going out to the pub. Their favourite time was the last week in May and the first in June.

They seemed extraordinarily content though it occurred to me that two men and a girl on a boat might present a problem, a 'television sit-com' in the making, and asked what happened if they became – I sought for the right word and came up with the wrong one, absurdly genteel in the circumstances – 'attached'.

'Romance on the high seas!' they laughed, but it turned out that this was exactly what had happened though I cannot remember if it was John or Colin who had fallen in love with Fiona. Six couples among the YCA staff had married after a summer's sailing – 'Eric's very proud of that' – but Colin, or John, admitted to me later that it was hell trying to make himself invisible in such an infinitesimal space.

As for the members, they denied there was a YCA type: 'Some are yachting fanatics used to hard sailing off England in oilskins who simply enjoy being out at sea. Blokes are usually very keen, the women aren't so keen. If it's too rough or tough the wife and children won't come back so you've got to get the balance right.'

Surprisingly, the actual skill needed for sailing seems to be within the scope of everyone though it helps to have some experience, or the three days' practice with the YCA course at Hamble. 'I wouldn't recommend it for a novice,' one of the wives at Olu-Deniz had told me, 'yesterday could have been terrifying. It was pretty frightening for us.' But she added, 'You don't have to be Admiral Benbow.'

Most of the members on the Turkish flotillas had sailed with the YCA in Greek waters, a good preparation for Turkey which is windier. Some yachts carry as many as six people, others two – and one in this flotilla was shared by a judge and an admiral. Occasionally two strangers team up and become friends for life. The yachts which look so small from the outside are designed especially for the YCA and the *Merlin* was perfect for four people. Even with my size and inexperience I did not feel in the way.

This was the first year that the YCA were operating full-time in Turkey and the crew applauded the move: 'Greek red tape is making life impossible. In Turkey common sense prevails and it's just beginning to take off.' They assured me, 'Where the YCA goes, other companies follow.' Their loyalty was admirable.

I needed no convincing. I am not inclined to follow my leader, nor do I particularly want to see familiar faces when I go ashore. That, at least, was my first reaction to such a yachting holiday. I was wrong. The sardine syndrome is largely of your own choosing, and the pilot boat is there literally to set you on the right course. The only provision is a genuine love of water, for once you are out at sea one coastline looks like any other in the world. It is only on land that you catch the flavour of the country. Even so, as we motored lazily towards Ekincek Bay, I found it hard to imagine a more perfect holiday than this.

As for those familiar faces, part of the fun would lie in making new friends – the most *awful*-looking people usually prove fascinating once you know them – with reunions on land as you swap experiences. Even a curmudgeon like myself who casts a jaundiced eye on bonhomie can recognise this, and as the crew moulded the meatballs – 'YCA burgers made of lamb' – I found that I was looking forward to the barbecue that evening, the only communal meal of the cruise. There was the promise of 'lots and lots of wine'.

The bay could not have been surpassed with pine forests falling to the water's edge and the absolute stillness broken only by the voices from the yachts mooring nearby, with laughter and greetings and invitations to come on board for a 'sundowner' – an exact description in that final glow which suffused the yachts with a last gasp of vivid light. We rowed ashore in the dinghy and I listened to the extraordinary antics of an octopus which had joined an earlier barbecue, venturing so close in the shallow water at the edge that one of the tentacles tested a pine cone in search of food before rejecting it. One yachtsman actually shook hands with the tentacle and gave it some pieces of cold fish which it stuffed into its mouth, like an elephant with its trunk. It was reddish in colour and 3 or 4 feet wide – though it is hard to estimate size where octopuses are concerned – and was followed by a younger, paler version, also hungry or attracted by the lights. All this sounded preposterous but was told me seriously.

The yachtsmen made me welcome at the barbecue but I was an intruder and every group forms its clique. Holidays are a form of snobbery to start with, each level looking down on the other, from the cultured ladies on the Swan Hellenic to the package tours shown on those television holiday programmes which put one off more countries than they attract one to, with hundreds of young British swigging back sangria and chanting *Viva Espanya!* The yachting enthusiasts are halfway in the pecking order but they indulged in their own communal singing. The chorus of 'She'll be coming round the mountain when she comes' shattered the tranquillity. Intoxicated by the air, so having no need of wine, I rowed back to the *Merlin* and read the last pages of Paul Theroux's remarkable *Mosquito Coast* in which a vulture rips out someone's tongue.

A cool dip in the bay at sunrise primed me for the excursion up the river to Dalyan. It proved one of the most exhilarating days in my life.

After saying goodbye to the pilot crew, who had seen it all before, I boarded one of the two Turkish caiques which collected the others from their yachts and headed out to the open sea towards the sandbank where the Dalyan river flows into the sea. This is an extraordinary place: unlike the strip of sandbar at outlets like Olympos, this stretches for a mile or two with water on either side. It is wide enough, a couple of hundred yards, to contain an unlikely settlement of shanty huts on stilts to protect them from sandstorms and the sea which sometimes flows across in winter. The huts are totally haphazard with no parallel lines, and until recently were painted in different colours which added to their rakish air. As most are used in mid-summer by families who escape from the heat inland, the place looks curiously deserted in the early morning as if it had been abandoned. No camera can capture the breadth of this landscape. Layers of perspective unfold from the sandbar towards the delta and a valley beyond with fields of cotton melting into distant hills.

The channel lies close to steep, forested land on one side with the sandbar on the other and it looks a perfect entrance. In fact it is so shallow that few boats can pass through it and when Freya Stark came here on her voyage along the Lycian Shore in the early 1950s her companion, David Balfour, had to coax the *Elfin* across, wading ahead with the water up to his waist in order to find the deepest currents. On the way back they found that the sand had shifted due to heavy rain and Balfour had to cast the anchor beyond the bar and winch the *Elfin* through: 'I felt a human pain with each blow of *Elfin*'s neatly painted bottom on the floor. It was over and she was through in a few minutes, with clouds of sand whirling about her.'

Balfour's example cannot be recommended because the currents are so unpredictable and the sand so shifting that it can suck you down like quicksand. I was told that two people have been drowned trying to wade the few yards across. It is safer to swim further out to sea, even out of your depth, if you want to reach the other side as I did, rewarded by a perfect, isolated beach surrounded by pines.

The shallow entrance was the reason for the two flat-bottomed caiques which took us through in seconds to the calm water on the other side of the sandbar before we entered the channels of the labyrinthine delta which stretches for miles.

I have taken a boat up the massive Danube delta to the Black Sea, but this is more beautiful if only because the bamboo reeds are low enough to allow constant views of the valley beyond and the hilltop of Caunus on the side.

The Danube delta is famous for its wildlife, though I failed to see one of the promised pelicans, and it is just as exhilarating here with flashes of a bright blue kingfisher and white egrets darting into the refuge of the reeds whose roots are structured under water. Even when the reeds surround you, the impression is so peaceful that I should find it hard to like anyone who found this journey boring.

We passed through the gates of the fish hatchery which gives Dalyan its name, with the mesh nets lowered from pulleys by two men on wooden platforms on either side, and soon we moored alongside a jetty further on and stepped ashore. The journey to Caunus had taken an hour.

31 Abidin Kurt

By now I was conscious of the striking figure who was guiding us, a huge Turk in small swimming trunks. This was my introduction to Abidin Kurt though at that time he called himself Kurt Abidin assuming that Kurt was a name which was instantly recognisable, creating a confusion he has since corrected. Even then he was known as 'Aberdeen', recognisable to us as a Scottish port though it made him sound like a retired Negro boxer. Like most Turkish words, it should be pronounced as spelt – Abb-idd-in. Women have told me that he was heartbreakingly handsome as a young man and he remains so today with a magnificently leonine head even if his stomach is a walking advertisement for the Turkish food he loves.

Since then he has become a friend, a strong yet gentle man who has never said or done a petty thing that I know of, nor have I seen his face look sullen or weak in repose. There are few people I would trust with my life, and he is one of them.

Much of Abidin's strength is derived from his native land, dominated by the ancient city of Caunus which we reached after a quarter of an hour's walk up the hill. He was born at Candir, a small village on the other side.

On a lesser scale than many ruins, Caunus suggests more mystery than most. It is still being excavated and the archaeologists have built themselves a sumptuous modern building which dominates the approach by caique, blending into the surroundings surprisingly well. Presumably it was constructed by the Turkish prisoners who assisted the archaeologists in the summer. 'It is really sad to watch them,' said the kindly Abidin, 'they are the slaves of today.' But I should have thought it a welcome release into the open air, performing a work which has the solace of taking them back to the past and away from their present misfortune. However, I have noticed a curious thing about excavations – I have never seen anyone excavate. All the sites I have visited have been deserted. That they do excavate is indisputable for the evidence is left even if the archaeologists are invisible. The shaded street with the curious circle at the end which might have contained a pool was restricted to visitors when I returned in 1984 though I walked along it that morning with Abidin.

Unlike Raif who was turned away at Heathrow, Abidin had been luckier when he came to London to visit his Australian girlfriend, and smartly found himself a job as porter in a large Paddington hotel. It did not take him long to realise that the other porters disliked the Arabs so he seized his opportunity to ingratiate himself with the visiting sheikhs who asked for his services exclusively when they discovered he was Islamic, rewarding him with such munificent tips that he was able to buy his first caique on his return to Dalyan. His stay in London had taught him English too.

Abidin's commentary is racy rather than academic, with references to a king called Caunus, alleged son of Miletus, whose sister Byblis fell in love with him and hanged herself when he deserted her.

Rediscovered as recently as 1842 by a Mr Hoskyn of *HMS Beacon*, Caunus was a Carian city though there is doubt over the population. Herodotus claimed that the Caunians came from Crete; George Bean believed they were indigenous. In the usual musical chairs of successive occupations, the town was captured by the Persians in 387 BC like other Lycian ports along the coast, by Antigonus after the death of Alexander the Great, and later fell under the jurisdiction of Rhodes, becoming a free city under Rome.

Apart from the Roman baths, always startling in their size and complexity, where you can actually see the outlet of the ancient water pipes, the outstanding attraction of Caunus is the ancient theatre in the familiar Greco-Roman style due to the Hellenising policy of Mausolus, provincial governor of Caria for the Persians. Writers claim that the theatre held 20,000 people though I should have thought that half that number would be closer; today it is pleasantly overgrown with five methuselahn olive trees renting the stone, but the spectacular bonus lies with the views when you walk along the top and see the lie of the land on every side. The panoramas help to put the history of Caunus in perspective. In particular you can appreciate the existence of the harbours which lay below when the sea surrounded the hill before the water receded for two miles.

The port was unique in paying a tax even higher than Ephesus which indicates an astonishing prosperity, probably due to the sale of salted fish, bass and mullet, from the hatcheries which existed even then though there is no actual proof that such an exorbitant tax was ever paid.

As for the placid lake which has been left there, the treasures it might hold for the archaeologists can be gauged by the marble dolphin dredged from the bottom, which I have not seen, and the splendid, white marble lion which stands in the nearby town of Koycegiz, one paw resting proudly on the head of a bull. I love that lion so transparently pleased with itself, and the thought of it lying submerged for 2,000 years yet emerging intact is deeply satisfying. What people they were to combine such strength with enhancements like this!

Yet the Caunians were not respected in their day. Looking over the lake it is possible to envisage the extensive marshland which bred the malaria which led to the city's decline. There is a well-known quotation which referred to the green complexions of the people, comparing them to leaves. When the Caunians protested, the writer assured them with mock solemnity that he would not dare to call their city unhealthy 'when dead men walk the streets'.

'Those stupid Caunians,' another critic called them, 'their misfortunes are due to their extreme folly and rascality, and if they are all but wiped out by fever it is no more than they deserve.' Because they made their home there in the first place? The judgment seems hard, but the fever did wipe them out and even when the late George Bean went there for the first time in 1946 he found the place 'singing with mosquitoes; and the least flaw in the mosquito-net meant a sleepless night.' Two years later the Turkish government started a vigorous campaign to eliminate the mosquitoes with newly invented DDT, and they succeeded – for a time.

When I was there I found to my irritation that the mosquitoes were making a return visit too, and though they may be fewer in numbers they are still a torment as the sun comes down and they come out like Dracula. They are the one drawback to Dalyan.

After showing us the ruins of Caunus, Abidin led us back to the caiques and we chortled past the village of Dalyan through a beautiful stretch of the river, with tall pine trees on one side and fields to the other, before we entered the massive, unspoilt lake of Koycegiz where the British leapt into the fresh water with squeals of delight and shampooed their hair, a ritual now replaced by taking them to the sulphur baths further on, under a covered dome.

Back at Dalyan where lunch was waiting in the garden of one of the restaurants, Abidin was revealed as a restaurateur, parading the choice of dishes for everyone to see with a cry of 'I show you the which is which, the what is what, and the why is wherefore!' And then it was time to leave the YCA and make my way back to Marmaris. Shaking hands with Abidin, I promised to return.

I had found my Turkish paradise. There was no doubt of that, though there were moments in the following year when I wondered if Dalyan could be as beautiful as the image in my mind confirmed. I wanted to find out what happens in a village like Dalyan after the tourists leave, remembering my father's description of a Russian river town called Ryazan when he sailed down the Volga on his way to climb the Caucasus as 'boredom personified'. His companion, an English eccentric, Alexander Wicksteed, agreed: 'Nothing but unmitigated and incessant vice could make such a place bearable!'

Was it possible that Dalyan would prove to be 'boredom personified' too?

I returned the following year, taking the bus from Marmaris to the end of the eucalyptus avenue where I hitched a lift in the front of a small van laden with vegetables whose driver dropped me off just as the dolmus was leaving Ortega for Dalyan, and squeezed inside although it was overcrowded as usual.

Though we stopped constantly while someone wandered into a nearby house to collect something or leave a message, the journey takes just fifteen minutes and I headed for the Aly Aktas Pension on the banks of the river which I had noticed the year before.

That evening I dined at the Denizati restaurant where I had paused briefly on my first visit and was welcomed by Ismet with such a beaming smile that it had to be genuine. 'Denizati' means seahorse, a lucky symbol for me as this was one of my nicknames when a child, and though the structure was simple with a concrete base and a latticed roof, the position beside the water was incomparable.

We could hardly speak a word of each other's language, though Ismet was struggling with the ramifications of a phrase book which proved alarming when he showed it to me: 'If John told you that last night, you can be sure that he lied to you' – 'Helen needs a lot of money' – and 'The doctor is drinking whisky'. What had they been up to? No wonder Ismet looked harassed as he tried to unravel the plot and I hoped he would never find himself in the situation where such phrases could be helpful.

As we sat and smiled in silence, I realised there are times when language can be a dreadful barrier to understanding. I thought of the dross of average conversation, which concentrates on platitudes about the weather and the morning gossip on television programmes seen the night before. If I was fluent, my tongue would risk offence even unintentionally, but silence leaves the benefit of the doubt. There is an innocence in sign language and though I could have spoken to an Englishman without a glance in his direction, it was necessary to look Ismet directly in the eye when I tried to make myself understood. If you cannot speak the language the vital element of mystery remains. How wise, how sympathetic, how humorous the man who cannot tell you everything!

After dinner, which Ismet would not allow me to pay for, I discovered what happens when the tourists leave – nothing! A few Turks watched a flickering television set, others played backgammon, the mosquitoes came out as the sun slipped behind the hills and I made my way back to the Aly Aktas pension to be in bed soon after nine, exactly what I needed after two weeks of constant travel.

The simple wooden verandah outside the pension has the sun behind it in the morning so I ate my breakfast of homemade yoghurt and dark local honey while I absorbed the scene in front of me. There is a small garden with some orange trees immediately below, and then the river. The only distraction in the night had been the gentle chugging of the passing caiques laden with bales of cotton picked by the women in the fields further up the valley – some distraction!

But the feature which makes Dalyan unique and this view unforgettable is the Lycian tombs carved high in the cliffs above the bend of the river as you approach the village. How they carved them several centuries before Christ remains a mystery, though it was probably from scaffolding lowered from above. You can reach the Lycian tombs at Fethiye and Demre by foot, but these remain inaccessible, their aloofness intact.

They are incredibly beautiful. A black and white photograph conveys their design and juxtaposition to the river, but cannot hint at the subtlety of their colouring. It is hard to describe: brown is insulting; beige is a colour from a textile catalogue; while apricot and peach sound like samples of paint. Sandstone is closest, but words are inadequate here as they are for Petra.

Abidin collected me by caique later in the afternoon, dropping me at the sandbar while he delivered the tourists to their yachts in Ekincek Bay.

The sandbar is wonderfully lonely in late October when the visitors have gone, and I walked along the edge of the surf cooling off every few hundred yards for it was still hot, or sitting down simply to watch the sandcrabs vanishing into their holes and the clusters of sandpipers scurrying together like a passing shadow.

Another time, at the end of May, I have seen the tracks like those of a miniature tank made by the turtles who wade ashore at night to lay their eggs, covering them with sand afterwards. Then they stagger laboriously back to the sea a few yards away by a parallel route which is why the tracks look mechanical. Sometimes the creatures are so exhausted after laying twenty or thirty eggs that they head inland before they realise their mistake and turn back.

One night I returned in the darkness with a torch in the hope of seeing one of the turtles and must have gone too early judging by the fresh tracks in the sand the next morning, yet I was glad I had not disturbed the animal at such a vulnerable moment. The wretched turtle has been decimated in recent years, so scarce nowadays that the Aegean is glutted with jellyfish, their usual prey. If Abidin happens to be there when the eggs hatch twenty days later he scoops up the baby turtles and carries them to the water before they are burnt by the blistering sand, but the turtle tracks in spring are becoming fewer.

On my way back from the shallow pond at the other end of the beach, I received a salutary shock when I saw a tortoise, which I assumed was the most fastidious creature, gorging itself on a lump of fresh manure left by one of the nine black cows, though what the animals find to graze on is hard to imagine. I saw two of them munching contentedly on cardboard.

With the sudden darkness the air became chilly after the heat of the day and the shanty settlement so ghostly that I wondered if I was alone until I saw the greeting of a naked light bulb in a primitive lokanta which was open for customers though the laconic owner, his son and dog were the only creatures there with the absurdity of a television set showing an early 'Star Trek' relayed from a Greek network across the water.

Waiting for Abidin's return as I drank an Efes beer and toyed with some octopus, I was joined mysteriously by an elegant English couple who appeared out of the darkness, walked up the wooden steps and sat down at the table opposite, immaculate apart from their wet feet having rowed ashore in a dinghy from their yacht which was moored under the island opposite.

The lady smiled and I flattered myself that she knew me from my old days in television but in fact she had seen the book I was reading and realised I was English. When we introduced ourselves, however, she recognised my name from my new column as TV critic for a Sunday newspaper and leant forward with exaggerated concern when she learnt that I had been travelling in Turkey for the past fortnight: 'Then you won't have heard the dreadful news. I hate to be the first to tell you. Elsie Tanner is leaving Coronation Street!'

A shock indeed. Ironically, my new job as TV critic was about to shatter my plans. My contract was due to be renewed and this was a job I wanted. The irony lay in having a job which provided the means to buy a place in Turkey but would keep me tied to England. It would be difficult to have both, even if I had the luck to find a piece of land for sale.

I was closer to this than I realised when a group of fishermen joined us for breakfast on the wooden steps of Abidin's hut the next morning, including one of the largest, swarthiest men I had ever seen. It turned out that he owned a piece of land beside the river, as Abidin told me when we returned by caique to Dalyan. Without the distraction of his usual group of tourists – for he ferries several thousand in the summer – Abidin was relaxed and spoke unashamedly of his pride in his birthplace: 'I like my country very much, the more and more every day. I work in Istanbul for four years studying but I cannot understand how people can live in a city. Whenever I go inland I am thankful to come back here for then I feel so *light* again.'

As we neared the Lycian tombs he pointed to a bare stretch of land on the Caunus side of the river which was owned by the large fisherman and might be for sale. I asked Abidin to moor alongside and as we walked across the plot for the next few moments I scrutinised every yard of earth, trying to visualise it as a home.

Abidin thought the land might cost around £13,000 which seemed a lot for Turkey with the need to build a house as well, though he assured me this could cost as little as £6,000, estimates which seem to have risen astronomically since then.

It was time to leave. I had to continue to Datca but apart from that the hospitality from Abidin and Izmet was proving an embarrassment. Neither would allow me to pay for anything. We lunched at the Denizati on Russian salad and a large *pal* fish, but when I produced my money Ismet said 'Okay', refusing to accept it.

'He says you are good man,' Abidin interpreted, and though this was far from the truth I felt better in consequence.

Their generosity persisted to the last moment as I climbed into the dolmus and discovered that Abidin had paid the driver already. Ismet hurried up as we were about to leave and dropped something into my carrier bag. As we drove off, I looked inside and found two apples, a stick of the wax-encased smoked roe of sea bass, pressed caviare which is a particular delicacy in Dalyan, and one slightly wilting marigold – 'the Turkish rose'.

Seldom have I been so flattered.

Information

The Yacht Cruising Association
Remarkable value: if the yacht carries four people, two weeks'
sailing can work out at roughly £400 each. The cost depends on the
type of boat and the time of year: if you take the smallest 28-foot
yacht on 1st May it can be as little as £279. I say 'little' because this
includes the air fare to Dalaman. Take the longest, 33-foot yacht in
the peak season and it will work out at just over £500. Yet May and
October are the perfect months if you are not tied down by jobs and
school holidays.

The YCA now have several flotillas along this coast; also, a
holiday which combines sailing with a villa on shore. An excellent
brochure will provide the details, obtainable from the YCA, Old
Stone House, Judge's Terrace, Ship Street, East Grinstead, Sussex
RH19. Tel: Reservations: 0342 311366.

Charter
The man who can help you with everything in Marmaris is Dogan
Tugay. His office is *Yesil Marmaris Travel* (P.O. Box 8, telex: 52528
gema tr), next to the *Kaptan Hotel* which is run by his father, and
opposite his ferry which goes every day to Rhodes. Dogan Tugay
has his own charter service of Turkish boats, with three cabins (two
berths each) and two lavatories, run by a Turkish crew. A large
table in the stern is perfect for meals in the open air under an
awning. Prices vary according to the time of the year etc., but it is
vital to check with him directly. There is now an international
telephone to Marmaris: 1033 1559. His agency is *Albatross*.

The *Moana Vahine* is the classiest yacht for charter along the
coast, a masterpiece of shining wood and brass, originally built in
Taiwan and sailed across the Indian Ocean and the Red Sea by Jim
and Jillian Anderson who have made their base in Marmaris where
they run *Charter Turkey*, the Aegean & Turkish Coast Yacht
Charter Group, in conjunction with Dogan Tugay who is godfather
to their son born in Marmaris in 1981. A charter licence is now
obligatory for yachts sailing commercially under a foreign flag, but
this ensures professional standards which comply with international
safety regulations at a realistic licensing fee. Charter Turkey received the first licence from the Turkish Ministry of Tourism. The
Andersons were lucky to sail into Marmaris Bay in 1980 after the
Greeks passed a new law forbidding foreign yachts to charter
between the Greek islands. Jill Anderson comes from New Zealand
(Jim is Australian) and says, 'As soon as we entered the bay of

Marmaris my tummy turned over. It was so like New Zealand it was just like coming home. I'd expected something barren like the Greek islands but it was green with great pine forests stretching down to the sea.' Since then the *Moana Vahine* has been available for charter. I had the luck to sail on her to the Island of Symi, after clearance in Rhodes, a luxury I could not have afforded myself, and it would be absurd to pretend that a charter cruise is the cost of an average holiday. This is an exceptional type of holiday exploring many places which can only be reached by sea, like Kekova or the island of Gemile which the Andersons discovered by accident: 'It's deserted with the ruins of an ancient city which the archaeologists have yet to disturb.' Ideal for six to eight guests, can accommodate ten. Windsurfer, snorkelling, etc. However, be prepared to pay around £350 a day in season, and this does not include food or the air fare.

Enquiries from Yesil Marmaris, or Halsey Marine, London. Tel: 01 724 1303.

Dalyan

Kurt Abidin can also advise you on charter cruises locally. He is indispensable if you need a caique to take you up the delta to Caunus. His office is in Dalyan itself: *Sardes Tourism and Travel*, Kordon Caddesi no. 26, Dalyan, Mugla. Tel: Dalyan 50.

Hotel
Aly Aktas Pension: Tel: Dalyan 42.

Restaurants
Denizati restaurant: Tel: Dalyan 21.
The *Piknik* pizza bar is run by Ismet, referred to in this book on page 209.

32 A rough road to Datca

The Datca Peninsula stretches beyond Marmaris and if I needed an alternative to the land at Dalyan I should seek it here. The peninsula runs parallel to the northern mainland which leads to Bodrum on the other side of the gulf of Gokova, with a southern arm which reaches down as if it is going to seize the island of Symi in its pincers.

On the map, the distance to Bozburun on this southern part is half that to Datca at the far end, but it takes over twice as long due to the rough track which sometimes gives up altogether.

The road from Marmaris starts encouragingly, slicing through woods and forests, but when you turn south it becomes a punishment though you are rewarded by entering another, wilder landscape. The hillsides are a mass of stones, with an occasional patch of earth such as one I saw ploughed by two cows rather than the usual oxen, which seemed typical of this land which has yet to be tamed.

In Turkey, a woman's place is the field and nowhere was this more apparent than here. Even if they were not carrying stacks of firewood, the women were bent double and looked incongruous as they wielded their heavy spades, walking barefoot down the rocky paths, their faces drained of all vitality. Down by the water's edge of one village, the men idled the day away contentedly, playing dominoes and cards in one of those ubiquitous cafés which sell remarkably little, and certainly no food. In contrast to the understandably disgruntled women, the men were sleek and smiling, greeting me warmly. The disparity between the sexes would have rendered a British feminist speechless and even I found it slightly shocking.

Though they are poor people in this area, they are outstandingly handsome, especially the younger women who still stand upright, and the young men with lustrous black hair.

I left Marmaris in a hired car at half past nine, turning south to Orhaniye after only half an hour, a pleasantly tranquil bay where I paused before we carried on to Sogut, famous for its almonds, and to Bayir, famous for honey. The road stopped before Selimye where we had to walk down to the beautiful bay and the small settlement of houses reached by sea from the village of Cubucak on the peninsula opposite. The stillness of the weather matched the atmosphere, for this was a place behind the back of progress and my own particular haste seemed ludicrous. As for such luxuries as the post, if a letter arrived there was every chance it might be collected by the next man who went to Bozburun a few miles further on.

Bozburun is the main town on this southern claw. It is a port of call for the YCA and famous for its boatbuilding yard, which makes it sound attractive. It proved a harsh little place with a quayside strewn with iron bars and rusting concrete mixers, while a noisy crane dropped boulders to form a mole. The glare in mid-summer must be painful and the heat unbearable due to the mountains which enclose the harbour and exclude the hope of any passing breeze. Yet the Liman restaurant provided an excellent sauté of lamb, one of the simplest and best of all Turkish dishes, and someone arrived with a red mullet almost as large as a lamb itself, with sad, yellow-orange eyes, caught by lowering a hook very deep near some rocks further out to sea, baited with the flesh of another fish.

I preferred the unpretentiousness of Datca, though my arrival in the evening could hardly have been more depressing, booking into a pension room which was little more than a downstairs cell with a broken glass door and a hostile lavatory. A few minutes later as the squalor penetrated, my instincts rebelled and I went to the hotel opposite the bus stop where a sullen receptionist sat behind his desk with a backdrop of keys in their cubby holes.

'Room!' he exclaimed, shaking his head indignantly, 'no room.' Walking across the road I found another pension beside a restaurant with a reasonable room with three beds, a cold-water tap in the corridor, and a friendlier lavatory. I collected my luggage from the cell, hanging my key on the nail beside the door as I crept out, and would have felt guiltier except for the lira notes left on the filthy pillow by some previous occupant, which suggest that the bedclothes were seldom if ever changed.

Datca out of season is as lively as any British seaside town of a comparable size. In the café where men played dominoes, I drank a beer and made some notes until the pictures on the television set, of mutilated victims from a coach crash became so depressing that I retreated to the restaurant opposite where some Germans were disputing their bill, loudly.

'Outside soup is 80. We pay 150. Not good enough. We do not come this place again' – a rash remark for this was apparently the only restaurant open. I wondered why they spoke English to the Turks, unless they were trying to discredit *us*. Then their dog, tied up outside, started to scream as if it had been hit – a sound which curdles my emotions – so when they appealed to me for support I told them, churlishly, to look after their animal instead, wondering afterwards why I had been rude to the only people who spoke my language. That, of course, was the reason.

I was bitten by mosquitoes in the night and woke in a rage to add the corpse of my predator to the blood-blotched concrete wall, amazed that such a tiny creature could have supped so much of my blood. In the morning my right eyelid was swollen, a favourite biting place, and after a breakfast on the balcony of the restaurant of fresh tangerine juice, yoghurt and honey, tea and two hardboiled eggs, overlooking the harbour and a range of distant mountains, I walked to the open-air mineral pool, a few hundred yards away. There used to be a mill here, replaced in 1984 by a concrete hut which serves as a small restaurant in the summer, but the wooden platform was deserted and after finishing my copy of *Robinson Crusoe* I lay in the sun, soothed by the mesmerising sound of the spring water flowing over a gap in the wall, running out to the sea. Then I spoilt it all by swimming in the sulphur water with my eyes wide open, hoping to reduce the swelling on my eyelid but gaining a slight infection in both eyes which lingered for a long time afterwards. If you swim there, do so with your eyes shut.

That evening I had another example of the Turkish generosity to strangers. Somehow I lost a 10,000-lira note, probably blown away as I sat down for a cup of coffee on the outside balcony. As I was relying on that money for the next stage of my journey, I went in search of Mahmut Gulbahar, the director of tourism, to see if he could help. I had seen him earlier in his office, flanked by Raif from Lake Van who was now his assistant and looked acutely homesick, and a young American painter and his New Zealand girlfriend, who were hoping to rent a place for the winter. The tourist office was shut so I continued round the corner and found the couple sitting outside a snack bar which I had failed to notice before. They were elated at having found a villa at a nominal cost, arranged for them by the lively young owner of the snack bar, Dogan Yalcinkaya. His place here was unpretentious, with a couple of tables inside and out, but he runs the grander Sandal restaurant in the season. He is a genius with food. I gathered this from the account of the banquet he had prepared for the couple the night before which was making me envious until he produced the best keftes I have eaten in Turkey, followed by another banquet improvised on his charcoal grill.

When I mentioned my loss, he produced a 10,000-lira note and thrust it into my hand.

'You don't know me!' I protested.

'That's all right. You come back to Datca and give it to me then.'

Footnote

I did so on an unexpected visit later. This confirmed that Dogan Omer Yalcinkaya is as bright as he is generous. His skill as a cook is self-taught for he was unable to make an omelette when he worked as a teacher in a remote mountain village enhanced by 'dogs, cats, goats and honey-bees' but dominated by the boys who never stopped feuding and finally drove him to food rather than drink. Today he is a true professional with instinctive flair. The Sandal, named after the small Turkish dinghys which decorate it inside, is not a smart place but he makes it fun. Realising that the cheap but delicious squid called *subye* is passed off as *calamares* by most restaurants who charge 1,000 lira accordingly, Dogan bills it unashamedly as *subye* and charges 1,200 serving it in the lightest batter. Octopus, which always sounds like a meal in itself, is cut into tiny pieces and tastes like succulent chicken. Best of all, and at lightning speed, he prepares a 'stew' with small pieces of veal simmered in oil, with onion, garlic, tomato paste, pepper and thyme in a heavy black pan known as a *sac*, a sort of Turkish *wok*. Sometimes this is varied with different meat and a lavish sprinkling of parsley and dill and is all the better because it is the height of simplicity and prepared with ease.

On this last visit I had the luck to coincide with groups from Ankara and Instanbul who were celebrating the public holiday which marks the end of the fast of Ramadan. They danced the night away and one girl was so brilliant that the waiter accompanying her on the drum continued to do so with such a violent beat that his fingers were bleeding by the time she stopped.

Like an impresario, Dogan sustained the atmosphere throughout, even placating a group from an English yacht who, to my astonishment, brandished an article I had written on Datca, as they complained that their chips were not hot enough. Soon they were dancing too, but they were the only other tourists.

On two successive evenings, the Sandal fulfilled my definition of a good restaurant – that you leave happier than when you arrived.

33 Cnidus – and the
sexy statue

The ruins of Cnidus (pronounced knee-dos) lie at the end of the peninsula where the Aegean meets the Mediterranean. They are reached easily by boat but the journey by road from Datca 35 kilometres away is a rougher ride though well worth it as you drive through primitive villages until you reach Cnidus where an army garrison of a dozen men and two simple-looking restaurants are the only evidence of the present. The rest is ruins.

There used to be two harbours, one for military purposes which is now silted up, and the other for commercial use. To sail inside on a hot day and moor here for the night would be an experience of a lifetime, though the archaeologists try to discourage it. Even when I went there by taxi in the middle of an overcast and lacklustre day, the ruins were dramatic.

There were two Cnidian cities originally. The first was situated close to Datca where the outlines are visible today, and when the Persian armies advanced the Cnidians tried to protect themselves by cutting through a narrow isthmus at the eastern end of the peninsula, turning their territory into an island. The sense of this is obvious when you study the map, but the hard rock splintered, cutting their bodies and endangering their eyes, so they sought advice from the Delphic Oracle who told them:

Dig not nor fence your isthmus: Zeus himself
Had made your land an island, had he so wished.

The Cnidians retreated to the furthest tip in the fourth century BC, a natural port for every passing merchant ship so that New Cnidus became a major trading centre of the time. As so often, the scale is overwhelming with a population reaching 70,000 at its peak. The city was guarded by a circular wall, with streets and houses built on a rectangular pattern inside, and the small island opposite was joined to the mainland by a causeway with the two artificial harbours on either side as they are today. Otherwise little is left apart from the foundations and the walls, the remains of the theatre, and the stones and terraces of former houses. It is the size of the place rather than the detail which impresses. This spot which seems so remote was a centre for the arts and sciences, the birthplace of Sostratos, the architect who built the lighthouse at Alexandria, one of the Seven Wonders of the Ancient World, and the astronomer Eudoxus, the designer of the first observatory known to the Grecian world.

Cnidus was visited, though ransacked might be a better word, in 1857 by Sir Charles Newton who delivered several hundred cases of sculpture to the British Museum in London. If you brave that impersonal building, you will see a great marble lion actually on display, instead of gathering dust in the vaults, along with the seated figure of the goddess Demeter, another item from Newton's loot. You will be doubly rewarded if you combine this with a look at the New Wolfson Galleries tucked away in the basement, filled with pieces of classical sculpture retrieved from the Mausoleum at Halicarnassus (Bodrum) and the Temple of Artemis at Ephesus. Unfortunately 'pieces' is the accurate description, and it is the massive scale of the Cnidus lion – the size of a car – which seizes the imagination so violently. Looking older and darker than the lions at Delos, the deep sockets of the eyes hold a remarkable depth of expression, as if they have witnessed all that there is to be seen.

Until I went to the Museum I believed the story which claims that this was one of two lions guarding the entrance to the southern harbour, perched on either side as if to spring on unwelcome visitors, and I cringed from the footnote which added that the other lion broke loose and fell into the sea as Newton transported his treasures back to the ship. But this is not the truth. This was the only lion, and it surmounted a massive tomb, rather like that of Mausolus, on a nearby headland. The tomb was in ruins by the time that Newton landed and transporting the lion down the cliff proved extremely difficult. At one point it got stuck, which might explain the apocryphal story of the alleged companion which tumbled into the sea.

This is the explanation given by the British Museum and I accept it unreservedly. I returned to see that lion recently and found it more compelling than ever. If you are going to Cnidius, or have gone, I urge you to see it too.

The most famous, or infamous, decoration was the statue of Aphrodite by the sculptor Praxiteles who made it between 365 and 360 BC. This had been rejected by the islanders on Cos because the naked form was considered too sensual, choosing a version which was modestly draped instead. The Cnidians had no such scruples, benefiting greatly from the notoriety of the statue which became a tourist attraction in its time attracting visitors who arrived by boat especially to see it. Pliny called it the finest statue in the world, Nicomedes, King of Bithynia, offered to settle the city's debts if he could have it in return, and it was said that one young man concealed himself in the temple one night and embraced the goddess so passionately that she bore a dark stain on the inner side of the thigh which remained on the marble forever. No one knows what happened to the statue in the end, though copies were made of the original.

The American archaeologist Dr Iris Love has excavated the ruins in order to find or prove the existence of the statue, and she has succeeded in uncovering the circular foundations of the temple to Aphrodite and the base for the statue itself. The temple had entrances around the figure so that admirers could see it from behind, apparently a most desirable view, and in 1970 the identification with Aphrodite was confirmed by the discovery of a block of marble nearby with the first letters of *Prax*(iteles) and *Aph*(rodite).

Coins have also been found with the statue of Aphrodite on one side, and that of the sculptor on the other. But Iris Love has met with opposition from the officials of British Museum who refuse to accept that a damaged marble head, which she rediscovered in the vaults, is that of Aphrodite. And some of the local villagers who own the land at Cnidus have witheld their permission which is needed for her work to continue.

So while the experts dispute and formalities obstruct, enjoy Cnidus for what it offers you today, the outline of a great city, and enrich it with the details of your knowledge and imagination.

Bodrum lies opposite the Gulf of Gokova, approximately three hours' sailing away.

A new ferry service is available in the summer, though it is vital to check the erratic sailing times in advance. The crossing on the small boat saves a day's bus journey, via Marmaris and Mugla unless you start out early.

34 Bodrum, and Dursun the sponge diver

Bodrum is a delightful town for a number of reasons. There is the satisfaction gained from a sense of history for this was the ancient Halicarnassus where Mausolus established his capital when he was king of Caria in 375 BC, marrying his sister Artemisia who built the massive tomb after his death which bore his name and was listed as one of the Seven Wonders of the World. A few years later, Halicarnassus fell to Alexander the Great who destroyed it completely.

This was the past. The present is dominated by the grand old Castle of St Peter built by the Knights of Rhodes in 1402 using stones from the famous mausoleum which is no more than a hole in the ground today. This makes the approach one of the most exciting in Turkey, first seen from above with the great fortress straddling the two bays on a rocky promontory that was once an island called Zephyria.

Bodrum is the right size, compact enough for the eye to absorb and easy to walk through once you have found your bearings. The shops are more elegant than most in Turkey with a surprising number of excellent cobblers though I discovered that my feet are immense by Turkish standards when I tried to buy a pair of shoes. I noticed also that the cobbler had a severe limp and wondered at the idiotic illogicality that this should distress me as much as an optician who wore pebble glasses or a dentist with false teeth.

Unlike Marmaris which has a single, and rather halfhearted bar, Bodrum sports a street of them, as lively at the end of November as I could have wished. A comparison is often made to St Tropez, and though this is one of those glib labels which don't really stick, the Hadigari Bar in particular has a cosmopolitan atmosphere which comes as a treat if you have been travelling in rougher parts of Turkey.

Reflecting the sophistication of Bodrum which even sports a French restaurant, the Hadigari fills up suddenly in the late afternoon with the atmosphere of a good party until everyone moves off around eight to other bars across the road, including one lined with large posters of film stars, such as Marilyn Monroe.

Though I was the only Englishman, some of the Turks had Belgian or German wives and most of them spoke English. It was in the Hadigari that I met Dursun the sponge diver. Dursun Mutlu is the main reason why I shall always come back to Bodrum. It is not surprising that I liked him on sight for his appearance is gleeful in itself: a short, wiry figure with a cluster of silvery curls and a grey beard, though he is only forty, which give him the mischievous look of an ancient satyr without his horns, or Neptune just risen from the waves.

The latter comparison is less fantastic when you learn that he was a sponge diver. Born in Bodrum, Dursun educated himself because his family were too poor to help him, and he started sponge diving at the age of eighteen. Of all the livings in the world, this is one of the most hazardous and when you see a man bent double on a Greek island like Symi or Kalymnos, or a Turkish town such as Bodrum, it is probable that he was a diver too. 'It is a difficult job. Many friends died or were paralysed.'

It is not so rewarding as you might imagine except for the owners of the boats and even then the Greeks have clung to the monopoly of exporting sponges around the world.

Yet the camaraderie must be enviable, as I sensed when I saw a fleet sail out of Kalymnos, six men to a boat, with their families waving them goodbye.

Dursun actually enjoyed diving and was one of the best. Most go down to a depth of 60 metres but he has gone to 80 and even 84 with scuba equipment and a tube, rather than a cylinder, which trails from the boat above.

'What is the world like down there?' I asked.

'Dark,' he replied. 'You do not see the sun.'

The danger comes in rising to the surface too quickly when the blood boils and paralyses a limb, the heart or the brain. After a dive of only two minutes it is necessary to pause below the surface for as long as fifteen minutes before the diver is hauled back on board.

Dursun compares the sponges to towns for they are alive, with the holes like streets crowded with activity. The largest he found weighed 12 kilos and was so old that the middle had gone. Once on deck the sponges are stamped on to get rid of their dirty-coloured juice and when they die the skin is pulled off and they are put back in the water in baskets to soak in the wake until they are taken up again, squeezed, and left to bleach in the sun before they are packed. They vary in size – the largest up to a metre wide – and the

Greeks cut them up into the shapes required.

Plainly the bucaneering life has its highlights, the celebrations when the fleets come together and drink themselves senseless, the homecoming as they sail into harbour with the baskets of sponges hanging from the masts, but ultimately these were outweighed by the scant reward for such horrifying risks as the 'bends'. He sums up the divers' philosophy: 'We work underwater without sweat, but we die without breath.'

I asked about such dangers as sharks, and he smiled. 'I've seen them off Libya. Well – it makes you frightened. I just came up to the surface. The man with me rose too quickly.'

'What happened to him?'

'He is making shoes in Bodrum.' He was the cobbler with the limp.

35 The *Maya* – available for charter

Dursun is a man with instinctive good taste as I realised when I visited his home off a pleasing, tree-lined back street in Bodrum. The main room is happily lived-in with a central staircase like a well surrounded by polished pine, piles of books, a music stand and paintings, reflecting the interests of his wife Lon. She is Dutch and they met when she came to Bodrum on her honeymoon. This did not prevent them from falling in love and she returned after her husband's death.

They have two sons and a daughter. The youngest boy was still a baby when I met him, called Derya, and the daughter's name is Maya. Dursun's yacht, built in the Bodrum boatyard in 1984, is named after her.

Of all the yachts I have seen along the Turkish coast, the *Maya* is the finest. The *Maya* took two and a half years to build, giving him some anxious moments when he ran out of money until the Turkish Touristic Bank helped him out. Near at hand, he was able to supervise the construction throughout: the decks are made of oak, the hull from pine which is more pliant, and he insisted on going to the Forestry Department himself to make certain that the resin had not been extracted from the wood. Unlike the gleaming white cocktail shelves with their profusion of polished brass and varnished wood, the *Maya* is painted a midnight blue.

Dursun designed the interior with three cabins with double beds and a spare bunk above, and another cabin with single berths. There are two lavatories, a shower and a big saloon on deck.

I have praised the exceptional value of the YCA if you want to go yachting in a flotilla, but for me a voyage on the *Maya* would be the ideal way to explore this incomparable coast. The crew consists of two young Turks, including the skipper Vasvi who speaks fluent French and has his master's ticket, but I should need the company of Dursun himself not only to act as guide and interpreter but because he would be the perfect companion.

'The only problem,' he says, shaking his head gravely, 'is when they don't drink. I hope they like drinks!' and his face brightens at the possibility.

The cost of chartering always seems prohibitive though Dursun's charges are lower than most, but if you sail out of season in the marvellous months of May or October you will enjoy one of the most rewarding experiences of a lifetime, far beyond money's worth. Even to quote the figure of £4,000 is misleading for this does not include the flight, though it is possible nowadays to take advantage of low-price fares to Izmir or Dalaman, and make your way easily from there by bus. Food and drink are extra too but these are still so cheap they are not a considerable item, unless you wish them to be so.

Even so the figure of £4,000 sounds forbidding at first. The moment you consider sharing it with one or two families you know, it becomes reasonable. If two of you share with four friends it would still work out at around £1,000 each depending on your tastes, but this is hardly excessive for such an opportunity, sailing down this incomparable coast on your own, in a 60-feet luxury yacht, with the benefit of Dursun to guide you.

On my last evening at the Hadigari, a Bodrum man who had returned from teaching in an American university told me he had never known Dursun do a nasty thing.

'If only he was more ambitious,' he sighed, 'instead of enjoying life as he does.'

'Come on,' I protested, 'you've just been singing his praises and now you want to change him!'

The Turk thought for a moment and nodded his head: 'You're right, of course. Dursun is a species that is almost extinct, we must preserve him as he is.'

Information

Datca

Restaurant
The *Sandal*.

Hotels

There are various pensions which need careful preliminary scrutiny. The modern *Dorya* hotel at the end of the point is in another category altogether, an attractive cluster of white buildings set in exotic gardens running down to the sea where you can swim. The blend of sophistication and naive informality is curious but pleasing, adding to the luxurious sense of tranquillity. £15 for a double room may be expensive for Turkey, but the Dorya is blessedly free from the curse of mosquitoes and creepy-crawlies. A fine place to relax.

Charter
The *Seheryeli* (*Morning Breeze*) carries twelve passengers and is a twin-mast 'goulette' type of boat, 17 metres long. Covers the so-called Blue Cruise around these waters, but could meet you at Bodrum though based in Datca. Tel: Office: Datca (9 6145) 1017. Home: 1051.

Shop
I found that the *Galeri Knidos*, beyond the tourist office, offered excellent Turkish silver goods, as did the *Abdullah*. *Huseyin Gunes*, on the harbour, has a fine selection of kilims from central Turkey.

Bodrum

Charter
Dursun Mutlu, Turkkuyusu Keles cik 5, Bodrum, Tel: Bodrum 1637. I recommend him unreservedly: for one thing, his prices are nearly half as much as those of other charter companies I have encountered along the Turkish coast. *Eti Seyahat Travel* offers a 10 per cent discount for charters of more than 21 days and a further possible 10 per cent discount out of season. Eti is a leading agency with its own traditional yachts and a crew of three. The manager, Alp, is extremely helpful.
The Eti offer a holiday villa service as well: a villa in *Aktur* ranging from $40 a day for six people in season, to $30 in low season. Address: Eti Travel. 10/B Kasaphane Cad., Bodrum. Tel: 1680. Telex: 52913.

Bars
Hadigari. Tel: 2962.

Restaurant
Boluk, French.

Accommodation
Heredot; Albatros. (Recommended, though not experienced personally. These are pensions, but judging by the hotels I have stayed in they may be preferable.)

What to see
The *Underwater Archaeological Museum* in the Castle of St Peter contains fascinating examples of objects dredged from the sandbanks not far from Bodrum itself where ships have foundered over

the centuries. Wrecks have disgorged Mycenaean pottery, dating from 1400 BC, perfume containers, bronze ingots from a wreck west of Antalya, with mirrors and razors, possibly on a boat from Cyprus, beautifully designed plates from a Byzantine wreck, in AD 12, and quantities of precious glass. Such wrecks are being discovered all the time. In 1984 a wreck was located near Kas with jars, glass, ivory, a gold goblet and a simple two-handled Mycenaean cup which helped to date this back to more than 3,400 years ago.

With underwater models, the *Bodrum Museum* is well worth a visit, and so is the castle itself.

Ferry to Cos
Check departures which should be daily in the summer, taking approximately one and a half hours. The Turkish ferry leaves Cos for Bodrum every afternoon at four.

Kusadasi (further up the coast, near Ephesus)

Hotel
Numerous people have told me that the *Kismet Hotel* is the best they have stayed at in Turkey.

Izmir

Hotels
I have stayed in the luxurious 5-star hotel, the *Buyuk Efes*, known as the biggest and the best with a rooftop restaurant famous for its smoked fish. It is luxurious, though not so expensive as its intimidating reputation suggests.

Cheaper but highly recommended hotels are the *Billur* and the *Anba*.

Restaurants
These can be chosen on sight if you walk along the quayside facing the Buyuk Efes. To the left they are simpler, to the right grander and more expensive such as the excellent *Deniz*. The *Alsancak* has been recommended to me for having local, Turkish atmosphere.

Transport
Izmir is a useful base to start from. On my last visit I flew from Istanbul but wished I had taken the weekly flight (winter) direct from London. Buses from the *garaj* on the outskirts go everywhere, even directly to Datca, six hours away, which I took on my journey back.

36 Aphrodisias, and the triumph of Professor Erim

From Bodrum I was driven to Aphrodisias, in many ways the most astonishing site in Turkey. When the excavations are complete, they promise to rival even those at Ephesus. Even at this stage, I found Aphrodisias more rewarding than Ephesus which I had seen on a dusty day shared with thousands of foreign tourists relayed by scores of coaches from their cruise ships at Kusadasi. If you can avoid it, never go anywhere in the middle of the day, especially not to a place as precious as Ephesus. This was one of the Seven Wonders of the World, the greatest city in Asia under Rome with a population which totalled 300,000 people at its peak. Nothing can diminish the magnificent reconstruction of the lovely Temple of Hadrian or the Library of Celsus, and you should make a point of visiting the simple house higher in the mountains where the Virgin Mary is alleged to have passed the last years of her life, but my visit was marred not only by dust and rain but the sight of folk dancers in national costume 'laid on' for the tourists, performing beside a vast plastic bottle advertising some mineral water in the remains of the theatre where St Paul preached to the Christians.

Because my stay was short, having taken the ferry to Kusadasi from the Greek island of Samos which lies opposite, I hired a taxi the following day to drive me across the plain to Miletos, and Didyma, where I photographed the cracked head of Medusa, stopping at Priene on the journey back at the honey hour before dusk when the light enhances the stone revealing colours which are killed by the midday glare. This was once a hillside port which welcomed Alexander the Great when he freed the area from the Persians, but the water has receded so far that Priene overlooks a plain today, and the ruins are minuscule compared to those at Ephesus, yet the five Ionian columns which were part of the Temple of Athena designed for Alexander while he lay siege to Miletos moved me more than the temples of Ephesus in their contrasting solitude. This proves that I am more of a sentimentalist than an archaeologist.

But it shows the power of Aphrodisias that the ruins exerted the same magic even though I saw them on a hot, dusty afternoon when I went there in the autumn of 1982.

The site of Aphrodisias is a visual sleight of hand, lying so flat you can hardly see it from the main road which runs across the valley, yet once you are inside, it does not seem flat at all. If I needed proof of the greatness of Greco-Roman civilisation I found it here, a hundred miles inland from Bodrum, a key position for the armies which marched through the Menderes Valley, such as Alexander's on his way to India, yet an extraordinary community in its own right. More than anywhere else in Turkey, I was impressed not just by the revelation of the ruins but the hint of the activity when Aphrodisias was the home for 50,000 people and larger than Pompeii.

The rediscovery is recent and due to the inspiration of one man, the distinguished archaeologist Kenan Erim who came across references to the city's famous school of sculpture when he was studying at Princetown in America, and determined to find out more. Starting his excavations in 1961, with subsequent help from the National Geographic Society, he struck lucky at once although the area was covered by earth and peasant villages, with little indication of what lay underneath: 'As I wandered down the narrow village streets, I noticed chunks of marble – some inscribed in Greek or Latin, some obviously sculptured – embedded in walls and houses. All about me, past met present. The residents used ancient sarcophagi as troughs for their livestock and as vats for making wine. Delicately fluted columns doubled as hitching posts, and many a temple lintel served as a farmer's doorstep.'

Even in 1982 I saw a trace of this with a white marble column used as a strut to support a modern wooden shack which will turn to dust long before the marble crumbles. And I found it daunting to overlook the 8,000 seats of the theatre and know it had been covered by earth with a couple of peasant huts above only seven years earlier.

Erim's initial luck came with his first dig: 'Suddenly I gasped at something I saw embedded in the side of the trench: "Look! There's a marble head!" ' It fitted a torso already recovered from an irrigation ditch, one of the statues which adorned a massive relief dating from the first century BC and named after Zoilos, a priest and magistrate of Aphrodite who gained a special exemption from taxes for the city from Augustus who stated, 'I have chosen this one city from all Asia as my own.' At the start of his reign, it seems likely that Aphrodisias was more imposing than Rome itself.

Understandably, Kenan Erim writes of Aphrodisias with a

partisan pride: 'October's breath cools me as I mount the acropolis of Aphrodisias and look out over the Greco-Roman city whose life for twenty years I have made mine. Twenty years earlier I stood on this same mount in summer's heat, full of anticipation – and apprehension. What would I find here within these unmanned ramparts and columned edifices, long untenanted and tumbled down? What lay under this raucous area of chickens, dogs and children?'

Since then, the village of Geyre has been transplanted and Erim has disclosed a moment of civilisation. To unfold a layer of history like this must be the most satisfying achievement of a lifetime.

The first impression today is one of space, but though the city stretched for 5 kilometres 2,000 years ago there is not a single monument to mark it from a distance. The magic of Aphrodisias is more subtle and enveloped me gradually. Excavations prove that Aphrodisias dates back to prehistoric times, a sacred site rather than a city until it came under the influence of Greece, and then of Rome when the name of Aphrodisias appears for the first time on silver coins.

The city's privileges were confirmed by Tiberius in AD 22 and continued until the Christians renamed it the City of the Cross and tried to kill the old traditions. The final decline was due to other acts of God, such as earthquakes, and the place was abandoned until the modern Turkish villages were built on top.

When Aphrodisias basked in prosperity for four centuries after the birth of Christ, the city was surrounded by a jumble of huts on the outskirts, noisy with children and animals, in contrast to the elegance inside with graceful avenues shaded by fig-trees and poplars that lined the cool stream which watered the city, one of the tributaries of the great River Meander, known today as Menderes.

Trees are still abundant: wild fig and pomegranate whose fruit is there for the picking, with birds darting in between the branches and the cooing of doves sacred to Aphrodite.

I walked across a bare field with the scent of thyme in the air and fragments of carved marble exposed in the newly ploughed earth and my first shock was the stadium, one of the largest in the Roman world, 250 yards long and 60 wide, with seats for 30,000 spectators who used to watch the gladiators encouraged by the roar of the crowd and the howl of the wild animals or Christians. Chariot races were held as well, here or in a hippodrome still to be uncovered.

Inevitably, Erim's excavations have revealed a temple to Aphrodite herself, the Greek goddess of love, beauty and fertility who gave this place her name. Immense columns rise to the sky today, but it is the modest odeum which conveys the distinction of Aphrodisias in particular. Compared to the massive theatre which looks across the plateau to the marble quarries in the distant hills of Baba Dag, the odeum is tiny and enclosed, with only 400 seats reserved for the most distinguished citizens who could relax in the comfort of marble chairs with arms. This was the peaceful setting where music was played on flutes, pipes and lyres by an orchestra on a sunken stage shaded by trees and decorated with marble statues. Sometimes the odeum would be taken over for the evening by a philosopher who read his latest work aloud while slaves waited with rolls of papyrus to record copies should it prove popular, using an ink made from resin, soot, wine dregs and cuttlefish. The six Baths of Hadrian ranged from hot to medium, with a steam hall and a cold plunge at the end, lined with white marble and heated by fires fed by slaves.

By now it was possible to sense the atmosphere: the elders in their white togas discussing the issues of the day, the avenues filled with people going about their business, children to school, athletes to the sports grounds, others to the markets, the noise from the smith's anvil and the sculptor's chisel, the clatter from the carpenter and tanner, and sing-song cries of merchants, and the voices of the storytellers. At night when the city was lit by torches and oil lamps, the theatre audience would greet the masked actors in a Plautus comedy with laughter while others danced or relaxed on couches, drinking the sweet wine poured from amphorae by their attendant slaves.

Though more than 1,000 miles from Rome, Aphrodisias must have shared the grandeur. This is evident from the museum where so many of the statues and decorations are displayed, having once adorned the odeum, and the great Zoilos Relief. Carved from the blue-grey marble quarried from the nearby hills, dozens of figures, many twice the size of life, have been unearthed though many of the torsos are headless, and the heads noseless, due to the desecration by the Christians who converted the Temple of Aphrodite into a church.

What remains is convincing enough: two immense figures of a philosopher and an unknown woman, whose drapery is sculpted so skilfully it seems to rustle with life; astonishing reliefs of Hercules releasing Prometheus; Leda and the Swan; and the young Augustus presented with a cornucopia of fruit by Earth and a twin-tailed mermaid. Marble faces, fragments of carved foliage and animals, indicate the wealth of decoration which enhanced every building. The faces of the philosophers are plainly taken from life, like that of the Emperor Trajan, though those of Achilles or the goddess of Aphrodite herself are the work of imagination. The finest I have seen in Turkey, they explain why the work of the Aphrodisian sculptors was admired in Rome, while the cases of pottery, glass and jewellery are a further indication of the quality of life.

One aspect is missing, yet that is typical of the Roman strong-holds in Asia Minor – that of war itself. Professor Erim has explained the lack of soldiers in Aphrodiasias thus: 'The legions were on distant frontiers guarding against Parthians in the east, Picts in Britain, Germanic tribes across the Danube, nomads in Africa. Within the Empire the Pax Romana reigns.' In Aphrodisias, only the watchmen carried arms.

Considering the extent of Aphrodisias the city remains surprisingly unknown though its fame is spreading due to Professor Erim. He uses a good phrase in referring to the 'husks of vanished cities' in western Turkey, adding Aphrodisias in the north-eastern corner of Caria to the chain of ports along the coast – Ephesus, Priene, Bodrum and Patara. Ports rather than forts, where the security was so complete that the excavations reveal theatres and odeums rather than prisons or barracks.

'Why do I keep returning here?' Professor Erim asked in the *National Geographic*. 'To bring a once great city back to the light of day is a privilege given but to a few' (vol. 160, no.4). Professor Erim is a fortunate man.

37 Pamukkale – Yusuf and the dead birds

From Aphrodisias I drove to Denizli and climbed into the mountains to Pamukkale. This is a merry freak of nature, an apparent ice floe around a hot water spa. From a distance the deposits of calcium from the hot springs above are less than spectacular, more a whitish stain down the cliffs, but once you arrive you step into a glacial fairyland of petrified waterfalls and dazzling white basins backed by a darkness of pine trees. It could be a winter sports resort and the source of the water at Hierapolis behind, founded by Eumenes II, King of Pergamum, in 190 BC, was adopted as a spa by the Romans, who considered it sacred due to the health-giving properties of the thermal water.

The Koru Motel where I was staying sported two hot water lakes on the edge of the cliffs, overlooking the vast plain of Denizli below, as well as a covered pool inside. Optimistic as ever, I had to go in the spacious open-air pool hoping to emerge rejuvenated but came out as limp as a lettuce leaf dunked in hot water. Even so, the mere promise that the water would perform miracles with my kidneys, liver and other damaged parts made me *feel* better if only through wishful thinking.

I would not recommend Pamukkale if going there involves a drastic detour, but the modern motels provide a pleasant enough pause and I was glad of an early night in a clean, quiet chalet which made good use of natural materials, such as wood, stone and marble, after a dinner where I was served the best Caucasian chicken I have tasted in Turkey, even though the dining room resembled an empty canteen, plainly between coach tours.

In the morning light, when the hot water from the mountains steamed in the early sun as I took another, optimistic swim, I admired the excellence of Turkish design yet again, simple and unfussy with the usual abundance of trees and flower beds and marble paths. Afterwards, in the Tusan motel behind us, I was peering into the Sacred Pool with broken marble columns when I was startled by a familiar voice as a man stepped out of the oleanders.

'I have been expecting you last night,' said Yusuf grimly. 'I wait for you.'

I could not make out if this was calculated or just coincidence, though the latter seemed more likely when he added that he had just said goodbye to a party of Japanese.

After the shock of his initial greeting, I was glad to see Yusuf again, my first guide to Turkey, and find him unchanged. He wanted to spend the day showing me some of the higher pools which are bathed in vivid colours but a lack of time prevented this and I accompanied him on a tour of the ruins of Hierapolis instead. It would be absurd to go to Pamukkale without doing so, as they are only a few minutes' walk away.

We came at last to a dip in the land near the Temple of Apollo, a bleak corner called the Plutonium, named after Pluto the lord of the underworld, and it was here that the real reason for Yusuf's presence was revealed – he was on reconnaissance preparing for his descent into a cave inside the temple which contains 'a treasure-trove of gold and jewels'. Apollo was one of the gods who did not welcome human sacrifice, Yusuf informed me, 'so crystals were brought to him instead. One, maybe two have been found. My friend who is jeweller tells me they are better than diamonds.'

My natural scepticism where Yusuf is concerned increased when he told me of his plans. He had contacted a mountaineering club and intended to lower himself inside the cave dressed either in a space suit or a diver's outfit complete with his own oxygen.

'That sounds rather dramatic,' I remarked, but Yusuf provided the explanation: 'It is poison inside, the air is sulphuric acid so your lungs are burnt. That is why no one finds the treasure.'

I enjoyed Yusuf's exaggeration, but then I noticed the barred entrance with a sign marked DANGER, warning people not to approach any further. I happened to look down and saw that the ground was dotted with the corpses of small birds. 'You see,' smiled Yusuf, having detected the note of cynicism in my voice, 'the birds fly inside at night and are killed by the poison as they try to escape.' The evidence was irrefutable, in front of me.

Nothing is new under the sun, as I discovered later, for Strabo witnessed the same phenomenon when he visited the Plutonium 2,000 years ago.

The Greek historian, who was born in 63 BC, described the Plutonium as 'an orifice under a slight ridge . . . large enough to admit a man, and very deep. Outside the enclosure the air is free of the mist, so long as no wind is blowing, and a man may approach safely; but for any living creature which enters inside death is instantaneous. Bulls, for example, which are taken in, collapse and are brought out dead; we ourselves sent in small birds which at once fell lifeless. The eunuchs of Cybele, however, are immune to the extent that they can approach the orifice and look in, and even penetrate for some distance, though not normally without holding their breath.'

I find it reassuring that so little should have changed between our two visits, spanned by 2,000 years, though the reference to the eunuchs is puzzling. Could it be that they were simply more inquisitive?

Though no eunuch himself, Yusuf hopes for worldwide coverage as he descends by rope dressed in his diving suit. I gathered at our last meeting that he has run into an official snag or two but I hope he prevails and emerges rich beyond the dreams of the gods, having had the last laugh as usual.

38 Return to Dalyan

After my previous visit to Dalyan, I wrote in my notebook, 'This is the fulfilment of a lifetime. Almost alarming, for something must go wrong or at least come to an end.' Why I indulged in such a dramatic note of pessimism I cannot imagine, unless the prospect of the land in Turkey seemed too good to be believed.

My friends greeted the news with derision. With some justification, my literary agent deplored the lack of an existing house or even a hut to provide a temporary roof. Francis Bacon warned me that Russia would invade Turkey within the next two years; others asked me what I would *do* there and how could I contemplate such a move when I was unable to speak Turkish. Nothing deterred me, not even the reference which I came across in my father's autobiography *The Way of a Transgressor* to his own visit to Turkey in the 1920s and the advice he received there from the Greek ambassador: 'There are three things, M'sieu, a man should not do: have a wife in Roumania, a ship in the Black Sea, or own land in Turkey – he will lose all three!'

I returned to Dalyan in May 1984 on a month's holiday from my job as television critic, taking the bus to Marmaris from Ankara, but as I ran out of the hotel to a waiting taxi the receptionist stopped me with a further fistful of bills which I disputed and by the time I raced through the *garaj* the bus had gone. As I stood forlornly between a phalanx of coaches apparently destined for every corner of Turkey except mine, someone heard me mention Dalyan and pointed to the bus beside me which was going to Koycegiz. The journey would take eighteen hours, but what the hell. I was there with my luggage and the thought of returning to the hotel was worse. It proved a journey full of the usual interest and I was astonished in the early light at dawn to see a signpost to Koycegiz, arriving there exactly twelve hours after leaving Ankara at a cost of less than £5. The luxury of a taxi to Dalyan cost the same but it was worth it to be welcomed at the Aly Aktas Pension, to shower and unpack, and let the peace of the place engulf me – a fish jumping in the grey river, doves chortling with contentment in a nearby tree – over my ubiquitous breakfast of yoghurt and honey.

I felt I was home.

This time I had allowed for a stay of several days but two things had to be done at once: to find out if the land was still for sale; and inspect it properly. Characteristically, I started in the wrong order, but instead of hiring a boatman to take me to Caunus at a cost of 1,500 Turkish lira, I paid 20 lira to two laughing men who were bailing out a leaking rowboat nearby and took me across in seconds to the opposite bank.

There is a track to the small village of Candir on the other side of Caunus and the absence of any through road impressed me as one of the advantages on this side of the river in spite of the practical difficulties of getting across, especially where building was concerned. However, the few houses which existed proved that this was not insuperable.

The walk to Caunus takes fifteen minutes but only five to the piece of land I had in mind, past the modern cemetery lined with eucalyptus trees below the Lycian tombs. A tractor passed driven by a farmer who called out 'Welcome!' but there was no one else in sight as I climbed over a ramshackle gate and stood on 'my' land. The earth was hard, covered with yellow ragwort soon to be replaced by cotton, but my imagination planted it with an orchard of lemon trees, orange, apricot and plum stretching down to the water. This daydream was encouraged by the actual existence of an ancient mulberry tree beside the river, a solitary male which looked forlorn, so it would only be right to plant a young, female mulberry as its companion. At the back there were several long-established trees, a poplar, a massive palm, and an overgrown fig, with a cactus and a grapevine, which is where I envisaged my house, surrounded by hibiscus and bougainvillaea, with space under the roof for swallows. There was even a disused well which could be restored to irrigate the land, for the water from the river was too brackish though eucalyptus seemed to prosper.

I planned a line of this most gracious tree to mark the boundary, with a fence of oleander. And several Corsican pine.

The existing trees were vital. Those on the edge of the river could shade the concrete landing stage which would be the first thing I should build, needed for materials shipped across and useful later as the basis for a possible riverside bar or small lokanta. Anyhow, it would be necessary for my boat. There would have to be a boat if only a rowboat to start with, made to my specifications with rowlocks and proper oars, instead of poles.

I saw it all.

Planning a garden is the next best thing to planting it, and this would be my last with enough time to see it grow, if I was lucky.

Roses flourish in Dalyan, but I had no intention of recreating an English garden. Instead I would take advantage of the climate and experiment with vivid colours, and a walnut tree and possibly an avocado. And I would. . . . At this point I remembered the reality – I did not even know if the land was still for sale, so I recrossed the river in search of Abidin.

On the way to the Denizati restaurant a few hundred yards away, someone approached me surreptitiously, offering a large silver coin covered in hieroglyphics presumably found at Caunus. It could have been priceless but I am no numismatist and could not afford it. Even if I had been interested, instinct warned me it would be disastrous to become known as the foreigner who bought up national treasures illegally. If I was to perch on this particular doorstep I should keep it clean. The muddiness would come.

Izmet greeted me as smilingly as ever but I noticed a subtle difference in the Denizati and he seemed in awe of a handsome, ebullient woman with dark hair and high cheekbones who might have been French but came from Ankara. Dramatising the innocuous, I cast her as one of those sophisticated women one meets the world over who have received a few knocks in life but persevere, making themselves indispensable. She appeared to be Izmet's assistant and I feared for the chances of such an innocent for it was obvious that she was superb at her job. Sensing that I wanted to meet the attractive woman sitting on her own outside, she introduced us.

This was my first meeting with Abidin's Australian girlfriend, and I liked Jan immediately. Young for her age, for she has two daughters and a grown-up son, she was instantly sympathetic with a humorous voice and just the faintest of accents. I could understand why the Turks like her so much, for she is totally loyal to Abidin, has bothered to learn Turkish, and accepted their standards however alien to her upbringing.

Abidin was in Ekincek sorting out a dispute with rival boatman, so she invited me to stay the night on the sandbar where I would be sure to find him, phoning Aly Aktas to say I might not return that night. At little more than a pound a day, I had no qualms at using the pension as a luggage room.

The sand was so hot when I arrived, even at the end of May, that my toes were blistered as I hopped across the bar to the sea and dozed briefly afterwards, tired from my sleepless night in the bus. I woke up baked by too much sun but revived with another swim in the shallow water and then it was dusk and the utter tranquillity returned.

As I drank a beer at the Yasar in Yehi lokanta, Abidin strode into sight in the same scandalous briefs, clutching a smart attaché case. I settled the bill – two beers, three double vodkas, two cherry juices, a fresh orange juice, and two bottles of wine to take away for dinner – at a cost of £5, and we settled down to business over a Turkish goulash prepared by Jan.

The land was still for sale, that was the good news, but the likeable, large fisherman was dead which meant I should have to deal with his brother instead. This led to several fraught days, accompanied by Abidin who was indispensable. Hiring a taxi we drove to Dalaman to the school where the owner of the land was a teacher, tracking him down at the opening of the annual embroidery exhibition which was a duplicate of the one I had seen at Adiyaman, with the same shy schoolgirls and civic dignitaries. The brother of the rugged fisherman was almost as large but a smartly suited, sleeker version, plainly neither a fool nor an innocent though it occurred to me that his position of responsibility as a government teacher could prove an advantage.

We continued to his imposing office where Abidin interpreted between us and the owner announced that the family wanted to retain a strip of the land to build on for themselves, which I conceded readily provided it was taken from the far side which I knew to be treeless. This would still leave me 5,000 square metres which was ample.

I am a Jonah where business is concerned but I excelled that afternoon, using my concession over the strip of land to beat the owner down until we reached a compromise and shook hands on a figure which I regarded as a bargain.

Bar the signing, I had the land!

The next morning I drove with Abidin to Koycegiz to see a lawyer who consulted his books in case there was any law preventing a foreigner from buying land in the area. Until 1984 you could do so on a 99-year lease, which seemed reasonable to me, but even this restriction was about to be lifted in Ankara. But – and there is always a but on such occasions – the fine print revealed that no foreigner could buy land where the population of the village was less than 2,000 and though my plot was directly opposite Dalyan it came under the jurisdiction of Candir, Abidin's village on the other side of Caunus, where the population was hardly more than 100.

'That's all right,' I told the lawyer. 'We shall have to ask for special permission from Ankara. If that fails, and Abidin agrees, I shall have to buy it in his name.'

From Koycegiz we drove to Mugla, the civic capital of the province, where my photograph was taken for the forms needed by a notary to give Abidin the power of attorney to act on my behalf.

On the drive back we passed a governmental farm where Abidin told me I could buy the trees and shrubs for the land. 'I want a lot of oleander,' I remarked.

'Oh no,' he exclaimed indignantly, 'They are everywhere. We need *special* trees.'

He was starting to plant the garden too.

Anxious to explore my new territory, I hired a boat from Aly Aktas's son the next morning to take me beyond Dalyan to Lake Koycegiz, a stretch which remains unspoilt. We tied up at a point under several tall pine trees and I turned round in time to see a fish jumping in the river, a huge, brown fish that I assumed was a carp, before I walked along a rough track beside some fields. Not having heard of it before, I was surprised by a natural hot spring spilling on to the track, roughly contained by a low wall so it resembled a steaming trough with curious floating cobwebs caused by the sulphur. In spite of them, I undressed and lowered myself inside hoping that the water would prove as miraculous as that in the Sultaniye Thermal Springs further up the lake, claimed in a local pamphlet to be 'the most radioactive in our country and the second one in the world. They cure roumatism (this was the spelling), neuralgia, gallbladder illnesses, liver disorders and women's diseases.' I would have been satisfied with a new mind or liver but came out much as I went in – worse for wear.

The peace is infinite in this lovely stretch of the water, soon to be broken by a new motorway which will plunge overhead directly from Dalaman to Marmaris. The whole area is poised for change, even the shanty huts on the sandbar which were painted in blue and green until now, or left in their natural wood, half-collapsing on to the sand as if the strain was too much, which was probably the case. Now a new law will spruce them up and discipline the settlement with every plank painted the same shade of brown and inside toilets instead of the outside boxes which worked, or failed to, on some principle I never understood, nor wanted to. The law makes sense; the place was becoming overcrowded for anyone was allowed to build there, but the primitive charm will go.

The most revolutionary change will come with a channel to be dredged through the sandbar in the next few years, allowing yachts and other boats to pour through into the delta, up to Dalyan and beyond to the lake. This will transform the area and spoil the simple fun of going up by caique with Abidin Kurt, though I suspect that many yachtsmen will prefer to do this anyhow. Inevitably, the power-boats will bring noise and pollution in their wake and, worst of all, the area will be *tamed*.

Such progress is unavoidable. I have seen the plans in Mugla which reveal that the entire area will be developed as a 'touristic centre' with hotels and marinas, and all their accessories. Yet, trying to rationalise as usual, this would provide the customers for my riverside bar which would, in turn, provide me with an income and English-speaking people to talk to. It would be a perfect place for yachtsmen to tie up and walk the short distance up the hill to Caunus rather than go by water. I was swayed by all the practical advantages in my paradise: half an hour from the airport, water and electricity available, the cooler evening in the shade of the Lycian tombs which provided another attraction for visitors who would give me a new livelihood.

Apart from the mosquitoes and the crucial lack of any temporary roof, Dalyan had more practical assets than any place I had seen, with the magic of the four waters: the sea, the river, the hot springs and the lake.

That afternoon I joined Jan who was guiding a 'Cricketer's Tour' to Caunus. There were several finely hewn English faces on the boat, one of them belonging to an elderly, elfin judge. Confiding my plans, I pointed to my plot of land as we sailed past.

'Well done!' he exclaimed, reassuringly. 'I've always acted on impulse. Things might go wrong, but if you don't have a go you will get nowhere.'

It was just what I wanted to hear.

Preferring the fantasy to the reality, I had pushed the greatest obstacle to the back of my mind – a lack of money. Buying the land was going to involve a punitive mortgage, though my well-paid job would be able to cover it. As for the house, I realised this would take several years to build but there was no question of any immediate move anyhow. I had my job and my dogs to tie me down in England, though the local vet had assured me they could be sedated for the flight to Dalaman and however horrible this might be, they would emerge unscathed. The problem lay in the quarantine, and once there they would have to stay. It would be hot, they would have to keep in the shade.

All such plans lay in the future, at least four years ahead. The first objective was securing the land; then building a landing stage and planting trees.

Even so, when I stopped in Marmaris on my way to the Greek island of Karpathos (via Rhodes), I asked for the name of a good architect and called at his office. I had sketched some ideas and I was heartened by his first questions which concerned the temperatures and the angle of the sun, especially when I learnt that he had designed a new house on the quayside which I admired for the attractive wooden balcony in the traditional Turkish style, just what I wanted for myself. When I suggested he should visit the site he asked if the owner of the land had a brother.

'No,' I told him, rather surprised, 'he died a few months ago.'

'But did the brother have any sons?'

'Several.'

'Ah!' He raised his eyes and examined the ceiling. 'Then I do nothing until I see the deeds in your hands.' His pessimism was confirmed by the message waiting for me in the hotel, sent by Abidin Kurt: *The brother's sons have changed their minds. Return Dalyan.*

The garbage lorries drive along the Marmaris quayside at the terrible hour of five, disgruntled vehicles, rasping as they pause, revving as they stagger a few more feet, with the hideous clatter as the men bang the rubbish of the restaurants from their bins. I found it impossible to sleep afterwards in my bedroom at the front, penalised for the view, and lay there in a torpor as I contemplated the loss of my land at Dalyan. At last I forced myself under the trickle of the shower and went downstairs as the ferry left for Rhodes, wishing I was on it, en route to Karpathos where I had intended to revel in a real holiday for once, without combining it with work.

But when I returned to Dalyan I found that Abidin had seen the nephews and talked them round. We drove that evening to see the fisherman's widow and finally to confirm the deal with his brother, shaking hands once again after sorting out the method of payment. That evening on the sandbar, Jan cried, 'Congratulations!' And then my luck ran out.

39 Bad news in England

After returning home, a friend phoned me from Soho to warn me that my job was in danger. The next morning I received a letter from my editor: 'I am afraid this is very bad news so I won't beat about the bush. As has happened so often in history the understudy has gone on stage and swept all before him . . .' etcetera. . . . 'I find this very distressing as you have done us so well, but I am afraid that all of us who are writers and performers know that we constantly walk a tightrope, liable to be pushed off at any moment by a rival. That is the angst from which we all suffer, not made easier when our fears become realities' . . . etcetera . . . for two more pages. It took several moments before I realised I had got the sack.

As my agent commented later, 'The answer, simply, was never to have gone to Turkey. But one cannot live like that.' Even so, there was a tone of reproach in her voice and if I am honest with myself I should admit that I jeopardised my job in pursuit of my paradise in Turkey.

The shock concentrated my mind wonderfully.

With a loan from my bank, I sent the deposit to Abidin, confirming that I would return with the rest of the money in September. The compensation from the newspaper would save me from the punitive mortgage which had been the alternative. Everything confirmed my wisdom in buying the land. At least I would have something tangible in the form of an investment to show for my time on the paper.

Then I received a phone call from Jan telling me that the owner had changed his mind once more. Not only had I lost my job, I had lost the land as well.

At the end of November 1984 I endured a nightmare flight arriving in Istanbul at three in the morning, nine hours late. From Istanbul I took a quick, internal flight to Izmir, an hour away, and continued by bus to Marmaris relaxing as the scenery grew familiar and the sun shone overhead. Abidin Kurt was waiting but he told me that the owner of the land remained adamant in his refusal to sell. What had gone wrong? Possibly I had struck too hard a bargain. Certainly I had talked too much, buttonholing every possible competitor with my good news. Abidin had warned me, 'Listen to everything, say nothing yourself,' but this sensible advice had come too late.

I was returning to Turkey in a last bid to find an alternative plot of land, preferably with some sort of a house already in existence, and I began by exploring the Datca Peninsula. Inevitably, there was nothing compared with the land I had lost, and I found myself drawn back to Dalyan as if by a magnet, even though I knew my chance had gone.

40 Farewell to Dalyan

People say one should 'never go back', and I think they are right.

We reached Dalyan in the dark around nine and Abidin with his usual speed managed to find someone to row us across the river in a few minutes' time. I seized the chance to visit Ismet having heard that he was now the owner of a fine new pizza parlour called the Piknik. Far from easing him out of the Denizati, the sophisticated woman from Ankara had bought this new place instead taking Ismet with her as a partner. He greeted me with his usual beatific smile and pulled me a glass of lager from a gleaming machine, then he showed me every detail of the cooling cabinet and the open pizza oven which was unlit. He looked extremely proud and I congratulated him warmly on his good fortune and looked around the small room approvingly, thinking he was smart to stake his claim before the avalanche of tourism descends.

We lapsed into silent smiles with a few abortive attempts to speak each other's language, and it was time to leave.

The rowboat slipped across the water and I turned up my trousers on the other side because of the muddy track, said goodbye to the boatman, and started the climb to Abidin's home in the village of Candir, no more than a cluster of houses on the other side of Caunus. It was a perfect night; I had never seen so many stars since those halcyon days in the north of Yugoslavia as a child when my father rowed me across Lake Bohinsko after a day's fishing. I remember the excitement in spotting shooting stars. I could only have seen a few yet my memory assures me that I saw them racing across the sky like fireworks. Tonight there were no shooting stars and little childish glee, and certainly no pleasure as we passed beside 'my land'. In my imagination I had planned many moonlight walks up to the ruins of Caunus in the coolness of a summer's night, and this was a bitter substitute. There was a crescent moon as new and slender as it could be, and I could make out the outline of the walls of ancient baths when we reached the top, but I scarcely looked as I allowed my self-pity to seep inside me, though I hoped I might glimpse the two bears who have returned to the district.

Then I heard the distant throb of drums and paused, suddenly alert. Turning to Abidin, he told me I was not mistaken, they were the drums for the wedding of one of the young men in the village which was taking place the next day, but the feasting had started already. The sound of the drums grew louder, reverberating in the stillness, urging me on, my self-pity forgotten.

Arriving at the celebration, I looked down on to groups of men dancing or sitting on planks balanced on empty beehives with tables in front of them strewn with food and bottles of raki. Other men sprawled across carpets laid on the bare earth of the open courtyard below the modern house which had two floors and a large open roof running parallel to the level where we were standing. This flat rooftop was crowded with the women of the village, traditionally kept apart from the men for no woman would dare to dance in front of them. They stood there watching intently like birds in trees, almost motionless.

The headman of the village joined us and I remembered having seen him with Aly Aktas in Dalyan. They were the same age and I realised that most of the men below were young, with their fathers keeping out of the way in order not to spoil their fun. Usually the sons do not drink in front of their fathers, so they were making up for it now.

'They will get very drunk,' said Abidin severely, 'and feel very brave and fight each other.' This sounded reasonable to me and I wished I could join them.

'Are they family friends of yours?' I asked Abidin, deceptively.

'But of course!' He laughed at my foolishness.

'They haven't invited you to join them.'

'I don't need invitation. Everyone is welcome.'

'They are?' I exclaimed incredulously. 'We are!'

Abidin believes that 'early sleep is the sweetest' but he was trapped into asking if I wanted to go down and join the wedding party and I agreed enthusiastically. The thought of going to bed at ten o'clock to the sound of that tantalising music was unbearable. The musicians were gypsies from Ortega, a traditional part of Turkish weddings in the countryside. If our gypsies played at our weddings we might like them more and treat them better, as symbols of good luck rather than bad. Two of them were standing, thwacking their drums with a persistent beat which grew in violence while the other two sat at a table and played instruments that looked a cross between a trumpet and flute but sounded surprisingly like bagpipes, and one tune did have a startling resemblance to 'Over the Sea to Skye.' Each dance lasted for ten or fifteen minutes after which they had a brief pause for a drink, and seeing my interest they showed me one of the 'flutes' carved from a hard wood, probably oak. I added 100 Turkish lira to the pile of notes on their table.

A plank had been arranged for Abidin, the headman and myself, the headman smiling benevolently, apparently oblivious to the drunkenness as the dancers staggered and fell around him. Many of the men came to welcome Abidin and myself, including the son of Aly Aktas and the groom himself, a young man of twenty-six with a bemused, humorous face, wearing a pale brown suit. Little wonder that he looked bemused for though he had seen his bride and even spoken to her at the formal ceremony of their marriage which had taken place two weeks earlier, they had not touched each other. Everything had been fixed by their families, including the all-important dowry; they had not even shaken hands.

Marriages of convenience seem strange to us because they are unfamiliar, but apparently 95 per cent of them work in Turkey, or so Abidin assured me, and on reflection I can understand why. The patience, the tolerance and sheer effort needed to make such an arrangement work must help it to do so.

The groom asked me to dance and I accepted eagerly for by now I have deluded myself into believing that I am rather good at Turkish dancing. There may be subtleties of steps I am unaware of, but the crazy-jumping-about-part with one's arms in the air is a whirl which even I can manage. In fact the groom danced as neatly and as nicely as he looked, with clever little sidesteps which I tried to emulate.

A few minutes later he reappeared with Turkish lira notes pinned to the lapels of his jacket. I asked Abidin what I should contribute and he told me 500 lira would be right. This seemed mean but I did not wish to appear patronising by giving more than anyone else. Unfortunately I did not have any large notes so tried to pin a clutch of small ones instead hoping they would not float away as he continued to dance with the notes swinging around him like a college scarf.

Yearning for a raki, I asked Abidin if I could buy a bottle, which was deceitful for I knew that one would be brought the moment the family realised I wanted to drink. The headman had given up the hard stuff twenty years ago but helped himself to the food which was laid in front of us: vine and cabbage leaves stuffed with rice, a bowl of white beans mixed with herbs, and a large chicken. While Abidin devoured one of the legs, he allowed himself a small raki too.

After a few more rakis we got down to the basic truths of life, one of the few advantages of alcohol and a dubious one at that. I told

Abidin he was blessed to lead such a life in surroundings like these. He agreed, saying, 'If you have a clean heart, then life is good,' or words to that effect. I thought of the rogues who prosper and all the decent people with the cleanest of hearts whose lives are marred by illness, accident and pain, but that is the pitfall of midnight conversations. Anyhow, I knew what he meant. He told me that when he is married he will have a traditional wedding like this with a dozen gypsy musicians and the feast will last for several days and nights. I gained the impression that the time is not far off when he will marry a Turkish girl and raise the family he plainly yearns for, so vital to his future too with sons to succeed him. At that moment his own family called, and he helped his younger brother back to their home just a couple of hundred yards away while I remained.

The dancing grew more frenzied. Like the young blades in Pamplona who caper in front of the bull, the dancers taunted the drum, sinking to their knees in front of it so they almost touched, while the gypsy advanced beating it to death, daring the dancer to attack.

Suddenly the party seemed to erupt. The groom was seized, covered with a striped sheet, and beaten as if he was a drum himself. Oh god, I thought for one split-second when he emerged, they've cut off his hand!

His right hand was covered by a bright red bandage knotted tightly round his wrist. In a few hours when the bandage was removed, his hand would be stained by the paste of henna which had been squeezed into it and the dye would linger for the next two weeks. The same ritual was taking place with the bride at Ortega.

The young men paraded the torn pieces of sheet above them like banners and the raki rose to my head as well. A vast log, placed over the open fire had assumed an extraordinary shape, with the head of an ostrich at one end and that of a pig on the other, or so I was convinced at the time. Whenever it was moved it gave off a firework display of sparks which added to the light and gave some warmth as well though this was hardly needed on the hot December night. The men danced in circles chanting 'Hok! Hok!' and the movement swung around me.

I woke in Abidin's house with cotton fields in front of it and the drums were still beating. When we passed the house later they were setting out for Dalyan on their way to Ortega to collect the bride, and the gypsies were still beating their drums, standing on the cart as the tractor pulled it away to take them over Caunus, the young men still gyrating, the women packed into separate carts behind.

I spent the morning looking for alternative sites of land helped by the faithful Abidin, and when we returned to the Denizati in Dalyan we coincided with the wedding party on their way back. They had filled the caiques which would carry them to the other side of the river to the track I had taken the night before, the musicians still playing and the men dancing. The only difference lay in the caique which carried the women for they were animated now, waving to the people on shore, and among them I could see the bride in white though her face was covered.

The groom had returned earlier to greet her at the entrance of their new home where they would touch each other for the first time. Then a goat or a sheep would be slaughtered and the meat distributed among the neighbours while the couple disappeared inside and the bride taken to the bedroom where the groom would lift the veil.

The event was one of unalloyed optimism. Even as an outsider I appreciated the warmth of their welcome and of course I could say that I danced with the groom.

I relished the exhilaration though this was at variance with my own frame of mind. I had seen new land at Datca and other parts of the coast nearby and I know I shall return for I love the country and the people, but I felt a tenderness for Dalyan that cannot be repeated.

Frankly, I have no idea what will happen. But in my search I have discovered what wiser people would have known from the outset: there is no such place as paradise – it lies fleetingly within oneself.

Index

Abas I, 57
Abdul Aziz, Sultan, 19
Abdul-Hamid-Khan, Sultan, 19
Abidin, Kurt, 169–75, 177, 202–13
Abraham's Pool, 89–90
Achilles, 196
Adam Kayalat, 108
Adiyaman, 92, 93, 100, 203
Aegean, 174, 182
Aga Khan, 116
Agri, 80
Ahlat, 73, 81
Ahmed, 12–13
Ahuramazda, 93
Akdamar Island, 72, 74, 75, 78, 82
Aktas, Aly, 200, 202, 204, 210–11
Akurgal, Ekrem, 29
Alantur, 123
Alanya, 101–2, 104, 107–8, 111, 125
Alcetas, 119–20
Alexander the Great: descent from,
    93; destruction of Halicarnassus,
    185; march to India, 193; at
    Perge, 126; at Phaselis, 119, 129;
    at Priene, 192; successors, 170
Alexandretta, 103
Alexius II, 50–1
Aliki, 4
Altindere Valley, 50
Anamur, 111
Anatolian Civilisation, Museum of,
    80
Anatolian plains, 58
Anderson, Jim and Jillian, 176
Ani, 57, 62–3, 73, 74
Anitkabir, Mausoleum of, 66–7
Ankara: Ataturk, 66–7; bus from,
    200; capital, 19, 66, 203; hotels,
    79; museum, 80; passing through,

66–7; restaurants, 80; traffic
    from, 107
Antalya: coastline, 128–9, 191;
    description, 126; failing to reach,
    24–5; hotel, 124, 127; Ibrahim,
    114–16; museum, 133; oil
    pipelines, 120; restaurant, 127
Antigonus, 119, 120, 170
Antiochus I of Commagene, 93, 95–
    7, 98
Antiphellus, 133
Aphrodisias, 192–6
Aphrodite, 105, 183–4, 193–6
Apollo, 93, 198
Arakli, 46
Ararat, Mount, 63, 74, 77, 79
Ares, 93
Argistis I, 72
Argistis II, 81
Arjesh, 81
Armenia, 46, 57, 72, 74, 81
Armenians, 62, 71, 73, 74
Arrian, 119
Artagenes, 93
Artemis, 183
Artemisia, 185
Aspendos, 125, 126
Assyrians, 41, 72
Atac, Inal and Gulen, 43, 53–5, 56
Ataturk, Kemal, 15, 19, 20, 26, 29,
    43–4, 46, 51, 54, 66–7, 132
Athena, Temple of, 192
Athens, 50, 147, 148
Athos, Mount, 154
Augustus, 193, 195
Avanos, 64

Baalbek, 25–6, 107
Baba Dag, 195

216   Index

Bacon, Francis, 200
Balfour, David, 167
Balian (architect), 19
Bari, 133
Barnabas the Blessed, 50
Basaran, Koksal, 47
Batum, 46
Bauer, William, 28
Bayir, 178
Bayram, 42, 44–5
Bean, George, 29, 170, 171
Beaufort, Captain, 130
Bellerophon, 131
Bithynia, 184
Bitlis, 82
Black Sea, 36, 39–40, 46, 52, 102, 168
Blue Mosque, the, 18–19
Bodrum: accommodation, 190; bars, 190; coastline, 101, 196; description, 185–6, 190–1; Dursun, 186–9; enjoying, 145; ferry, 147, 191; Halicarnassus, 183, 185; location, 184; museum, 190–1; restaurant, 190
Bogsak, 104, 113
Bohinsko, Lake, 209
Bosphorus: description, 38–9; ferry across, 65; fish from, 18, 36; Istanbul, 17–20, 26; sailing up, 38–9; Tarabya, 22
Bozburun, 178, 179
British Museum, London, 183
Bryce, James, 79
Buchan, John, 7, 57
Burnley, C.A., 29
Buyukbendi, Ibrahim, 114–17, see also Ibrahim
Buyukdere, 39
Byblis, 170
Byzantines, 41, 46, 60, 126

Caesarea, 59, 63
Canaan, 90
Candir, 169, 201, 203, 209
Cappadocia, 36, 59, 63, 64
Caracalla, 98
Caria, 170, 185, 196
Castellorizon, 133, 134–9, 140, 149
Caunus: ancient city, 169–71; buying land near, 175, 201, 209;

journey to, 168, 177, 201; visitors to, 205
Celal, 135–7, 140–1
Celsus, Library of, 192
Cendere, 98
Charan, 90
Chimera, 131
Chrysanthos, Abbot, 152
Cilicia, 107
Cleopatra, 102
Cleopatra's Baths, 145
Cnidus, 182–4
Colin, 164–5
Commagene, Kingdom of, 93, 98
Comnenus Empire, 45, 51
Constantine, Father, 156
Constantine, feast for, 151
Constantinople, 7, 23, 26, 39, 46, 66
Constantius, Emperor, 83
Cos, 147, 148, 153, 183, 191
Cousteau, Jacques, 116
Cowen, Malcolm, 56
Crete, 170
Cubucak, 179
Cunaxa, battle of, 52
Cybele, 199
Cydnus River, 102

Dalaman, 203, 204, 205
Dalaman airport, 67, 162, 176, 189
Dalyan: Abidin, 169–70, 173–5, 177; buying land near, 175, 200–9; description, 171–2, 173; first visit, 164–8; hotel, 177; Ismet, 172–3, 175; restaurant, 177; second visit, 172; third visit, 200; wedding near, 212–13
Damascus, 125
Danube, 40, 168
Dardanelles, 39
Darius I, 93
Datca: buses, 191; Cnidian city, 182; cruises from, 162, 164, 190; description, 179–81; hotels, 189; lunch at, 35; Peninsula, 178, 208, 213; restaurants, 180–1; shop, 190
David Comnenus, Emperor, 46
Delos, 105, 183
Demre, 132, 173
Demurcili, 106

Denizli, 197
Derinkuyu, 60
Didyma, 102
Diocaesarea, 107
Diyarbakir, 82–5, 86–7, 88, 90–2
Dnieper, 40
Dodecanese Islands, 134, 150
Dogubayazit, 63, 80, 81
Dolmabahce Palace, 19–20, 39
Don, 40
Dracek, 109
Dursun, 186–7, 188–9, 190

Edirne, 7
Edward VIII, 19
Egypt, Sultan of, 134
Ekincek, 202
Ekincek Bay, 166
Enver Pasha, General, 57
Ephesus, 170, 183, 191, 192, 196
Ercis, 80, 81
Erciyers, Mount, 59
Ergen, Fatin and Ayser, 145
Eric, 94–5
Erim, Kenan, 193–6
Erkman, Yusuf, 20, *see also* Yusuf
Erzen, Professor Afif, 29
Erzerum, 50, 56
Erzincan, 58
Eski Kale, 98
Eudoxus, 183
Eumenes II, 197
Euphrates, 93, 96
Eurymedon, River, 125
Evren, President, 67
Eyupoglu, Captain Huseyin, 40–1, 43

Fellows, Charles, 144
Fethiye, 145, 146, 164, 173
Finike, 131, 132
Fiona, 164–5
Firat, 93
Flecker, Elroy, 44
Flower Seller's Alley, Istanbul, 9–13, 27
Fortune, Goddess of, 93, 95
Freely, John, 29, 72, 81

Gaigik I, King, 73
Galata, 17, 65

Galata Bridge, 17–18, 27
Gallipoli, 43
Gavustepe, 77
Gemile, 177
Gerger, 95, 96
Geta, 98
Gevas, 73, 76, 81
Geyre, 194
Giresun, 42, 55
Glazebrook, Philip, 29, 56–7, 58
Gocek, 145
Gok Medrese, 59
Gokcul, Kaptan Kembal, 135–8
Gokova, Gulf of, 178, 184
Golden Horn, the, 17, 26, 38, 65
Goreme, 60, 63
Gotch, Paul, 74
Grace, Princess, 116–17
Grand Bazaar, Istanbul (Kapali Carsi), 18, 27, 86
Groombridge, Maureen and Alan, 162
Gulbahar, Mahmut, 180
Gulluk Dag, 118
Gumushane, 43, 51, 53–5, 58
Gunes, Huseyin, 190
Gurkan, Anthea, 144
Gurpinar, 76
Guzelgoz, Mustafa, 63
Guzelsu, 77

Hadrian, Baths of, 195
Hadrian, Emperor, 131
Hadrian, Temple of, 192
Haidar Pasha, 38
Haik, 74
Hakkari, 77
Halime Hatun Turbesi, 73
Halicarnassus, 183, 185
Hannay, Richard, 7, 68
Harran, 88, 90
Harsit Cayi, 53
Hasan, Kemmoni, 11–13
Haydarpasa Gari, 65
Helios, 93
Hera, 105
Hercules, 93, 98, 195
Hermes, 93
Herodotus, 143, 170
Hierapolis, 197, 198
Hittite Museum, Ankara, 80

Hittites, 59, 80, 93
Holy Cross, Church of the,
    Akdamar Island, 73–4, 78
Homer, 131, 134
Hopa, 46
Hopkirk, Peter, 76
Hosap Kale, 77, 78
Hosap River, 78
Hoskyn, Mr, 170
Hugo, 152–3
Hurrians, 72

Ibrahim, 114–24, 140–1, 146, 162
Imrie, Evelyn, 38–9
Iran, 69, 77, 80
Ishak Pasha, 63
Iskenderum, 22, 36, 103, 125
Ismet, 172–3, 175, 177, 202, 209
Istanbul: baths, 49; coach to, 7;
    Dolmabahce Palace, 19–20, 39;
    flights from, 127, 191, 207;
    Flower Seller's Alley, 9–13;
    Galata Bridge, 16–17, 27; Grand
    Bazaar (Kapali Carsi), 18, 27, 86;
    hotels, 28; Naval Museum, 20;
    New Mosque, 18; nightlife, 27–8;
    Pera Palas Hotel, 8, 14–16;
    restaurants, 23, 31–2, 35; Santa
    Sophia, 18, 25–6; Spice Market,
    18, 27; Topkapi, the, 18, 19, 26–
    7; Tourist office, 31
Italy, King of, 135
Izmir, 12, 24, 36, 146, 189, 191, 207

Jan, 202–3, 205, 207
Jerry, 68–70, 75
Joe, 83, 87–8, 91–2
John, 164–5
Joy, 68–70, 75
Julia Domna, 98
Justinian, 26

Kahta, 94, 95, 100
Kale, 141–2
Kalkan, 142–3
Kalogiannidou, Mrs, 6
Kalymnos, 186
Kapali Carsi (Grand Bazaar)
    Istanbul, 18, 27, 86
Kaptan, the, 135–8
Karabelen, 96

Karakoy ferry, 65
Karanlik Kilisse, Dark Church of,
    60
Karpathos, 206
Kars, 10, 50, 56–7, 62, 74, 87
Kas: Castellorizon and, 134, 137,
    138; cruising to, 164; description,
    133; excursions from, 141, 142;
    hotels, 142; wreck near, 191
Kastellorizo, see Castellorizon
Kavala, 3, 5, 6
Kaya, Sahin, 63
Kaymakli, 60
Kayseri, 58–9, 63
Kekova, 102, 140–1, 147, 162, 177
Kemer, 129, 142
Keramoti, 7
Kilic, A.E., 29
Kiz Kalesi, 104
Koksal, 108, 109, 111
Konstantinos, Ayios, 151
Konya, 107
Korikos, 112
Korkuteli, 118
Koycegiz, 171, 200, 203, 204
Kummuhu, 93
Kurban Bayram, 42
Kurt Abidin, see Abidin
Kusadasi, 49, 147, 191–2

Lanciewicz, General Mariau, 38
Laodike, Queen, 98
Lapeski, 105
Lapriak, Major, 152
Lassen, Anders, 152
Layard, Julian Henry, 39
Lazes, 45
Ligos, 103
Limenas, 5, 6
Lindos, 141
Love, Dr Iris, 184
Luke, St, 50
Lycia, 132, 134, 144
Lycian coast, 128, 129, 133, 140
Lycians, 140–1, 173, 175

Macaulay, Rose, 29, 44
Macka, 50
Mahmudis, 78
Maiden's Castle, 108, 112
Makryammos, 3

Malatya, 99, 100, 103
Manavgat, 125, 126
Marc Antony, 102
Marcus Aurelius, 130
Marmara, Sea of, 36, 38, 39, 65
Marmaris: bar, 185; bath, 49; buses, 172, 184, 200, 207; coast at, 128; cruising from, 162, 164, 171, 176–7; description, 164; enjoying, 145; ferry, 147, 148, 176; *hammam*, 49; Holiday Village, 67, 146, 158–9; honesty in, 3; honey, 35; hotels, 158–9, 206; kilims, 86; restaurants, 159; roads, 146, 178, 204
Mary, Virgin, 50, 192
Mausolus, 170, 183, 185
Meander, River, 194
Medes, 72
Mediterranean, 39, 62, 101, 102, 124, 182
Medusa, 105, 121, 122
Mehmet the Conqueror, 26
Mehmet II, Sultan, 27, 46
Mejingir, 76
Menderes Valley, 193, 194
Mentes, Ridvan, 33
Menua, King, 72, 77
Mersin, 62, 101, 102–3, 107, 112
Mesopotamia, 82, 88, 96
Miletos, 192
Miletus, 170
Misir Carsisi, 18
Mithradates I of Commagene, 93, 98
Mithras, 93
Modiano, Mario, 138–9
Moltke, Helmut von, 95
Mouvarieff, General, 57
Mugla, 146, 204, 205
Muradiye, 81
Mustafa, 44–5
Mutlu, Dursun, 186–7, 188–9, 190
Muyla, 184
Myra, 132, 134
Mytilene, 149

Naples, King of, 134
Narince, 95
Narlikuyu, 104, 112
Naval Museum, Istanbul, 20

Nemrut Dagi, 69
Nemrut, Mount, 93, 94, 95, 99, 100
Neveshir, 60, 62, 64
Newby, Eric, 26
Newton, Sir Charles, 183
Nicholas, St, 132–3
Nicomedes, 184
Nimrud, Mount, 93
Nineveh, 72
Noah, 74, 77
Nympheos, River, 98

Olba, 107
Olu-Deniz, 115, 144–5, 162–3, 165
Olympos, 102, 129, 130, 167
Olympos, Mount, 130
Orhaniye, 178
Orient Express, 15, 21
Ortega, 172, 210, 212
Osman (driver), 47, 51–3, 58, 107–9, 123, 143
Ottoman Empire, 26, 41, 66, 72, 78
Ozkal, Ahmed, 159

Pamphylia, 126, 129
Pamphylian plain, 120
Pamukkale, 36, 197–8
Panayia, 3
Panormitis, 153, 154–8
Panormitis, Abbot of, 152
Papadoyannis, Yannis, 6
Patara, 101, 102, 129, 133, 143, 196
Patnos, 76, 80
Paul, 124–5
Paul, St, 102, 134, 192
Pegasus, 131
Pergamum, 197
Perge, 125, 126
Persians, 41, 46, 144, 170, 182
Phaselis, 119, 126, 129, 130
Phoenix, Mount, 130
Pits of Heaven and Hell, 112
Pliny, 131, 184
Pluto, 198
Plutonium, 198–9
Polo, Marco, 53, 81
Potamia, 4
Praxiteles, 183–4
Priape, 105, 107
Priene, 192, 196
Prinos, 3, 4–5

Prometheus, 195

Raif, 71, 73–7, 82, 170, 180
Rainier, Prince, 116–17
Red Tower, Alanya, 111
Rhodes: Castellorizon and , 134;
    Caunus and, 170; cruises from,
    162, 177; description, 147–8;
    ferries, 139, 147, 150, 159, 176,
    206; flights to, 148; knights of,
    185; Lindos, 141; settlers from,
    130
Richardson, Eric, 161–2, 164
Rihtim Caddesi, Istanbul, 18
Rize, 33, 46, 53
Ro, 139
Romans at: Aphrodisias, 194–6;
    Caunus, 170; Kayseri, 59; Patara,
    143; Perge, 126; Phaselis, 130;
    Sinop, 41; Termessos, 120;
    Uzuncaburc, 106–7
Rock Men, 108
Rumbelow, Donald, 30
Russians, 43, 46, 57, 71
Ryazan, 172

Sacred Pool, 197
St John, Knights of, 134
St Luke, 50
St Nicholas, 132–3
St Paul, 102, 134, 192
St Peter, Castle of, 185, 190–1
St Sophia, see Santa Sophia
Salonika, 3, 6
Samos, 4, 147, 192
Samsun, 42
Santa Sophia, Istanbul, 18, 25–6
Santorini, 105
Sardur I, King, 72
Sarduris II, 72
Sari Suleyman Bey, 78
Sassoon, Sybil, 74
Schneider, Dux, 29
Scot, Samuel, 39
Scutari, 38
Seleucus I, 107
Selim II, 7
Selimye, 178
Seljuks at: Ahlat, 81; Alanya, 125;
    Avanos, 64; Gevas, 73; Gok
    Medrese, 59; Goreme, 60; Kale,

141; Van, 72
Semiran Suyu, 77
Seneca, 131
Septimius Severus, Emperor, 98
Side, 121, 126
Sikalos, Nikos, 160
Silifke, 104, 105, 107, 112, 113
Sinan (architect), 7, 19, 27
Sinop, 40, 41
Sinova, 41
Sivas, 58–9, 63
Skala Potamias, 4, 6
Sogut, 178
Solymus, Mount, 118
Sophia, Church of Ayia,
    Trebizond, 45–6
Sophia, Santa, Istanbul, 18, 25–6
Sostratos, 183
Sotiris, 153
Spice Market, 18, 27
Stamboul, 17, 18
Stark, Dame Freya, 29, 130, 131,
    135, 167
Stevenson, R.L., 102
Strabo, 198
Suleyman the Magnificent, 7, 19,
    149
Sultaniye Thermal Springs, 204
Sumela, 50–1, 53, 60, 74
Summerton, Muareen and Bill, 162
Sumner-Boyd, Hilary, 29
Susanoglu, 108
Suzer, Hasan, 15–16, 88
Sylvana, 152
Symi: description, 149–53; divers,
    186; ferries, 159; hotels, 159;
    monastery, 154; Panormitis, 154–
    8; sailing to, 177; villas, 160

Tackin, Erkut and Figen, 142
Tarabya, 22, 31, 32, 36
Tarsus, 62, 101, 102, 106
Tasucu, 113
Tatvan, 69, 80, 82
Taurus Mountains, 93, 124
Telmessos, 145
Termessos, 117, 118–22, 123, 126
Thassos, 3, 4, 5, 6, 149
Thatch, 12–13
Thera, 105
Tiberius, 194

Tigris, 82, 88, 96
Tomb of the Fearless King, 104, 110–11
Topkapi, the, 18, 19, 26–7, 39
Trabzon (Trebizond), 44–7, 48
Trajan, Emperor, 196
Trapezus, 45, 52
Trebizond (Trabzon), 42, 43, 44–7, 53
Troy, 134
Tugay, Dogan, 147, 164, 176
Turkmenusagi, 108
Tushpa, 71–2

Ucagiz-Theimesa, 140
Ur, 90
Urartians, 72, 77, 78, 81
Urartu, 71–2, 74
Urfa, 87, 88–91, 92
Urgup, 60–1, 63, 101
Uskudar, 38, 39
Uzuncaburc, 106–7

Van, citadel of, 77, 78
Van, Lake: Armenia, 74; description, 69, 71; floods, 71, 77, 81; hotel, 80; journey to, 65; legend of cats, 73; transport, 80

Van, Province of, 72, 76, 78
Van (town), 70–2, 74, 77, 80, 81–2
Vespasian, Emperor, 107
Victoria, Queen, 19
Volga, 172
Voyantzis, Lina, 160

Wicksteed, Alexander, 172
Williams, General Sir Fenwick, 57

Xanthi, 7
Xanthos, 144
Xanthus Valley, 33
Xenophon, 52
Xera Cove, 140

Yalcinkaya, Dogan, 180–1
Yeni Cami, 18
Yusuf, 20, 21–5, 114–15, 124, 198

Zelve, 59
Zephyria, 185
Zeus, 105
Zeus, statue of, 93, 96
Zeus, Temple of, Uzuncaburc, 107
Zigana Pass, 51, 52, 53
Zoilos, 193, 195

Page 37 Chicken & Walnut recipe.

The IZMIR recommended to up up Bosphorus to B.S.

Page 42. Kissing hand, raised to forehead by younger person. Greeting: "I obey you also a

Page 59 Kayseri (Caesarea) homes & churches in rocks
DERINKUYU - KAYMAKLI (underground dwellings
7 centuries.
URGUP - good centre. (not the holiday village to stay in
TURBAN OTELI
too touristy.)

Muezzin. Minaret

Pictures P. 31.